# The Writing Kaleidoscope
## Writing, Reading, and Grammar

Kathryn Benander

*Porterville College*

Prentice Hall, Upper Saddle River, New Jersey 07458

*Library of Congress Cataloging-in-Publication Data*

Benander, Kathryn
   The writing kaleidoscope : writing, reading, and grammar / Kathryn Benander.
      p.      cm.
   Includes index.
   ISBN 0-13-530957-3
   1. English language—Rhetoric.  2. English language—Grammar.
   3. Report writing.  4. College readers.  I. Title.
PE1408. B474  1999
808'.0427—dc21                                                      97–38865
                                                                        CIP

Editorial Director: Charlyce Jones Owen
Acquisitions Editor: Maggie Barbieri
Director of Production
   and Manufacturing: Barbara Kittle
Senior Production Manager: Bonnie Biller
Production Editor: Joan E. Foley
Copyeditor: Virginia Rubens
Editorial Assistant: Joan Polk
Manufacturing Manager: Nick Sklitsis
Prepress and Manufacturing Buyer: Mary Ann Gloriande
Marketing Manager: Robert Mejia
Cover Art Director: Jayne Conte
Cover Designer: Bruce Kenselaar

This book was set in 11/13 New Baskerville by The Clarinda Company
and was printed and bound by Hamilton Printing Company. The cover
was printed by Phoenix Color Company.

Printed in the United States of America
10   9   8   7   6   5   4   3   2

**ISBN 0-13-530957-3**

Prentice-Hall International (UK) Limited, *London*
Prentice-Hall of Australia Pty. Limited, *Sydney*
Prentice-Hall Canada Inc., *Toronto*
Prentice-Hall Hispanoamericana, S.A., *Mexico*
Prentice-Hall of India Private Limited, *New Delhi*
Prentice-Hall of Japan, Inc., *Tokyo*
Pearson Education Asia Pte. Ltd., *Singapore*
Editora Prentice-Hall do Brasil, Ltda., *Rio de Janeiro*

In memory of

**Lillian Belle Wright**

a woman of great strength

11/14/12–10/15/91

# Contents

## Chapter 3: *Giving Your Ideas Form*, 58

## Chapter 4: *Making Sense*, 85

## Chapter 5: *Developing Your Ideas*, 110

# *Preface*

## TO THE INSTRUCTOR

Teaching English is a challenging and wonderful profession because it allows us to influence the quality of our students' lives in profound and exciting ways. In courses where students may have few writing skills, this becomes even more important, as literacy can easily determine the quality of our students' lives and their children's lives as well. The goal of this text is to supply you with a variety of instructional materials and choices to use as you encourage your students to learn to write, read, and use grammar more proficiently. We already know that students who read often tend to be better writers, so applying this easily observed connection in a writing class makes a lot of sense. Furthermore, connecting grammar instruction and practice to writing and reading makes grammar seem more useful and important.

This text purposely emphasizes communication, not correctness. This may seem, perhaps, to be a small distinction, but for students, this is often an unfamiliar concept. If students do not see writing as communication, how can they see it as important to every facet of their lives? If they do understand that writing is self-expression and communicating ideas, how can they see it as anything but vital to their lives? A focus on correctness can be destructive to fledgling writers just learning to communicate their ideas on paper. They need time to experiment with language, especially the use of language to communicate a purposeful message to an intended audience. Without this "transaction," as William Zinsser calls it, what purpose is served by learning to write well? The unexpected bonuses, of course, are even more valuable to many students: self-confidence and self-respect.

This book is designed, both in layout and in content, to communicate clearly and without intimidation the connection between writing, reading, and grammar and the activities they allow us to do well. This approach is based on the belief that our use of language directly affects the quality of our lives and that learning to read and write well involves many stages that are discursive and individual. Because no single approach can be applied with equal benefit to every student, this book is designed to be used for the personal and in-class exploration of language, including reading, writing, and grammar. These skills are so interrelated that none of them can be truly learned and understood without the others. As an instructor, you can use whichever parts of this book you consider necessary for your class; at the same time, the book provides enough information, quality readings, exercises, and guidance so that students will be able to use it on their own as a multifaceted resource to build the skills for a lifetime of reading, writing, and thinking.

All the chapters follow a similar plan to assist you in making assignments and to assist students in finding them. Each chapter is structured in the following manner:

## Opening Discussion

The first section in each chapter discusses a writing, reading, or grammar topic that gives the student a foundation for the topics to be explored in the rest of the chapter. Each opening section emphasizes the connections between writing, reading, and grammar, and how the student can become a more proficient learner, thinker, and communicator. In addition, each introduction relates the skills in the chapter to real-life academic, job, and personal goals.

## Reading an Essay

Each chapter includes an essay written by a professional writer that addresses some aspect of reading, writing, or grammar. The essays purposely include more than one paragraph and may seem more difficult than choices typically included in a text of this type. Students, however, are likely to enjoy these longer essays more than short, stilted paragraphs that leave them uninspired and really do not reflect the type of reading many of them need to learn to do more effectively. To help them with comprehension and interest, each essay is preceded by a reading strategy to aid students in establishing goals and a context for reading. Additionally, each reading is accompanied by prereading questions and a "Building Your Skills" section that includes vocabulary and comprehension questions. The exercises that accompany each reading make good starting points for classroom discussions, individual or journal exercises, or small-group activities. They purposely challenge students to read beyond the literal level. Literal thinking, of course, also affects their writing and their ability to comprehend the world around them, so as students read and discuss these essays, they are likely to begin to see the differences between passively reading the words printed on a page and actively reading for meaning, ideas, and applications to their own lives.

## Techniques for Writing

Each chapter includes a writing section that focuses on a writing skill or technique, such as paragraph and essay structure, rhetorical strategies, techniques for introductions and conclusions, and other specific instruction for improving writing. This section includes demonstrations, questions to promote active reading, and ideas for individual and group activities. The sequence of writing techniques throughout the chapters will help students move from getting started to writing shorter works to writing essay-length works. "Building Your Skills" includes writing and essay assignments that encourage students to write with a process and to practice ideas from each chapter. Assignments vary in their difficulty and scope to allow students to gain experience with various kinds of writing, including paragraphs, essays using different rhetorical strategies, letters to the editor, summaries, and job application materials. Most of the writing assignments also offer opportunities for exploration of topics that can easily be used for group or collaborative activities. Much of the rewriting suggested encourages students to work with others and to allow others to read what they have produced. Students understand the connection between writer and audience much better when they have played both roles by responding to other students' writing and seeing others responding to theirs.

## Reading a Student Essay

This section includes a peer review strategy that identifies a specific focus for students as they read. The student essays also demonstrate techniques the student has read about, and this can promote a stimulating small-group or class discussion. The "Building Your Skills" questions following each student essay encourage evaluation, and they include a section where the student can list three positive characteristics and three possible improvements for each essay. This set of questions forces students to look for something positive to say about another student's essay rather than being overly critical. Since the student essays are well-written, the questions also force them to think about what could be changed without sacrificing quality. The instructor's manual offers vocabulary and comprehension questions if you prefer a different approach.

## Using Grammar

Each grammar section explains a grammatical concept by means of demonstrations and then discusses its relationship to writing and reading. Each presents common grammatical problems for writers who are developing their skills. In these discussions, students learn what grammar is, how it affects the writing process, and specific guidelines for using punctuation, parts of speech, and improving sentence structure. The "Building Your

Skills" section following each discussion provides grammar exercises that help students observe the use of grammar in other people's writing as well as in their own; they learn to use grammar skills in their assignments and everyday life rather than simply filling in a workbook full of blank lines. Many of these segments refer to reference materials in the Appendix and cross-reference other sections of the book. You may want to photocopy the Appendix or have students photocopy it for themselves for easy reference in class or during assignments. In addition, the first chapter introduces an idea for developing a grammar journal and many of the assignments in "Seeing the Connections: Applying Your Skills" ask students to use and develop a grammar journal.

## Seeing the Connections: Applying Your Skills

This final section in each chapter offers three assignments that can be used in addition to or instead of the other assignments in the chapter. Each assignment includes a reading, writing, and grammar component to help students see the connections between the skills they are developing and to give them an opportunity to apply their skills.

Most of the students in basic skills or developmental courses need help in reading, writing, and grammar that prepares them for college require-ments or job goals. This text includes writing assignments that give students opportunities to express themselves better and more professionally. Some assignments work on developing specific types of writing, such as college admission essays, resumés, cover letters, and other assignments in practical writing. Other activities encourage students to find reading and resource materials in newspapers, magazines, dictionaries, and other commonly read resources. Chapter 10 includes a discussion of the various types of library resources and how to use them. Students who read about and use these resources will not only become better writers in particular situations, they will gain a better understanding of the resources available to them and of the many opportunities that many students simply do not know exist.

## Acknowledgments

I owe much of my philosophy of teaching and approaches in the classroom to two of my teachers who later became dear friends, Kim and Michael Flachmann. Their lifetime commitment to learning and to teaching others has influenced my teaching and writing in ways too numerous to name. I admire them both and aspire to their level of excellence and stamina. In addition, I would like to thank my colleagues at Porterville College for their support and their contagious enthusiasm for teaching and learning—especially my colleagues in the Language Arts Department: Beverly Richardson, Ted Wise, Othel Pearson, Jacinto Gardea, Nancy Whitman, Ann-Marie Wagstaff, Laurie Buchholz, Susan Regier, Kathleen Bennet, and the newly retired Howard Waters. In addition, I'd like to thank the many staff members who make the excellent teaching environment at Porterville College possible, especially the library staff members, who are always incredibly helpful. Most of all, I wish to thank the many students I have taught over the last ten years, who have brought enthusiasm and even skepticism into my classes. The most exciting aspect of teaching has been the opportunity to see students progress from being unsure of themselves to gaining a foundation for learning and for living. I am always amazed at the level of thought, the degree of dedication, and the determination so many of my students bring to my classes. My students have taught me so much and provide the real rewards for teaching.

Throughout my life, home has provided the most significant foundation for me. Throughout this project, my husband, Ron Benander, demonstrated patience and offered encouragement only possible through sainthood or true love. I want to thank him for his faith in me and his unwavering support for my teaching and writing. I am also thankful for the foundation my wonderful parents provided for me. I miss my late father, Elwood Harvey, and am reminded of his words as I teach and write: "Books are free at the library and so is learning." My parents prepared me for the many challenges in life by helping me to see that learning, determination, and self-direction were necessary for self-fulfillment. I'd also like to thank Mary Lamb, my mother, who has always believed in me and provided me with an example of great motivation and accomplishment, and her husband, Ralph Lamb, who through his humor and personality has brought a lot of joy into my mother's life and into mine. I am also grateful to the rest of my family, especially Vicki, Virgel, and Dale Standfill, Dennis and Lynn Mattocks, David and Lynn Mattocks, and Elsie, Dick, and the entire Lee family.

The many supportive people at Prentice Hall also deserve my lifelong devotion for their encouragement, guidance, and friendliness. I greatly appreciate Maggie Barbieri, Senior English Editor, for guiding me through the process of drafting this book, helping me maintain a sense of humor, and helping me to do my best work: Rob Mejia, Senior Marketing Manager, for his knowledge and help in marketing this text; Harriett Prentiss, Developmental Editor, for her experience and valuable insight; Joan Foley, Production Editor, for her attention to detail, foresight, and her guidance through the production process; Virginia Rubens, Copyeditor, for her brilliant and thoughtful advice and editing; and Joan Polk, Editorial Assistant, for her friendly assistance; and the following reviewers: Janet Bacon, De Kalb College; Nancy Barlow, Brookhaven College; Therese Brychta, Truckee Meadows Community College; Mary Caldwell, University of Texas at El Paso; Stanley Coberly, West Virginia University at Parkersburg; Elaine Chakonas, Dominican University; Terry Hite, Columbus State Community College; Thomas Mozola, Macomb Community College; Bonnie Ronson, Hillsborough Community College; Annamarie Schlender, California State University at Hayward; and Karen Standridge, Pikes Peak Community College.

## TO THE STUDENT

This book is not designed to teach you how to pass a particular course; it is designed to teach you the skills that will give you the opportunities to read, write, and learn throughout your life. It will prepare you for a job, for college-level work, for writing to friends, writing to the IRS—anything you do that involves writing, reading, or speaking (which, by the way, is just about everything!). If you have not done much reading or writing, you may not be aware of the richness and opportunity they can bring to your life. You may even believe that reading and writing are boring or frustrating activities that are unrelated to your everyday life. As a writer and reader, you can express yourself better and understand what others want to communicate to you more easily. But reading and writing have some important effects on a person that may not be immediately obvious. As you learn to read better, you begin to understand not only what people say, but how they are communicating that message. You begin to think and interpret the world for yourself. Although this may seem like an unimportant reason to read, think about the many ways you must interpret the world for yourself. Each day you are bombarded by messages from people around you, from television, newspapers, billboards, and so on. Interpreting the world and making good decisions are developed through reading, while expressing those views and decisions is a function of writing. Through becoming a better writer, you will gain an ability to communicate your ideas better, to identify and speak to different audiences, and to write appropriately for a variety of situations. Most important, you will gain confidence in your ability to read, write, and think that will affect all areas of your life. People who are confident and think for themselves are able to speak with others and write to others, as well as to express their feelings and opinions without feeling embarrassed or silly. They have learned the value of what they have to say and write, and they know how to persuade others to see their opinions too.

This book will help you to build the skills and background to become a better student, writer, reader, speaker, and listener. You will read what many other writers think about language and other interesting topics; you will learn to use processes and techniques for writing that will help you get your ideas on paper so that you can organize and work with them. You will learn about grammar and the effect grammar has on language and self-expression. You will learn how to construct sentences, paragraphs, and essays, and how to use marks of punctuation. You will also learn about the many resources available to you for a lifetime of learning and success. Try to begin using this book with an open mind and allow your skills to build. Sometimes students begin with a feeling that they will not do well in a writing or English class—but try to avoid giving yourself these negative messages. Instead, wait a few weeks before you make up your mind about how well you will do in this writing course. This book is designed for your success and was class-tested with many students like yourself who needed to build their language skills and confidence. Work to build habits and routines that will make you more comfortable with reading, writing, and studying.

The title of this book—*The Writing Kaleidoscope: Writing, Reading, and Grammar*—hints at the important focuses of the book. Each chapter includes instruction in writing techniques, reading, and grammar. You will be asked to examine your own writing, reading, and grammar routines and techniques and to make adjustments to improve your ability to express yourself and to increase your ability to read and write different types of material to satisfy a variety of goals. As a student, you may find this intimidating and sometimes even frustrating. Learning to use language well and to think well is not the easiest thing in the world, but it is certainly one of the most rewarding and it affects practically everything else you do. This book takes each of these factors into consideration by offering you detailed instruction and guidance, interesting and thought-provoking reading and writing assignments, clear grammar instruction, and practical writing skills that relate to the real world and to the personal and professional goals you may have.

As you use this book, work to develop routines, habits, and styles that you can take with you into jobs and other classes and academic settings. As you learn to read better, remember the benefits you will receive in school, on the job, at home, or in learning to read for pleasure. Most of all, commit yourself to a course of study that will allow you to make informed, thoughtful decisions so that you can be your own person. Until you have learned to read, to write, to think, and to communicate to your greatest potential, you will never know what you are missing.

Kathryn Benander

# Introduction

A kaleidoscope—a tube filled with colored glass—reflects the elements to which it is exposed. It performs in a constantly changing pattern. In fact, a kaleidoscope is very much like a writer. A writer reflects the elements to which he or she is exposed. In addition, a writer performs in constantly changing patterns that are influenced by writing tasks, reading, grammar, thinking, and new experiences. Because of the versatility writing allows us, self-expression is possible. The way we reflect our experiences and thoughts in writing allows us to produce something completely individual. Just as the kaleidoscope gives the viewer an infinite number of color combinations, writing gives us an infinite number of opportunities for expression, learning, and influence.

Thinking is the core of writing and reading. When we write or read, we learn to think, to concentrate, to actively pursue an idea, and to persuade others through our expression. Activities like reading and writing contribute to what we know, who we are, and who others perceive us to be. Whenever we use or improve these skills and abilities, we also change and expand our thinking, feeling, and being. Without reading or writing, we would probably never learn to truly ponder or consider an idea; we probably would not know the history of ideas either.

Thought creates opportunities and frustrations, but it leads us to a well-reasoned life. It allows us to interpret the world around us and to share that interpretation in a meaningful way. As you begin a course of reading and writing, and perhaps even college, you will be challenged often to identify your beliefs and to support them, sometimes in writing, sometimes in speech. Writing, reading, and grammar are integral to your expression and your ability to identify, convey, and support your beliefs. They are also imperative to building the confidence that will allow you to express your beliefs. Think of a speaker you have seen recently or of a public figure whom you admire. What is it about this person's presentation that makes him or her convincing or persuasive? What makes you believe this person's message or respect his or her view?

Rhetoric is the art of persuasion. Throughout history, many different characteristics have been identified as being important to the art of persuasion: integrity, honesty, specific types of speech or gestures. Ultimately, three factors decide whether a writer or speaker effectively persuades others. One factor is the audience. Each listener or reader decides what is persuasive and believable and what is not based on his or her own experience and knowledge. The second factor is purpose. The writer or speaker must have a purpose and must make this purpose clear to whomever he or she plans to persuade. The third factor is the way the speaker or writer uses language. The use of formal or informal language, certain phrases, grammar, and vocabulary all determine how effectively a speaker or writer presents his or her message and how well that message will be received by the audience. Even though rhetoric as an art form is thousands of years old, people still study ways to speak and write better.

Why do colleges require writing courses and courses to help students read better? Communication (and rhetoric) are at the heart of the human experience. We all have beliefs and ideas; we all think and want to be heard. With this common goal and need, many of us learn to use language to fulfill this human need for expression. As you use this text, keep in mind the benefits that expressing yourself well can have for you. Notice when you struggle to express an idea and when you are able to help someone understand your message. Most of all, remember that learning to think clearly and express your ideas effectively is part of what makes our lives most rewarding, fulfilling, and human.

# Chapter 1

## Building Confidence in Your Writing

In this chapter you will learn

★ to write using a process approach rather than a product approach;
★ to use SQ3R to improve your ability to read and remember;
★ to recognize the target audience in reading and to identify your own audience in writing;
★ to identify the writer's purpose when you read and to focus on a specific purpose in your own writing;
★ to define the word *grammar*;
★ to choose a grammar handbook.

Take a moment to answer the following questions:

1. What is "good" writing?

_____

_____

_____

2. Who determines when writing is "good" or less than good?

_____

_____

_____

3. How do you feel when you are writing something you know other people will read?

_____

_____

_____

4. What experiences have you had with writing and with writing classes?

_____

_____

_____

## TAKING THE FIRST STEP

Writing involves vulnerability—putting a piece of yourself on paper. Many writers, though they may not realize it, fear putting words on paper because they are afraid they may be criticized or that their way of putting words on paper may not communicate what they have to say effectively. Sometimes, students simply fear an unsatisfactory grade. Unlike speech, which can be changed, repeated, denied, softened, or emphasized by voice or gesture, writing implies permanence. In this chapter, you will learn techniques that will help you become more comfortable with writing—writing to yourself, to your friends and family, and to your instructors. The most important first step, however, is actually to write something. You must be willing to take that risk before the learning process can really begin.

Almost all writers at some time suffer from a fear of writing or a feeling of being unable to write; often, this is called writer's block. Have you ever tried to write when you were sad, really excited, or angry? You may have found that you had difficulty concentrating on a writing task or communicating your message. Usually, a little time and relaxation takes care of an occasional setback like this. When we are frustrated—with the subject matter, with another person, with a real-life situation—we may feel "blocked" or unable to write, but with practice, these blocks are easier to overcome. Perhaps the hardest "block" to overcome, though, is the inexperienced or reluctant writer's fear of writing (and handing in) the first paper. Obviously, part of this fear comes from not knowing the reader—usually the instructor. Another concern may arise from past bad experiences with writing or speaking. Of course, the first step in writing is allowing yourself to be vulnerable. Are you willing to express your ideas or life experiences to a total stranger? How about to an acquaintance? If you are not comfortable in these situations, then it is no surprise that you might be uncomfortable sharing your ideas in writing, especially knowing that an instructor will respond to your writing, perhaps grade your writing, and certainly use your writing as a tool to evaluate your ability or performance on an assignment. You must take a chance on writing the first essay or assignment in a class and think only about communicating what you want to say to your instructor in order to succeed in that class.

Each student has his or her own fear about what may happen when turning in that first essay or paragraph. The worst fear is often that the instructor will view the student as unintelligent or incapable of writing. As a general group, though, teachers tend to value people and to like reading people's ideas. If you are not sure whether this is true of your instructor, ask him or her. In addition, almost everyone can write and can learn to write well, so chances are very good that you can become a proficient writer in a reasonable amount of time. Again, though, you must be willing to take that first step: writing and turning in the first assignment.

Anxiety about writing can come from a variety of sources and can be overcome in many ways. Each person's feelings are different, so some methods will work for some students, some for others. The important thing is to find what works for you. The following are some suggestions for overcoming common "blocks" that writers face.

## ❏ Relax.

Sometimes the fear of writing produces counterproductive, inhibiting stress that makes a writer so nervous he or she finds writing impossible. Relaxation through exercise, listening to music, visiting with friends, or some other pleasurable activity can reduce your stress and make putting words on paper an easier and more rewarding experience. For example, if you sit down to write and feel it is impossible for you to write anything, one way you might relax is to take thirty minutes and do something you've been wanting to do for a while. However, this technique only works if you have the discipline to stick to thirty minutes of relaxation followed by a set amount of time for writing.

## ❏ Gather Ideas.

Sometimes, the problem is not stress, but having too few ideas. The feeling that you have nothing to write about is usually derived from one of two sources: either you have not given the assignment or topic enough thought or preparation time, or you feel that other people will not value what you have to say on the subject (perhaps *you* do not even value what you have to say). If you have not given enough thought to your topic, you may be trying to write when you should be generating ideas, outlining, or using other invention strategies (this is discussed further in Chapter 2, pages 39–45). Sometimes writers need to write ideas freely on paper; at other times they need to write freely for a specific amount of time; some even use mundane activities like washing dishes, raking leaves, or straightening a desktop as thinking time for writing. In fact, many experienced writers go through regular routines of performing mundane tasks before they ever put a word on the page. Some sharpen every pencil in their house or office; some prepare a work station; some brew a pot of coffee. These routines help signal the brain that it's time to do some serious thinking and writing, and they seem to work very well for some writers. Try using an activity every time you write as a way to signal your brain that it is time to start the writing process.

## ❏ Value Your Message.

Another common problem for inexperienced writers is the feeling that they really have nothing to say. This is a bit harder to overcome; if you feel others will not value what you have to say, writing can seem like a dull, meaningless exercise. If you think that what you have to write is not worth writing, ask yourself the following questions:

> Why would my instructor ask for an essay or written response to this topic?
> What is he or she hoping to accomplish with this assignment?
> How can he or she relate to what I know about this topic?
> What do I know about this topic that the instructor will not?
> How can I learn more about this topic so that I can write about it?

When people feel they have nothing meaningful to say it is usually because they lack confidence. You can develop more confidence in your ideas by discovering what you have to say and then identifying how those ideas can be meaningful to you and to others, including your instructor. Recognizing that you have an audience is one of the most fundamental steps in writing. Unless you are writing a note or journal entry just for yourself, every part of your writing (the message, the style, the organization) must specifically address the needs of your reader. After all, if communication is your goal, then the person or people to whom you are writing must be able to receive your message.

## ❏ Test the Waters.

Yet another fear of the inexperienced writer is the perception that the instructor assumes that each student has a high level of skill. A student who lacks confidence is likely to feel that a written assignment will not meet with his or her instructor's approval. Several techniques can help you if you feel this way. First, take a sample of your writing to the instructor or to another student who has attended that class and ask for suggestions about writing appropriate responses for the assignments in your class. What should your response include? What format should you use? Seek out assistance by asking the instructor to clarify directions, show you an example paper, or read rough drafts or early versions of what you have written. If your instructor is not available to do this, ask a tutor or trusted friend to evaluate your work. However, when working with a tutor or another student, remember that you are ultimately responsible for what goes on the page. They can assist you by acting and reacting as a reader, but you are still the writer, and the written product should employ statements and techniques with which you feel comfortable.

## ❏ Be Yourself.

In addition, be careful that you do not assume too much about the instructor—for example, that the instructor expects you to write in an unheard-of form of English or without any personality or individual thought. Be yourself. Though you should not write as though you were talking, you certainly should communicate your ideas. With communication as your focus, you should be able to avoid trying to use an exaggerated, overly sophisticated, or phony style.

## ❏ Focus on Communication.

With your first paper, focus on communicating and writing to the instructor rather than on achieving a specific grade. Don't be intimidated by trying to get an A or the highest grade in the class. By writing to express your ideas, you can avoid any anxiety or difficulties that may arise from trying to achieve a specific grade.

Also, when all else fails, perhaps the best way to get through the first writing assignment is simply to write what comes to mind and worry about perfecting what you have written later. Ultimately, getting words on the page will help you to relax and find your message within what you've written; perhaps the most frightful part of any assignment is staring at a blank page. If you find yourself doing this, take a walk, mow the lawn, or call a friend, and then write for thirty minutes to loosen up and get ideas on paper. After that, if you like what you have, work with it and turn it in; if you do not like what you have written, toss it aside and start again. However, do not take this as a fault or as evidence that you cannot learn to write well. Once you have written words on the page, been frustrated, and thrown a few pages away, you have joined the ranks of experienced writers who know that this is part of the process of learning what they know and think and expressing it to others. Now you can face your second essay with the confidence of knowing that you *can* get words on paper!

## READING AN ESSAY

### Strategy for Reading: SQ3R

SQ3R represents a five-part process that helps readers to better understand and remember what they read.

| | |
|---|---|
| **SURVEY** | Look over the material to be read, observing the format, sub-headings, length, pictures, and any other special features. |
| **QUESTION** | Formulate a few questions that you think reading this essay will answer: What is the purpose of this essay? What does the title mean? |
| **READ** | Read the essay or paragraph completely, preferably with a pencil in your hand so that you can take notes on paper or in the margin. |
| **REVIEW** | Try to remember the major points this essay makes and answer your own questions. Review notes you made about this reading assignment. |
| **RESTATE** | Write a brief statement about the purpose and meaning of the essay in the margin or on a separate sheet of paper. |

When you read the essay by Amy Tan that follows, use SQ3R. Follow each step and write your notes either in the margin of this book or on a separate piece of paper. Guidelines for each step are printed in italics and parentheses along the way.

(***SURVEY:*** *Look over the whole essay.*)

(***QUESTION:*** *Answer the following questions.*)

---

### BEFORE YOU READ

1. How much does language influence the way people see you? How are others influenced by the way you speak?
2. Who helped to form the speech patterns you use?
3. Have you ever felt embarrassed about your own speech or about the way that someone else speaks? What do you think caused your embarrassment?

---

(***READ:*** *Read the essay and make notations or mark specific words.*)

---

## Mother Tongue*

### by Amy Tan

As you know, I am a writer and by that definition I am someone who has always loved language. I think that is first and foremost with almost every writer I know. I'm fascinated by language in daily life. I spend a great deal of time thinking about the power of language—the way it can evoke an emotion, a visual image, a complex idea or a simple truth. As a writer, language is the tool of my trade and I use them all, all the Englishes I grew up with.                                   1

A few months back, I was made keenly aware of the Englishes I do use. I was giving a talk to a large group of people, the same talk I had given many times before and also with notes. And the nature of the talk was about my                 2

writing, my life, and my book *The Joy Luck Club*. The talk was
going along well enough until I remembered one major difference that made the whole thing seem wrong. My mother
was in the room, and it was perhaps the first time she had
heard me give a lengthy speech, using a kind of English I
had never used with her. I was saying things like "the inter-
section of memory and imagination," and "there is an
aspect of my fiction that relates to this and thus." A speech
filled with carefully wrought grammatical sentences, burdened to me it seemed with nominalized forms, past perfect
tenses, conditional phrases, all the forms of standard English that I had learned in school and through books, a form
of English I did not use at home or with my mother.

Shortly after that I was walking down the street with my          3
mother and my husband and I became self-conscious of the
English I was using, the English that I do use with her. We
were talking about the price of new and used furniture and
I heard myself saying to her, "Not waste money that way." My
husband was with me as well, and he didn't notice any
switch in my English. And then I realized why: because over
the twenty years that we've been together he's often used
that English with me and I've used that with him. It is sort
of the English that is our language of intimacy, the English
that relates to family talk, the English that I grew up with.

I'd like to give you some idea what my family talk                4
sounds like and I'll do that by quoting what my mother said
during a recent conversation which I videotaped and then
transcribed. During this conversation, my mother was talking about a political gangster who had the same last name
as her family, Du, and how the gangster in his early years
wanted to be adopted by her family which was by comparison very rich. Later the gangster became more rich, more
powerful than my mother's family and one day showed up
at my mother's wedding to pay his respects. And here's what
she said about that, in part, "Du Yu Sung having business
like food stand, like off the street kind; he's Du like Du
Zong but not Tsung-ming Island people. The local people
call him Du, from the river east side. He belong that side,
local people. That man want to ask Du Zong father take

him in become like own family. Du Zong father look down on him but don't take seriously until that many become big like, become a Mafia. Now important person, very hard inviting him. Chinese way: come only to show respect, don't stay for dinner. Respect for making big celebration; he shows up. Means gives lots of respect, Chinese custom. Chinese social life that way—if too important, won't have to stay too long. He come to my wedding; I didn't see it I heard it. I gone to boy's side. They have YMCA dinner; Chinese age I was nineteen."

You should know that my mother's expressive command of English belies how much she actually understands. She reads the *Forbes Report,* listens to *Wall Street Week,* converses daily with her stockbroker, reads all of Shirley MacLaine's books with ease, all kinds of things I can't begin to understand. Yet some of my friends tell me that they understand 50 percent of what my mother says. Some say maybe they understand maybe 80 percent. Some say they understand almost nothing at all. As a case in point, a television station recently interviewed my mother and I didn't see this program when it was first aired, but my mother did. She was telling me what happened. She said that everything she said, which was in English, was subtitled in English, as if she had been speaking in pure Chinese. She was understandably puzzled and upset. Recently a friend gave me that tape and I saw that same interview and I watched. And sure enough—subtitles—and I was puzzled because listening to that tape it seemed to me that my mother's English sounded perfectly clear and perfectly natural. Of course, I realize that my mother's English is what I grew up with. It is literally my mother tongue, not Chinese, not standard English, but my mother's English which I later found out is almost a direct translation of Chinese.

Her language as I hear it is vivid and direct, full of observation and imagery. That was the language that helped shape the way that I saw things, expressed things, made sense of the world. Lately I've been giving more thought to the kind of English that my mother speaks. Like others I have described it to people as broken or fractured English,

5

6

but I wince when I say that. It has always bothered me that I can think of no other way to describe it than broken, as if it were damaged or needed to be fixed, that it lacked a certain wholeness or soundness to it. I've heard other terms used, "Limited English" for example. But they seem just as bad, as if everything is limited, including people's perceptions of the Limited English speaker.

I know this for a fact, because when I was growing up          7
my mother's limited English limited my perception of her. I was ashamed of her English. I believed that her English reflected the quality of what she had to say. That is, because she expressed it imperfectly, her thoughts were imperfect as well. And I had plenty of empirical evidence to support me: The fact that people in department stores, at banks, at supermarkets, at restaurants did not take her as seriously, did not give her good service, pretended not to understand her, or even acted as if they did not hear her.

My mother has long realized the limitations of her          8
English as well. When I was fifteen she used to have me call people on the phone to pretend I was she. In this guise, I was forced to ask for information or oftentimes to complain and yell at people that had been rude to her. One time it was a call to her stockbroker in New York. She had cashed out her small portfolio and it just so happened that we were going to New York the next week, our very first trip outside of California. I had to get on the phone and say in my adolescent voice, which was not very convincing, "This is Mrs. Tan." And my mother was in the back whispering loudly, "Why don't he send me check already? Two weeks late. So mad he lie to me, losing me money." Then I said in perfect English, "Yes, I'm getting rather concerned. You had agreed to send the check two weeks ago, but it hasn't arrived." And she began to talk more loudly, "What you want—I come to New York, tell him front of his boss you cheating me?" And I was trying to calm her down, making her be quiet, while telling this stockbroker, "I can't tolerate any more excuses. If I don't receive the check immediately I'm going to have to speak to your manager when I arrive in New York." And sure enough the following week, there we were in front of

this astonished stockbroker. And there I was, red-faced and quiet, and my mother the real Mrs. Tan was shouting at his boss in her impeccable broken English.

We used a similar routine a few months ago for a situation that was actually far less humorous. My mother had gone to the hospital for an appointment to find out about a benign brain tumor a CAT scan had revealed a month ago. And she had spoken very good English she said—her best English, no mistakes. Still she said the hospital had not apologized when they said they had lost the CAT scan and she had come for nothing. She said that they did not seem to have any sympathy when she told them she was anxious to know the exact diagnosis since her husband and son had both died of brain tumors. She said they would not give her any more information until the next time; she would have to make another appointment for that, so she said she would not leave until the doctor called her daughter. She wouldn't budge, and when the doctor finally called her daughter, me, who spoke in perfect English, lo-and-behold, we had assurances the CAT scan would be found, they promised a conference call on Monday, and apologies were given for any suffering my mother had gone through for a most regrettable mistake. By the way, apart from the distress of that episode, my mother is fine.

But it has continued to disturb me how much my mother's English still limits people's perceptions of her. I think my mother's English almost had an effect on limiting my possibilities as well. Sociologists and linguists will probably tell you that a person's developing language skills are more influenced by peers. But I do think the language spoken by the family, especially immigrant families, which are more insular, plays a large role in shaping the language of the child. . . . [While this may be true, I always wanted, however,] to capture what language ability tests can never reveal—her intent, her passion, her imagery, the rhythms of her speech, and the nature of her thoughts. Apart from what any critic had to say about my writing, I knew I had succeeded where it counted when my mother finished reading my first book and gave me her verdict. "So easy to read."

9

10

*(**REVIEW:**   Think about the main points of the essay. What is Tan trying to communicate? Answer your own questions about the essay or write answers to the questions below.)*

*(**RESTATE:**   Test your recall and improve your ability to remember this essay by writing a short statement about the meaning and point of this essay.)*

## Building Your Skills

### Focus on Words

Look up the following words or parts of phrases in a dictionary. Consult the preceding essay and identify the meaning that best fits the way the author uses the word in this essay. Each word or phrase is followed by the number of the paragraph in which it appears.

| | |
|---|---|
| intersection (2) | belies (5) |
| nominalized (2) | empirical (7) |
| Standard English (2) | impeccable (8) |
| expressive command of English (5) | linguists (10) |

### Focus on the Message

1. What does Tan mean when she writes that she uses "all the Englishes" she has learned (para. 1)?
2. Why is Tan self-conscious about speaking in Standard English while her mother is present?
3. In what ways does Tan think the term "Limited English" inadequately describes the language her mother speaks?
4. How well do you understand people who speak differently from you? What point does Tan make about the way people treat her mother based on the way she speaks English? Is it fair to judge someone's ideas based on the way he or she uses language? Why or why not?
5. What overall point does Tan make about the power of language? Does she discuss any other issues concerning language?

---

### READING STRATEGY NOTE

How does using SQ3R differ from the way you usually read an essay?

In what ways did it help you to understand and remember Tan's essay more effectively?

---

## TECHNIQUES FOR WRITING: BEGINNING TO SEE WRITING AS A PROCESS

Many students view writing as a one-draft process: they sit down, write words on paper, and then hand the paper in to an instructor. Most experienced writers, however, wouldn't dream of turning in a first draft. They see writing as a process. By viewing writing as a process—a set of steps leading to a final product—we can more easily see how writers create a readable, thoughtful final product. Writing, though some people may make it seem easy, is work.

Every writer beginning the writing process must have two things: a purpose and an audience. The purpose may include a reason for writing and certainly should include what the writer hopes to accomplish by writing. For example, a student writing to a friend about a vacation may want to communicate how enjoyable or disastrous the vacation was. A student staring at a blank page often is searching for a reason to write—a point or idea that he or she needs to communicate. Only after a writer has decided what to say will he or she begin to feel a sense of purpose and a reason to write. If you do not know why you are writing, then you have missed a major step in the writing process. Communication is indeed difficult if even *you* do not know what you are trying to say.

**Purpose** and **audience** control the writing process. They help writers decide what to include and what to leave out; they also help identify goals, grammar usage, and how formally or informally the writer should address his or her readers. Prewriting, drafting, and rewriting are part of all writers' processes, but writers use these parts of the process at different times and with different emphasis within their writing routines. The first step in the writing process is to identify the purpose—what the requirements of the writing task are (i.e., letter or essay format, a shopping list, a demonstration, careful directions, and so on)—and the audience who will be reading the final written product (i.e., a friend, a teacher, the readers of a newspaper). With these two determining factors, the writing process leads you through a set of steps that produce a written product that communicates your message to a particular audience.

To begin using a process in your writing rather than trying to write the final draft of a work, begin by prewriting (follow the directions in the section titled "Prewriting—Turning Off the Censor in Your Head" in Chapter 2, pages 39–45). If you begin by determining your purpose for writing, you will have goals for your writing and a reason to write.

Furthermore, if you decide who you are writing to, you will have a clear idea of how much information is necessary or what can be omitted to accomplish this purpose. Many students struggle because they do not feel they have a reason to write. Following a process, though, helps you to build a feeling that you have something to communicate and a reason to write; most writers use this feeling to motivate themselves to sit for the length of time that it takes to write a good essay or even a good book. By following this process, you will begin writing by producing a draft without expecting perfection; then, hopefully, you can put that draft aside for a few hours or a day and when you read it again, you will begin to see your ideas taking shape and creating meaning, and you will have ideas for changes that can make your next draft a better version than your first.

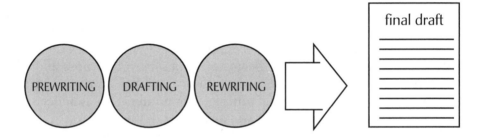

Generating ideas and organizing those ideas are the major activities of **prewriting,** the first step in the writing process. This beginning process helps a writer to clarify his or her ideas, choose a clear topic, and decide how best to present that topic. Prewriting can include a variety of activities to get the writer thinking and warmed up for writing. Some writers like to list ideas randomly; others need thinking time in the form of a mindless activity that allows them to let their ideas build until they are ready to write.

**Drafting** includes all of the false starts, the crumpled pages, the erased lines on a computer screen—everything that writers produce only to later delete or throw away. Essentially, drafting is the process of creating sentences and paragraphs that present information in a readable form. During the process of drafting or putting words onto page or screen, writers work to record their ideas in language. Some writers write two or three drafts, while others write twenty or more. The number of drafts, and the amount of time spent drafting, is always determined by the writer's purpose or goal, the time available, and the audience who will be reading the final product.

Each of these factors motivates the writer to produce pieces of written work and to work with what is written on the page to determine what should be added, taken out, or changed.

This brings us to the third part of the writing process: **rewriting.** Rewriting is the rethinking, reorganizing, redoing that all writers do to produce a final product. It is not simply checking spelling; it goes much deeper than the surface of the written work. Rewriting is the process of reorganizing ideas into their most effective order for clear and persuasive presentation. Rewriting may include getting the opinions of other readers, or allowing time to lapse before rereading. The process of rewriting should always include reading back the essay. To perform this task, the writer simply reads the essay from start to finish, preferably out loud. While the writer reads, he or she can decide if what is included is sufficient for the reader, is worded effectively, and is presented in a way that achieves his or her overall goal.

Each of these steps in the writing process is governed by purpose and audience. What a writer wants to say and the person or people with whom the writer wants to communicate determine the process he or she uses. A grocery list requires less prewriting, drafting, and rewriting than a letter to a friend. A letter to a friend requires less of this process than a letter to the IRS. The writing task, the writer's purpose, and the audience decide the level of detail, the approach, and every other decision the writer makes.

Work on seeing writing as a set of steps rather than a high-pressure situation that must produce perfection. Relax and enjoy communicating something you feel, or think, or have learned. Keep your mind on communication, and even if you are unsure about your writing now, you will begin to enjoy the results of your hard work.

## Building Your Skills

### Assignment 1

Define the following terms in your own words, and include examples where possible.

1. purpose  _____

_____

_____

2. audience  _____

_____

_____

3. SQ3R  _____

_____

_____

4. writing as a process  _____

_____

_____

5. prewriting  _____

_____

_____

6. drafting  _____

_____

_____

7. rewriting  _____

_____

_____

## Assignment 2

I really enjoy spending time alone. When I am alone, I listen to music, read magazines, and cook whatever I like whenever I like. I work a lot. I think the best is watching TV until late at night.

Can you identify the purpose of this paragraph? What do you think is the point the writer is trying to make? Can you tell who his audience is?

Rewrite the paragraph identifying a particular audience and purpose for the paragraph. Make any changes necessary to rewrite this paragraph so that it accomplishes *your* purpose for *your* audience.

purpose _____

_____

_____

audience _____

_____

_____

rewritten paragraph _____

_____

_____

_____

_____

_____

_____

_____

_____

_____

_____

### Assignment 3

In a letter to your instructor, describe the experiences you have had with writing or how you feel about being a student in a writing class. Then, reread your letter and look for changes you would need to make to send this letter to a close friend or family member. List the changes you would make, and beside each change, identify the reason it would be necessary. How did audience and purpose influence your decisions to make changes in this letter?

# READING A STUDENT ESSAY

## Peer Review Strategy: Reading for Purpose and Audience

When we edit or review the work of other writers, we also improve our ability to edit our own writing. As you look at another student's essay, you will be functioning as a reader and noticing the techniques that work, as well as those that do not work, for you as a reader. As you read this student essay, you will be reading to get your general reaction first, and then you will be looking specifically at how well this essay establishes its purpose and appeals to you as an audience. In addition, you will be increasing your ability to detect when your own writing has a clear purpose and appeals to a particular audience, as well as when it is not accomplishing your purpose or making your ideas clear for your reader.

The purpose in an essay is usually the author's point or reason for sharing his or her idea or experience. As a member of the reading audience, you may or may not understand this purpose. Furthermore, the essay may be intended for an audience that does not include you. Read the student essay below in two steps: first, read the entire essay and write a personal reaction or comment about the essay on the lines that follow; second, reread or skim the essay to determine the main purpose you think the author has in writing this essay and then try to determine the audience for whom she is most likely writing this essay.

### Unrealistic Images

#### by Candice Mayer

Most of today's women's magazines geared toward 17–38-year-old readers suggest by their articles that they promote feminist ideas. Most of the articles can be entertaining, informative, and interesting. Then why, when I look at the covers of these magazines and the                    1 many pages of advertisements, do I feel that they are really just trying to sell me an image of what I should look like?

Why do the owners and editors of these magazines feel they must bombard us with advertisements and photographs of women who aren't representative of most women? Many of the models have had breast augmentations or some other form of cosmetic surgery. Do most women assume if they buy this product or that product that they will look like the women selling the product? These women spend many hours with a professional makeup artist and hairstylist to look the way they do. 2

Many young women who may have poor self-images or who are vulnerable to anorexia or bulimia may be encouraged to try all the tricks for losing weight that are well-known in the modeling industry. They may believe the idea that in order to be successful, they have to be thin and beautiful. 3

When boys see these magazines starting at a very young age, they may also begin to believe that this is what all women should look like. All they see is the image of a beautiful woman—and this is all they see! They don't see women as real people with different personalities, shapes, and sizes. They begin to believe that women are only to be looked at and that their value is equal to their attractiveness. 4

The impression I get when I read these magazines is that all successful women must, as a prerequisite, be beautiful. They do not use pictures that reflect the kind of people reading their magazine; they always use pictures of beautiful models. 5

Who decided that these models are the standards to which we hold ourselves anyway? Is it the owners or editors of these magazines? Is it the consumer? Obviously beauty sells; the cosmetic and hair care 6

industry is a multi-billion dollar industry and growing
every year.

    I picked up a magazine at the supermarket rack          7
the other day and scanned the article headlines. One
of the headlines read, "What It Means to Be Neurotic."
How appropriate coming from a magazine that helps to
perpetuate phobias about how women should look.
Maybe if these magazines used a variety of women
who represent the women from different walks of life
and experience, we wouldn't be so neurotic—at least
not about our looks anyway.

## Building Your Skills

1. What reaction do you have to Mayer's essay, ideas, or point?

_____

_____

_____

_____

_____

_____

_____

_____

_____

_____

_____

2. What is Mayer's main point, and what does she want you to believe or understand about this point? What do you think is her reason for writing this essay?

_____

_____

_____

_____

_____

_____

_____

_____

_____

3. Describe the people who would be most likely to read and understand Mayer's essay. Do you think she is appealing more to one gender than to another? Find and list specific words or phrases that lead you to believe this.

_____

_____

_____

_____

_____

_____

_____

_____

_____

4. As if you were discussing Candice's paper with her, list three features of her essay that work very well or that really appeal to you as a reader. Then, recommend three changes she could make to improve her essay. Two examples have been provided for you.

---

### FEATURES THAT MAKE THIS ESSAY EFFECTIVE

1. Uses questions to stimulate reader interest
2. Example of standing in supermarket reading headlines

---

Describe three features that are effective for you as a reader:

a. _____

b. _____

c. _____

---

### IMPROVEMENTS OR CHANGES FOR A MORE EFFECTIVE ESSAY

1. Use statistics to demonstrate the number of readers
2. Use an example of an actual reader who was affected by these magazines

---

Describe three improvements or changes Mayer could make to create a more effective, interesting, or informative essay:

a. _____

b. _____

c. _____

# USING GRAMMAR: WHAT IS GRAMMAR?

When you hear the word *grammar,* what associations do you have with it? Do you have mostly negative or mostly positive feelings? Many people react negatively to this word. They feel as if grammar is a secret code they just cannot learn. Grammar is perhaps the most intimidating concept a student of writing faces, but it really does not need to be. First of all, the average student already knows a lot about grammar from reading and exposure to language. Second, **grammar** is simply a set of rules—nothing more, nothing less.

Language can be viewed in two ways: prescriptively or descriptively. A **prescriptive** view of language is one that tells speakers or writers how they *should* speak or write a specific language. A **descriptive** view describes how people *do* speak or write a specific language. A handbook that teaches Standard English is prescriptive because it tells readers how they should use punctuation, sentence structure, and so on. A dictionary, on the other hand, is descriptive. It defines words and offers information about how a word is currently being used. For example, the dictionary offers two pronunciations for the word *either.* If dictionaries were prescriptive, only one pronunciation of *either* would be given. But because people pronounce this word differently, the dictionary gives the language user a choice.

Learning Standard English grammar requires finding a prescriptive source and learning the recommended grammatical forms, but it does not require that you leave your old ways of expressing yourself behind. In fact, correcting others or trying to be grammatical all of the time will probably take away from your ability to communicate easily with others rather than enhancing it. Think of the process as adding to, not getting rid of, what you already know about language. In some cases, learning to write in Standard English can seem like learning a new language altogether. But remember, Standard English will help you communicate effectively with those who are accustomed to reading and writing it—teachers, employers, lawyers, businesspeople, and so forth.

Beginning to see grammar as a set of rules that change as language changes will help you understand that not only does grammar change, but the rules are determined by language use and language users. All languages have a grammar. Each one has acceptable and less acceptable forms. In fact, most languages have dialects that are simply changes in the "standard" rules. In this text, we will focus on Standard English as it is currently used—but a hundred years from now, the advice this book offers could be inaccurate.

Changes in language and grammar take place over long periods of time and often are the result of speakers of a language trying to express themselves more effectively. Since the goal of language is communication, grammar adjusts its conventions or rules to meet the needs of the speakers or writers who are using a specific form of a language such as English. If you are outside of a language group or if you have mostly practiced a different form of a language, you must use a common form of the language to communicate effectively with speakers or readers belonging to other groups. In almost all writing situations, the writer must use a language common to most of his or her readers. Most readers expect a form of English that is easy for them to understand; thus, if you are writing to an instructor, you should use a form that the instructor will find easy to comprehend. If you are writing to a close friend, a different form of language may be appropriate.

Although grammar is an important part of your writing, it is not the most important part of any piece of writing. If you were to read the words "I don't like he," you would easily recognize this as ungrammatical or nonstandard, but you would probably know basically what the phrase meant. Clear communication is influenced by grammar, but it is not wholly dependent upon it. More important, the focus of your efforts when you write should not be wholly on grammar or spelling. Many people who are not experienced with writing assume that if their writing is grammatical, it is good. They also assume that ungrammatical writing must be bad. The following passage, taken from Maya Angelou's book *Wouldn't Take Nothing for My Journey Now,* demonstrates effective writing:

> Content is of great importance, but we must not underrate the value of style. That is, attention must be paid to not only what is said but how it is said; to what we wear, as well as how we wear it. In fact, we should be aware of all we do and of how we do all that we do. (Angelou 27)

A handbook that teaches Standard English would recommend that a semicolon be followed by a complete sentence and that "to not only what" be changed to "not only to what is said but to how." Notice in the passage above that Angelou chooses to use a semicolon and to use the phrase "to not only what" even though they do not follow Standard English conventions. If effectiveness in a piece of writing is judged by how well that writing communicates an idea, then clearly this passage by Angelou, which communicates an idea, is effective even though to some it may not be grammatical.

Revising or editing your writing for grammar allows you to make choices such as the choice demonstrated by Angelou, who is a world-renowned writer and speaker. She uses grammatical conventions to suit the needs of her audience, and given the success of her books, she is doing something that works. Following the guidelines of a good grammar hand-book will keep your writing from being misunderstood by an instructor—but you should never mistake grammatical correctness for "good" writing, because writing need not always be perfectly grammatical to be effective.

As you begin writing for your class, try to focus first on what you want to say, organize and write down your ideas, and then look at whether or not what you have written follows the conventions of Standard English. Deter-mining whether or not something you have written is grammatical can be done by having a friend, tutor, or instructor read your paper, but ulti-mately, your goal should be to begin to see necessary changes yourself. Learning grammatical rules and conventions can benefit you if you learn to apply grammatical concepts to actual writing. For example, in this book you will learn about sentence parts that influence punctuation. By learning these concepts, you will more easily be able to determine whether or not a sentence requires a comma. You will learn how to use punctuation marks such as the semicolon and colon. By actually applying these ideas to your writing, you will have gained grammatical skills that can be used in essays for school, on the job, when applying for a job, or in writing a letter of complaint or a letter to the editor. In addition to learning punctuation in your English class or directly from an instructor, you can use other meth-ods to improve your own understanding and use of grammar.

### Using a Handbook

One of the best ways to learn about your own use and understanding of grammar is to look at your papers when they are returned by an instructor. If the instructor marks a grammatical problem, you can learn about that grammatical concept by looking it up in a handbook. All writers can bene-fit from a good handbook. Handbooks serve a variety of purposes:

> they define and describe parts of speech and grammatical concepts;
>
> they demonstrate rules of grammar so that writers can learn and apply them in their writing;
>
> they help students avoid plagiarism (the use of others' words or ideas without giving them proper credit);
>
> they provide other guidance, such as helping students distinguish between homonyms (words like *there, their, they're*).

Not all handbooks offer exactly the same options, so finding one that meets your needs as an individual writer is important. A handbook should also offer explanations and examples you find relatively easy to under-stand; otherwise, the guidance you receive really will not be very helpful.

The easiest way to find a good handbook is by browsing through the handbooks your school bookstore carries. Another way is by finding the handbooks your library has available and checking out one or two to see which is the most helpful. If you are using a word processor, many programs even have grammar checkers. Whatever source you choose, be sure to use it to review information about grammatical concepts that an instructor marks several times on one essay or a problem that is repeatedly marked on a series of papers.

For example, if your instructor marks "fragment" on your papers frequently, you could look up the word *fragment* in the index of your handbook; turn to the pages on fragments; read the discussion about fragments; then do the practice exercises to test your comprehension. If the section is not very clear, you might also consult another handbook or ask your instructor, a tutor, or a trusted friend for help. Whatever you do, do not simply keep repeating a usage pattern that is ineffective. If one instructor reacts negatively to the same grammar problem several times, other instructors or readers may as well. You might as well look up the concept and learn it now rather than waiting until later.

### Using Notecards or Rule Guides

Another helpful technique for learning grammar is using notecards or pages posted at your desk or favorite writing place that demonstrate concepts you find particularly difficult. For example, if you have trouble using commas, keep the rules and examples for using commas close by while you are writing. But, again, do not worry about grammar until your ideas are already on the page. Expect that all of your writing will need to be edited for ungrammatical usage. Everyone who writes—professional and novice alike—does this kind of editing. When you read your own writing for the appropriateness and clarity of what you have said, you become a more experienced and better writer almost immediately, not to mention a better reader.

### Keeping a Grammar Journal

A final idea for improving your use and understanding of grammar is to keep a grammar journal. Create a notebook, either on disk or in traditional form, and whenever you get a paper back, write down the sentences that include grammatical problems. Rewrite the sentences and write any rules or grammatical information that you need to know to write the sentence grammatically. For example, if a sentence has a comma problem, write the sentence, write the comma rule and any examples, then rewrite your sentence applying the rule. In addition to rewritten sentences, you might include any wording problems or rules that have been difficult for you in the past. The grammar journal eventually becomes your own personal handbook for writing.

## Building Your Skills

### Assignment 1

In the following sentences, test your knowledge of Standard English grammar. When a sentence is grammatical, write "G"; when a sentence is ungrammatical, write "UG." Then try to identify the problem. If you have difficulty, do not worry, because all of these concepts will be discussed in this text.

1. _____ When I think about the good times we have had.

2. _____ I don't have no more money to buy books; my books cost $120.

3. _____ Everyone ought to do their own homework.

4. _____ I like to fish and swim I don't like to eat fish and clean pools though.

5. _____ If only he could stay she would be much happier.

6. _____ Floyd enjoyed his job however he did not make much money.

7. _____ Los Angeles is enormous fun to visit and expensive.

8. _____ We went to the store, come home, and waiting for you to arrive.

9. _____ Henry bought a car from his mother that never ran.

10. _____ She wanted to not remember this day again.

### Assignment 2

For several days observe the different Englishes you use in your daily life. Notice especially the differences in the ways you speak or write to friends, family, employers, customers, teachers, and so on. When do you use speech that some of these groups would consider to be ungrammatical or inappropriate? When do you adjust your language to meet another standard? To understand the differences between the way you use grammar in speech and the way you use it in writing, make a list of the types of differences between your speech and writing by observing some of your writing and making notes after observing how you speak for a day or two. Identify one or two goals for improving your speaking or writing over the next few months. Make a note of this on an index card that you keep with your writing supplies. An example might be avoiding the use of double negatives such as "Don't got none" in your speech and writing and replacing this with "Don't have any." Making commitments such as "I will write properly" are not specific enough—try to focus on something you can change that will help you to communicate more effectively with a wider audience.

### Assignment 3

Which rules of Standard English confuse you the most? Identify a rule you want to learn more about (some possible topics include how to use commas or semicolons, how to use apostrophes, how to avoid writing sentence fragments or run-ons—or ask your instructor for a topic that best suits your writing ability), and then keep a journal or notebook that includes the rule or rules, examples from your papers, practice sentences, and/or examples from magazine or newspaper articles. Consult a handbook or ask your instructor to clarify the rule or rules, and try some examples in your own writing so that you can become more comfortable using whatever you have chosen.

## SEEING THE CONNECTIONS: APPLYING YOUR SKILLS

### Assignment 1

Read the following paragraph carefully and note the underlined words indicating ungrammatical usage.

> Choosing a new car can be a daunting task. Not only do you have to learn to deal with salespeople, but one must understand the whole financing process. If you are naive, a buyer may end up with the worst car on the lot for the most money. If you want a good deal a buyer must do his or her homework.

Find at least two handbooks, either by sharing with friends, going to a local or school library, or using books supplied in class by your instructor. Look up "person" or "shift in person."

Write the definition that each book gives for shifts in person on a piece of paper. Then evaluate each explanation. Which one is written so that you can understand it the easiest? Which one provides the best examples? Which seems to be the best choice for a writing student who may need assistance with this concept? Rewrite the paragraph following the advice one of the handbooks offers for eliminating the shifts in person.

Finally, write a short explanation answering the following question:

Which handbook would you choose to use for guidance in writing your future papers?

### Assignment 2

Find three examples of writing (magazine articles, essays from this book, newspaper articles). Compare the audience for which each of these pieces seems to be written. To determine the intended audience, look at the grammar, the complexity of the sentences, the words, and the length. Write a sentence or two that summarizes the point of each article and then comment on how persuasive or convincing this essay or article is for you as a reader. Are you part of the intended audience? How does this affect your reading?

### Assignment 3

Read Amy Tan's "Mother Tongue" (p. 9) and answer the following questions in a group or on your own: What process do you think Tan used to write her speech? What does she tell us about her writing process in her speech? What dialects or grammars does Tan discuss? How many different forms of language does Tan use in her presentation? Write a discussion in one or two pages based on one of the options below.

**Option 1:**  Write a description of the Englishes you have learned to use (family language, baby talk, special words or commands for pets, language including gestures, language within a love relationship, moving between two or more languages); identify the ways each of them communicates effectively; then discuss any biases you think people may have against some of the language you use.

**Option 2:**  Have you ever judged someone based on that person's use of language? Describe some of the judgments you have made about someone else's use of language and identify the reasons for your judgments, as well as the reactions these judgments caused in you and others. After reading Tan's essay, do you think your judgments were justified or unfair?

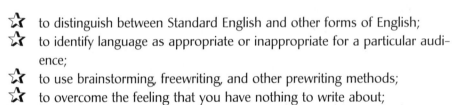

# Chapter 2

# *Getting Started*

In this chapter you will learn

★ to distinguish between Standard English and other forms of English;
★ to identify language as appropriate or inappropriate for a particular audience;
★ to use brainstorming, freewriting, and other prewriting methods;
★ to overcome the feeling that you have nothing to write about;
★ to distinguish between sentences and nonsentences;
★ to identify nouns and verbs in sentences.

Take a moment to answer the following questions:

1. Describe the language used most often in your community or school.

_____

_____

_____

2. What words and phrases do you use the most?

_____

_____

_____

3. How comfortable do you feel when you speak with your friends and family? How comfortable are you when you speak with professionals in a particular field (lawyers, doctors, teachers, interviewers/employers, and so on)?

_____

_____

_____

4. On what occasions do you adjust the language you speak in some way?

_____

_____

_____

# LEARNING AND USING LANGUAGE

Language is such an essential part of our everyday lives that we tend to forget or ignore its complicated nature. Language has many varieties: verbal and nonverbal, standard and nonstandard, socially acceptable and socially unacceptable. Each speaker/writer determines how appropriate a form of language is for addressing his or her audience. Most cues for using, evaluating, and distinguishing language are learned. We learn language from our surroundings, from people, from reading and writing, and from our culture.

### Verbal and Nonverbal Communication

**Nonverbal** communication includes our mannerisms, our body language, our cultural understanding of gestures and facial expressions, and, of course, our presentation of ourselves to the world. Sometimes we even communicate ideas or thoughts we would rather keep to ourselves.

**Verbal** communication can be spoken or written in nature and shares some characteristics with nonverbal communication in its ability to be understood. In order for a person to understand another person, verbal or nonverbal signals must be interpreted correctly. If we misinterpret an angry look, we might think the person with whom we are communicating is not angry at all. Likewise, if we fail to understand a word or concept in a letter, we may completely misinterpret what the person who wrote the letter meant to say. Being unable to communicate or understand meaning is one of the possible frustrations inherent in all language—written or spoken.

The major difference between what we say or hear and what we read or write is that the spoken word allows us to use nonverbal cues to accompany our spoken message. A speaker may use hand gestures or facial expressions, for example, to make a joke funnier than it would be on paper. A writer, on the other hand, has only his or her words on the page to express meaning. What does this mean for the writer? While writing tends to have more permanence than spoken words, the writer must also be more specific and clear because readers cannot ask for clarification or restatement. The writer must use language and techniques that make his or her point clear. Unlike a listener, who may feel compelled to listen politely, a reader is unlikely to keep reading for the sake of good manners.

### Standard and Nonstandard Language

English as a language varies in the ways is it spoken, pronounced, and communicated. Each of us speaks English in a slightly different way, using different words and techniques to communicate our message. We also share patterns of speaking and writing with others; sometimes we use patterns of a small group with which we identify, sometimes patterns of a larger, more universal group. Depending on where a person lives, how well-educated a person is, and whether a person grew up speaking English, a speaker may use a variety of words, phrases, or grammatical constructions that may or may not be common to most speakers of English.

When you are with family and friends, which would you be most likely to say?

> I don't have any.
> I ain't got any.
> I don't have none.

Each of these is used by people to express basically the same idea, but different groups of English speakers would have clear opinions about which "sounds right" or is the "proper" way to communicate this idea. Their choices (and yours) reflect the types of language experiences they (and you) have had, as well as the richness of our language, used by many speakers with many different results. Is there a right way or wrong way to communicate this idea? Many would say with fervor, "Yes!" But, if our goal is truly communication, each of the above statements communicates the idea adequately. So if communication does not determine which is "correct," what does? The appropriateness of a statement or phrase to a given situation or audience actually determines what is or is not an acceptable method for communicating an idea. If you said, "I ain't got any" to a parent who also uses this phrase regularly, obviously this would be an acceptable method of stating your idea. If, however, you used this phrase in a formal essay for your English class, your instructor might have another reaction. Which phrase do you think would be appropriate in an essay? Why?

**Standard English** is the form of English most students are taught in school. It is a language used in the media, in government, and in business; thus, a person wanting to write for a large audience at work, in school, or in a profession would need to communicate in the most widely accepted form—Standard English. Does this mean you should unlearn, erase, or try to forget the other dialects or forms of English you have learned to use? Should you force yourself to use Standard English at absolutely all times? Of course, that would be impractical; besides, you would not want to use Standard English when it is more appropriate to use your dialect or the form of communication with which you are most comfortable, especially with family and friends. And you certainly wouldn't want to correct family and friends if they did not use Standard English. All forms of language have a place and purpose; the key is learning the appropriate forms to use in a given situation. If the goal of language is to communicate, then using the form of language that allows you to communicate most effectively is the best policy.

With communication as our ultimate goal, then, how do we determine whether a statement "sounds right"? What, for example, makes one set of words work together and another seem jumbled or nonsensical? Rules of grammar we have learned through listening, reading, and writing make this decision. When you hear the word "grammar," how does it make you feel? Many people feel nervous or insecure about grammar and think of it as the *right* way to speak or write. But this brings up several important questions—Who decides what is the *right* way? Is there one *right* way?

**Grammar,** when we take all the right and wrong out of it, is simply a set of rules that govern the way words are combined in a language. Each language has a grammar; for that matter, each dialect has rules or acceptable and unacceptable methods of making a statement or asking a question. We learn grammar from parents, friends, teachers, television, and reading materials. Many times, teachers present a different grammar than we have learned elsewhere. Whose is the right grammar then? Grammar is a set of rules—but just as you might break a speeding law in an emergency (some would say this is an appropriate response), different grammars (or sets of rules) are appropriate in different situations. In this text, we will be studying Standard English grammar, a grammar used in writing for business, school, professional or legal documents, and, less frequently, in speaking.

Most people use slang, shortened forms of words and phrases, and even some incomplete sentences when they speak; speaking is almost always less standardized than writing. Why study grammar at all, then? One reason is that understanding Standard English grammar will be important to revising your essays for a general audience and will help you use the appropriate forms to address your audience. Essentially, grammar, like the other concepts we've learned in this chapter, is a matter of knowing the appropriate form in a given situation.

Appropriate forms in English grammar can sometimes be difficult to determine because they change over time, they depend on the audience, and they even depend on your location. A good handbook, though, can recommend the form that is currently understood as Standard English. A dictionary can also be a good resource for finding the most appropriate form of a word. But remember, language is always in a state of change, so follow what you know to be the expectations of your audience.

Learning language can be challenging for a very ironic reason—most people are to some extent learning what they already know. In other words, most people have a variety of language skills, but in a language class they learn terms, grammatical rules, and techniques that may seem unfamiliar because the language they are used to may be somewhat different from the form of English they are being taught. To benefit the most from a book like this one or from taking an English class, you must be willing to study language open-mindedly and to learn new methods even though you already know a great deal about the language. A reasonable goal might be to add to your existing knowledge to gain greater language opportunities and options.

# READING AN ESSAY

## Strategy for Reading: Annotating as You Read

Sometimes reading can seem like a dull activity; in fact, you may find your mind wandering or you may find that after you have read an entire essay, you have no idea what it says. One way to read actively and remember what you read is to annotate. Annotating means taking notes in the margins that tell you important points or ideas in the essay. For example, the words written in the margins here summarize this paragraph in a few words.

Annotating means taking notes in the margins

To annotate an essay, write a comment in the margin for each paragraph. The comment can be any form of reaction, but the most helpful annotations are probably summaries of each paragraph or important definitions or questions. Anything you want to remember should be part of your annotation. In addition, annotations are most helpful when they are written in your own words rather than copied straight from the paragraph. To write something in your own words, you have to understand it. If you prefer not to write directly on your book, you might also try using Post-it notes that you stick in the margins and remove later.

As you annotate, you may also want to include quick reference notes in the margins where major points are presented or where major ideas are connected. Develop a system for note-taking where "ex." means example, "imp." means important idea, and so on. Your system can be whatever is easiest for you to remember.

In the essay below, space has been provided for you to annotate each paragraph. In the space, write a point that Roberts makes in his essay, a summary of each paragraph, a question that you have as you read, or anything else that will help you understand or remember the essay.

---

### BEFORE YOU READ

1. Of what communities do you consider yourself to be a member (school, family, neighborhood, city, state, ethnic group, gender, etc.)? How does the language used in these communities differ?
2. How do you treat people who speak differently from you? Do you ever find the way someone else speaks funny or irritating?
3. Do you find people who speak differently from you more or less believable?

## Speech Communities*

### by Paul Roberts

Speech communities are formed by many features: age, geography, education, occupation, social position. Young people speak differently from old people, Kansans differently from Virginians, Yale graduates differently from Dannemora graduates. Now let us pose a delicate question: Aren't some of these speech communities better than others? That is, isn't better language heard in some than in others?

Well, yes, of course. One speech community is always better than all the rest. This is the group in which one happens to find oneself. The writer would answer unhesitatingly that the noblest, loveliest, purest English is that heard in the Men's Faculty Club of San Jose State College, San Jose, California. He would admit, of course, that the speech of some of the younger members leaves something to be desired; that certain recent immigrants from Harvard, Michigan, and other foreign parts need to work on the laughable oddities lingering in their speech; and that members of certain departments tend to introduce a lot of queer terms that can only be described as jargon. But in general, the English of the Faculty Club is ennobling and sweet.

As a practical matter, good English is whatever English is spoken by the group in which one moves contentedly and at ease. To the bum on Main Street in Los Angeles, good English is the language of other L.A. bums. Should he wander onto the campus of UCLA, he would find the talk there unpleasant, confusing, and comical. He might agree, if pressed, that the college man speaks "correctly" and he doesn't. But in his heart, he knows better. He wouldn't talk like them college jerks if you paid him.

If you admire the language of other speech communities more than you do your own, the reasonable hypothesis

1

2

3

4

---

*\*Source:* Roberts, Paul. "Speech Communities." From *Understanding English* by Paul Roberts. Copyright © 1958 by Paul Roberts. Reprinted by permission of Addison Wesley Educational Publishers, Inc.

is that you are dissatisfied with the community itself. It is not precisely other speech that attracts you but the people who use the speech. Conversely, if some language strikes you as unpleasant or foolish or rough, it is presumably because the speakers themselves seem so.

To many people, the sentence "Where is he at?" sounds bad. It is bad, they would say, in and of itself. The sounds are bad. But this is very hard to prove. If "Where is he at?" is bad because it had bad sound combinations, then presumably "Where is the cat?" or "Where is my hat?" are just as bad, yet no one thinks them so. Well, then, "Where is he at?" is bad because it uses too many words. One gets the same meaning from "Where is he?" so why add the *at?* True. Then "He going with us?" is a better sentence than "Is he going with us?" You don't really need the *is,* so why put it in?

5

Certainly there are some features of language to which we can apply the terms *good* and *bad, better* and *worse.* Clarity is usually better than obscurity; precision is better than vagueness. But these are not often what we have in mind when we speak of good and bad English. If we like the speech of upper-class Englishmen, the presumption is that we admire upper-class Englishmen—their characters, culture, habits of mind. Their sounds and words simply come to connote the people themselves and become admirable therefore. If we knew the same sounds and words from people who were distasteful to us, we would find the speech ugly.

6

This is not to say that correctness and incorrectness do not exist in speech. They obviously do, but they are relative to the speech community—or communities—in which one operates. As a practical matter, correct speech is that which sounds normal or natural to one's comrades. Incorrect speech is that which evokes in them discomfort or hostility or disdain.

7

## Building Your Skills

### Focus on Words

Look up the following words or parts of phrases in a dictionary. Consult the preceding essay and identify the meaning that best fits the way the author uses the word in this essay. Each word or phrase is followed by the number of the paragraph in which it appears.

| | |
|---|---|
| noblest (2) | hypothesis (4) |
| oddities (2) | presumably (4) |
| lingering (2) | obscurity (6) |
| queer terms (2) | vagueness (6) |
| ennobling (2) | comrades (7) |
| contentedly (3) | disdain (7) |

### Focus on the Message

1. What does Roberts mean when he writes that each of us likes our own language or dialect the best?
2. What does Roberts mean when he states, "if some language strikes you as unpleasant or foolish or rough, it is presumably because the speakers themselves seem so" (para. 4)?
3. What is a speech community? How is "correctness" relative to speech communities?
4. What is Roberts's purpose in this essay? Who seems to be his primary audience?
5. Do you believe people have language prejudices and judge others based on their language? In what ways are these judgments fair or unfair? Accurate or inaccurate?

---

### READING STRATEGY NOTE

When did annotating help you to read more effectively?

Did it ever distract you?

Do you think this technique may be helpful for reading your other textbooks?

---

# TECHNIQUES FOR WRITING: PREWRITING— TURNING OFF THE CENSOR IN YOUR HEAD

Everyone who writes at some time has a feeling that what he or she writes may not be good enough or clear enough. Sometimes this is productive and helpful, but when this takes place before a writer can write a draft or even start writing, this fear becomes unproductive. Imagine for a minute that just as television stations have a censor, your head also has a censor who keeps your ideas from coming out. The censor sends messages like "this isn't good enough," or "that's a silly idea," or "people will laugh at this idea." In other words, the censor in your head keeps you from producing any ideas for fear that the ideas you do produce will not be good enough.

Before a writer can begin to write seriously, he or she must have something to say. Without a message or purpose, a writer cannot be fully prepared to write. But getting ideas sometimes requires turning off or suspending the censor in your head because having ideas is necessary to the process of writing. A writer need not know exactly what to say in a whole paragraph or essay, but a clear idea or topic (often called a thesis or thesis statement) makes the writing process more rewarding and easier. However, rarely does a writer begin easily with a developed idea. Instead writers use invention techniques to generate ideas before beginning to write. In fact, many writers consider this a vital part of their writing routine and use prewriting or invention strategies before beginning any writing project.

Many prewriting or invention techniques can help you generate and develop ideas during the writing process. You may want to try each of the techniques described in this chapter to see which one works best for you, or you may want to use a combination of techniques as a part of your writing routine.

### Listing
Listing ideas is a process many writers use when they simply want to get a sense of possible topics or ideas within one topic. A topic or idea list may be created gradually over a few hours or with a three- or five-minute time limit. To create, write down your ideas freely in list form. Even if an idea seems off topic, it might be a good idea to list it anyway to preserve it in case you change your topic later. Another listing technique is to create multiple lists about different parts of the same topic to narrow down the focus or thesis of an essay or paragraph. Look at the following examples:

| TYPES OF MUSIC | DESCRIPTION OF ROCK 'N' ROLL |
|---|---|
| rap<br>alternative<br>rock 'n' roll<br>country<br>classical | years (1950s–now)<br>very loud<br>classic and current forms<br>offshoots include heavy metal,<br>alternative |

A student could begin with music as his or her topic, and then by listing ideas that student could write about the current forms of rock 'n' roll or the similarities and differences between classic and current rock 'n' roll.

### Brainstorming and Clustering

Brainstorming and clustering are similar to listing and to each other in technique and result. Both involve jotting down ideas on paper, can be used with a time limit, and help get ideas flowing. You might try challenging the linear or top-down look of the list by beginning in the middle or lower corner of a page.

To brainstorm, write a topic (an assigned topic or one you choose on your own) in the center or lower half of a blank piece of paper. Give yourself five minutes and write literally everything that comes to mind. This exercise works best when you allow yourself to write freely whatever comes to mind. Envision that a censor lives inside of you and prevents you from writing whatever you feel, either because of fear or because of a desire for privacy. This censor also prevents the free flow of ideas. To get beyond or past this censor, allow yourself in this very safe environment to write anything and everything that comes to mind for five minutes. No one should ever read this, so you really can write anything you want! After five minutes, stop writing and look at your brainstorm for possible writing ideas. Choose several possibilities. If you still are not sure about your thesis or topic, choose one of the ideas and brainstorm further by breaking it down or narrowing it into a more specific topic.

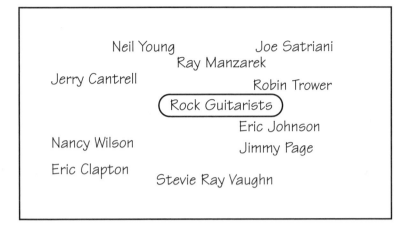

The brainstorm above shows a variety of guitarists. The writer could then create a new brainstorm focusing on one guitarist, a comparative brainstorm about two of the guitarists, or a brainstorm on guitar playing styles that classifies the artists into categories. Or the writer could have an idea and simply sit down to write a first draft.

Clustering is just like brainstorming except that the writer groups ideas into categories while brainstorming. The brainstorm above, if it were done as a cluster, might look like this:

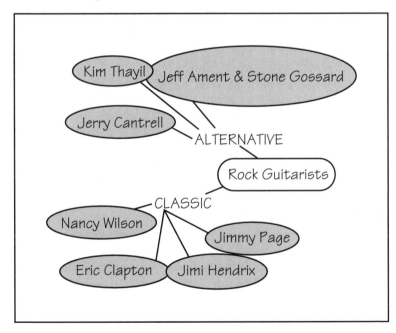

Clustering works best for writers who begin categorizing and figuring out a form while generating the topic. If you are intimidated by writing or are unsure about what to write, try brainstorming without clustering, and then when you become a bit more comfortable with generating ideas and beginning the writing process, try clustering.

### Freewriting

Freewriting is an exercise that many writers do to loosen up and start writing. Initially, sometimes writers feel nervous about beginning to write; freewriting helps them begin writing without worrying about form and punctuation. In fact, some writers allow themselves to freewrite without using any punctuation at all as a way of focusing purely on their ideas. To freewrite, begin with some paper and a timer or a friend who can time you. For ten minutes do nothing but write. You might find it helpful to begin with a topic or idea you came up with in brainstorming, but you can simply begin by writing anything that comes to mind. In fact, once you begin, do not stop to correct your writing in any way, and if you do come to a point where you have nothing else to write, literally write "I do not know what to write" or some other phrase until something comes to you.

> I'm not sure what to write but I think beginning with the topic for our class assignment may be a good idea. We are supposed to write about an important choice we have made in our lives. My best idea is to write about the experience I once had with choosing whether or not to move away from home to a four-year university. I really wanted to move away but I knew that I would have to work a lot harder to pay the extra costs such as more tuition, rent, my own food, etc. Even though I'm not always happy that I chose to keep living at home with my parents, I do feel that I am safer and better off than I would have been at a large school.

Freewriting allows you to express your ideas just as they come to you. Notice that the freewriting sample above addresses a specific topic. Of course, writing an essay to turn in to an instructor would be somewhat different; however, the idea or focus for that essay could be the major idea discussed here. The goal of freewriting is to get ideas on paper and to loosen up, not to write your essay more quickly. Using freewriting, though, will help many writers begin essays with less hesitation and with greater ease and comfort. Try freewriting for ten minutes before starting your next essay to see if this prewriting technique works for you.

### The 5W and H Questions

Journalists ask themselves *what, when, where, who, why,* and *how* to make sure that they have answered the pertinent questions for their reading audience. When you are writing about an actual event that took place, you might try answering these questions to get your ideas on paper and then forming these facts into an essay designed for your audience. The other way to use this technique is to test what you have already written to see if it answers these vital questions—but this technique would fall into the realm of rewriting, rather than prewriting.

```
What:   a car accident
When:   January 15, 1995
Where:  on the highway (Interstate 10)
Who:    me
Why:    the roads were slick because of rain; I was driving too
        fast
How:    I smashed the left side of my car when I ran off the road
```

The example above demonstrates this technique in its simplest form; however, if you wanted to develop your ideas more fully, you could add many details, creating an outline of the facts and descriptions necessary for your essay. This technique, of course, works best for essays written to describe an event.

### Outlining

Another technique for generating ideas and structuring them at the same time is outlining. An outline can be traditional, illustrating the relationship of major and minor topics using capital or lower-case letters and numbers, or an outline can be informal, using any system that works for you. For prewriting, the informal outline is adjustable so that you can add or delete ideas without worrying about formal outline structure, thereby promoting the free flow of ideas. Look at the example below:

---

### GOING BACK TO SCHOOL

Introduction
    many emotions:   frightened, excited, overwhelmed
    starting on the right foot:   getting an advisor, learning about the school

Body
    describe my sleepless first week and then how I began to like school

Conclusion
    describe how my first semester was a success: grades, learning, making friends

---

Notice the way this outline prepares the writer for the overall structure of ideas, as well as the progression of ideas within the essay. It could, however, just as easily take the form below:

---

### GOING BACK TO SCHOOL

Describe my feelings at first:
    I was frightened, excited, overwhelmed
    I needed an advisor, a map, and a tutor
Describe my sleepless first week and then how I began to like school
Describe how my first semester was a success: grades, learning, making friends
Describe how the benefits of school outweigh the disadvantages

---

This outline, unlike the first one, emphasizes the overall point of the essay over the actual form of the essay. Another technique that outlining is particularly good for is working out relationships between ideas. You can use outlines to determine the best sequence for your ideas either before or after writing a draft.

### Interviewing/Talking to a Friend

One technique for building your interest and knowledge base about a topic is interviewing or talking with others. Formal interviews typically consist of asking predetermined interview questions that help you gain knowledge and a professional perspective from an authority in a particular field. Informal discussions may take place among friends or could be induced by surveying fellow students' opinions or reactions to a subject. This can be an especially helpful technique when you must write about a topic with which you are not very familiar or comfortable.

### Reading

Like interviews, reading can assist you when you need more information or background about a topic. By reading about a topic you may gain new insight or develop a greater interest in that topic. In addition, reading will help you begin to see the variety of approaches to a particular topic. Writing responses to the materials you read might produce the beginnings of an essay or at least provide a direction you can use for guidance in writing your essay.

Be careful, when you use other people's research or ideas, to give them credit by mentioning their names and the source for your information (for example, an interview, a magazine article). Some instructors may require a specific way to give credit, so ask your instructor for guidance if you plan to use this technique or if you plan to use information you have acquired from a source (see Chapter 10, pages 309–311).

Prewriting can take many forms and can produce many different results. Each writer will prefer to use a couple of techniques that work best given his or her writing routine. As you respond to the writing assignments in this book and in your class, experiment with these techniques to find which are most comfortable and productive for you. Try to incorporate at least one of them into your regular writing routine, and work to establish a routine for essays written in-class and out-of-class.

## Building Your Skills

### Assignment 1

Brainstorm about the choices you have made in your life. For five minutes, write down every idea just as it comes to you. When you have written for five minutes or longer, choose one of the ideas you have listed.

Divide a piece of paper into two columns and list the benefits this choice has brought to your life; on the other side, list the difficulties this choice has caused in your life. Write a paragraph or a page (or more) that describes this important choice you have made in your life. Discuss how your life or views have changed because of this choice.

### Assignment 2

Freewrite for seven minutes about a challenge that you have recently faced. As you write, remember that in freewriting you should write everything as it comes to you, and you should not pay attention to spelling, grammar, or the structure of what you are writing. Allow your ideas to flow freely and without any particular order. When you have completed this task, read what you have written. Look for the feelings you expressed about this event and the reasons it was so challenging. Write a paragraph or more that addresses the following:

> Describe a recent challenge you faced, how you felt about it, and how you dealt with this challenge. Include specific details about your feelings and the reasons this was a challenge.

### Assignment 3

Spend time observing a place or incident on your school campus. Have another person (perhaps someone in your class) observe this same place or incident. Write down your perceptions in a short paragraph or page, and have your partner do the same. Discuss your perceptions with your partner, comparing the feelings and events each of you observed. Write a paragraph or page that explains to your partner why you had the perceptions you did. For example, if you witnessed an argument and your partner witnessed a discussion, explain to your partner why this was an argument or at least why you thought it was at first. When you finish, compare paragraphs and highlight or underline the *what, when, where, who, why,* and *how* you describe.

## READING A STUDENT ESSAY

### Peer Review Strategy: Using Sensory Details

When a writer tells us about a place, event, or situation, he or she must describe the scene or event so that we become involved and interested. The easiest and most effective way to create interest for a reader, in fact, is to involve his or her senses. The senses of sight, smell, hearing, touch, and taste can evoke memories and associations and can spark curiosity and reaction.

When you help another person rewrite by reading and reacting to what he or she has written, you may think "this essay is okay, but it needs more . . . more something." Often what is missing is the very thing that makes an essay work for the reader—the emotion. The essay is probably missing an appeal to the reader and to the reader's senses. The sensations the writer felt during the experience must be communicated on paper so that the reader can read, relate to, and feel these sensations too.

Some sensory words are listed below for each sense.

| | |
|---|---|
| **sight** | bright |
| | glistening |
| **sound** | blasting |
| | chirping |
| **touch** | tingling |
| | velvety |
| **taste** | syrupy |
| | bittersweet |
| **smell** | roses |
| | rotten fruit |

How do these words communicate a sensation? Can you identify with the sensations each of these evokes? Writers often use more than one word to communicate a sensation—they describe sensual details so that we actually begin to experience what it is that they are describing.

As you read the following essay, underline or list on paper the details that appeal to your senses and that set the scene for this essay. Think about how these details make you feel while you read this essay.

A Time to Listen

by Lorenzo S. Cruz

Everywhere I have ever gone, or will ever go,                    1
there has always been one thing in common with these
places. I have spent my entire life around trees,
plants, things of nature. Many different shapes and

sizes. I have even worked in the profession of landscaping during my younger years. I have seen trees, lots of trees, with their limbs and leaves. Not too long ago though, on my walk to and from class, I took a second to stop and pick up a fallen leaf that caught my eye. On the ground it seemed like just a plain green leaf, but as I took a closer look, I noticed there was more to that single leaf.

I remember as a kid drawing many crayon pictures of trees and bushes that were made up of one-color leaves: green for live leaves, brown for dead leaves. As I looked closer at the leaf in my hand, I noticed something different. The coloring on the outer edge of the leaf was a deep burgundy. Moving toward the center, though, the dominating color changed to a shiny green. A two-colored leaf—if I had known that information as a kid producing crayon pictures, I would have been very frustrated.

2

The shape was a lot simpler, a basic round with a little point at the top. Toward the top on the sides ran little ridges, nice and uniform. I wondered why they were there. Maybe these served as protection or as special distinguishing markings that made it look different from the other leaves nearby, similar to the shapes and sizes of humans when compared to other humans. Some tall and others short, all features help us to establish individualism and set us apart from others. Maybe this leaf is making its own unique fashion statement, or perhaps, it's just a plain, ordinary, everyday Joe. Nothing special or extravagant, so why was this leaf so noticeable to me? I really do not know why.

3

I wonder if it decided to call my name, and I merely responded. Whatever the leaf was thinking or not thinking at the time intrigues me. I ponder the thousands and millions of leaves that go unnoticed. I think about the leaf that is falling at this very

4

moment outside this classroom. Is there more to it than just a plain old leaf that has grown weary and is now joining the ground from which it came? Was there more to it that I will never know because I did not take the time to look or listen? Will I ever hear what the leaves are trying to tell me, what they may be trying to show me, or will they always be "just leaves"?

## Building Your Skills

1. How many words or phrases did you underline or list? Divide them into categories of sight, sound, touch, taste, smell. How does Cruz's use of sensory details affect your ability to read and relate to this essay?

_____

_____

_____

_____

_____

_____

_____

_____

_____

2. What is Cruz's main point? What do you think is his reason for writing this essay?

_____

_____

_____

_____

_____

_____

_____

_____

_____

_____

3. Who do you think is Cruz's primary audience? Find and list specific words or phrases that lead you to believe this.

_____

_____

_____

_____

_____

_____

_____

_____

_____

4. As if you were discussing Lorenzo's paper with him, list three features of his essay that work very well or that really appeal to you as a reader. Then, recommend three changes he could make to improve his essay. How could he add more sensory details and where would more details be effective?

Describe three features that are effective for you as a reader:

a. _____

b. _____

c. _____

Describe three improvements or changes Lorenzo could make to create a more effective, interesting, or informative essay:

a. _____

b. _____

c. _____

# USING GRAMMAR: DEFINING THE SENTENCE

A sentence is a group of words that makes a complete thought. Many people learn this statement as a definition for the word *sentence*. Using this method to tell a sentence from a nonsentence (a group of words that is not a sentence), however, can be difficult because it does not specifically tell you what to look for or what must be included for a group of words to be a sentence. You might ask, "How do I tell when my sentence is complete?"

Perhaps a better way to look at a sentence is to observe its essential parts. Look at the following group of words:

Bob parked his car on the street.

What does this group of words have that a group that is not a sentence is missing? First, this sentence has a **subject.** "Bob," the subject, is the focus of the sentence or the person the sentence is about. This sentence also has a **verb**—a word showing what the subject did or the subject's physical state. What did Bob do? Bob "parked."

subject   verb

Bob parked his car on the street.

This sentence contains other parts, but notice that these two words could stand as a sentence without the other parts:

subject   verb

Bob parked.

A **sentence,** then, can be defined as a group of words with a subject and verb that presents a complete thought. It may also have other parts, but it must have these essential parts to be called a sentence. One way to remember this definition is by writing it on a 3″ × 5″ notecard so that you can refer back to it while you are learning this concept. In addition, learning more about subjects and verbs might make detecting these items in a sentence an easier task.

The subject in a sentence is often a one-word noun, such as "Bob" in the sentences above. A **noun,** as you may already know, is a person, place, or thing. Sometimes sentences have more than one noun, but not every noun in a sentence serves as a subject. In the following examples, look at the subject or subjects and also notice the other nouns in the sentences.

subject                        noun

The car was parked in an alley.

"Car" in the sentence above is the subject or what the sentence is about, but "alley" is not in a subject position and could be taken completely out of the sentence. "The car was parked" would make sense and stand alone as a sentence. Thus, "alley" is a noun, but it is not a subject in the sentence.

Sentences can also have more than one subject or verb and sometimes have combinations of subjects and verbs. Notice in the following sentence that two of the nouns are subjects, while a third is not a subject in the sentence.

subject        subject                        noun

The car and the bus were parked in the alley.

Since both the car and the bus are parked, they are both subjects in this sentence. As with subjects, we can have more than one verb in a sentence. In the following sentence, notice that both verbs tell what the subject did.

subject   verb        noun        verb        noun

The man parked his car and took the bus.

Both verbs tell what the man (the subject of the sentence) did. The number of subjects and verbs may vary, but the key is to look for subject and verb groupings when there are two or more subjects, two or more verbs, or both. Punctuation rules sometimes depend on this. In the next example, observe the subjects and verbs in both sentences.

| sentence one | | sentence two | |
| --- | --- | --- | --- |
| subject | verb | subject | verb |

Sue prepared her letter. Kathy mailed her letter a day later.

| | one sentence | | |
| --- | --- | --- | --- |
| subject | subject | verb | verb |

Sue and Kathy prepared and mailed their letters on the same day.

The first example has two sentences, each with a subject and a verb. The second example has a single sentence with multiple subjects and verbs. Each is equally correct.

Another way that you can learn to see the essential parts in a sentence is through observing what you read a bit more carefully. Most writers use a variety of sentence types in their work, so as you read, you get a chance to see how writers actually use sentences and sentence structure in their work.

In the following example paragraphs taken from the essay "Aria: A Memoir of a Bilingual Childhood," the writer, Richard Rodriguez, uses a variety of sentence types. Some have single subjects and a verb; others have subject and verb combinations. Read the paragraphs and observe the subjects and verbs, as well as how the sentences are constructed. One paragraph has the subjects underlined and the verbs printed in bold. Notice that there are several sentence parts that aren't marked. These will be the focus of chapters to come. For right now, try underlining the subjects and circling the verbs in the second paragraph, and check them with another student or with your instructor. Also notice how the grammar and structure of the sentences influences how easily you are able to read these paragraphs.

An <u>accident</u> of geography **sent** me to a school where all my classmates were white and many were the children of doctors and lawyers and business executives. On that first day of school, my <u>classmates</u> **must** certainly **have been** uneasy to find themselves apart from their families, in the first institution of their lives. But <u>I</u> **was** astonished. <u>I</u> **was** fated to be the "problem student" in class.

The nun said, in a friendly but oddly impersonal voice: "Boys and girls, this is Richard Rodriguez." (I heard her sound it out: *Rich-heard Road-ree-guess*). It was the first time I had heard anyone say my name in English. "Richard" the nun repeated more slowly, writing my name down in her book. Quickly I turned to see my mother's face dissolve in a watery blur behind the pebbled-glass door.

Sentence structure is a vital part of writing and communication. You already know a great deal about it, even if you may not be familiar with the terms and concepts we will study in this book. While you speak and write, you use these concepts without even realizing it. As you practice using them and learning the technical terms in this text, you will become a better writer and reader and develop a better understanding of the language you use daily and the standard form that is its counterpart.

## Building Your Skills

### Assignment 1

<u>Underline</u> the subjects and ◯circle◯ the verbs in the following sentences.

1. The cat knocked the flowerpot over.

2. Henry and Philip saw a movie with their friends.

3. She knew that it was true love.

4. The owner wrote a big check and made a lot of money.

5. Susie and Blanca were good friends and enjoyed going places together.

6. Movies are fun to watch, but I hate when other people talk during a movie.

7. A good writing handbook provides grammar rules, gives advice about research papers, and identifies writing pitfalls to avoid.

8. The desk and the table need to be cleaned and delivered by tomorrow.

9. We went for a ride in the park, and then we went home.

10. We went for a ride in the park, took a walk at the mall, and then came home.

Fill in your own subjects and verbs in the following sentences.

After the concert, _____ had a good time.
subject

_____ and _____ had a lot of fun.
subject                                          subject

They all _____ to the park and _____
verb                                                 subject

took them to a fancy restaurant. Whenever _____
subject

and _____ go out, they _____ fun.
subject                                     verb

When we _____ to the park, _____
verb                                             verb

concerts, and _____ time together, we have a
verb

great time.

## Assignment 2

Define the word *sentence*. Write a sentence. Find the features that make this group of words a sentence. List reasons for calling this group of words a sentence. To test your understanding, write a list of ten sentences. Trade lists with another student and practice identifying the subject and verb for each sentence. Remember that some sentences may have more than one subject and verb, and if you cannot find a subject and verb, look to see if what your classmate has written is indeed a sentence. If not, rewrite the group of words to make it a sentence.

## Assignment 3

Find three different definitions for the word *sentence* in three different handbooks or English textbooks. (Most school libraries have handbooks and textbooks for student use.) Compare the definitions provided. Write your own definition on a 3″ × 5″ notecard, include a good example sentence, and then practice identifying subjects and verbs in sentences from a recent essay you have written or in Lorenzo Cruz's student essay in this chapter.

## SEEING THE CONNECTIONS: APPLYING YOUR SKILLS

### Assignment 1

Brainstorm about an event that happened to you recently. Write down anything you recall about the specific event—including how it made you feel. Write a letter to a friend or family member telling this person the details of this event and the effect it had on you.

Once you have finished the letter, write a paragraph describing this event to your instructor. Because your instructor is a different audience, adjust your language, grammar, writing style, and word use to meet the needs of this new audience.

Exchange your letter and paragraph with a friend. Read each other's letters and paragraphs and discuss or write answers to the following questions:

1. To what speech community is each of these written?
2. Which phrases and words did the writer change? Why did he or she make these changes?
3. Which is better, the letter or the paragraph? Why?
4. Which do you think was easier to write? Why?
5. Does each use vivid sensory details? How could each be rewritten to appeal more to each reader's senses?

### Assignment 2

Read and annotate Paul Roberts's "Speech Communities" as directed earlier in this chapter.

How well does Roberts address his audience?

What is his point, and how well does he communicate this point?

What makes his essay easy to read?

What makes it difficult to read?

Using your annotations and your reactions to the essay and the questions above, put yourself in the role of a reviewer or critic for a student guide to great essays about writing, and write a review of this essay. A review usually discusses how readable, informative, interesting, and worthwhile a written work is for a particular audience. Your review should be at least a paragraph long, should include examples from the essay, and should discuss how much students would enjoy reading Roberts's essay.

*Assignment 3*

Read "A Time to Listen," the student essay by Lorenzo Cruz included in this chapter. Choose an object with which most people are familiar—preferably something you see all the time. Brainstorm about the features of this object and then brainstorm a second time to discover ways this object might relate to your life. For example, if you chose a candle, you might describe the candle as burning strongly at times and weakly at other times, and then think about how your energy flickers in a similar way.

Choose one or two features of the object you brainstormed about and write a page about this object and the way it compares to your life, some aspect of your personality, or a value you hold.

When you have finished the first draft of your essay, write each sentence on a 3″ × 5″ card. Examine each sentence and mark the subject(s) and verb(s). Does each group of words include a subject and a verb? If not, add whatever is missing to make this a sentence. Also make any changes that would make the individual sentences better or stronger (change at least five sentences in some way), then rewrite your paragraph or essay. While you have your sentences on cards, you might also see whether they can be placed in a different order rather than simply putting them back as you had them.

# Chapter 3

# Giving
# Your Ideas Form

In this chapter you will learn

★ to develop a writing routine;
★ to distinguish between a paragraph and an essay;
★ to recognize major and minor points;
★ to identify and use topic sentences and thesis statements;
★ to distinguish between independent and dependent clauses;
★ to recognize prepositions.

Take a moment to answer the following questions:

1. How do you usually begin writing assignments or writing tasks?

_____

_____

_____

2. Do you enjoy writing? How do you usually react when you have to write?

_____

_____

_____

3. Are there any writing situations that make you extremely uncomfortable?

_____

_____

_____

4. What are the requirements for writing a paragraph or essay? What experiences have you had writing either paragraphs or essays?

_____

_____

_____

## ESTABLISHING A WRITING ROUTINE

A writing routine means different things to different writers. Generally, a writing routine is what you do before, during, and after writing that allows you to gain a sense of control and reassurance while writing. Some writers have a very set, elaborate routine; others have less rigid routines. Beginning writers who work to bring a routine into their writing process often find that when they do this, writing becomes less intimidating and easier to start. Almost all routines involve generating ideas and resolving difficulties in expressing an idea. Some writers begin their writing routine by organizing their writing desk or table; some sharpen pencils and brew coffee or tea; some put their favorite CD on the stereo. Most begin by doing some activity that they find relaxing. Though some stress or tension is necessary for motivating most writers, relaxing with a routine that tells your brain "It's time to write!" allows a writer to get "in the mood" to write. Writers also typically use a process that includes generating ideas (thinking, writing ideas down, and so on), producing a piece of writing, and revising what they have produced. Think about the last time you sat down to write something. What steps did you take to begin? How did you know when you were finished? How comfortable were you with writing and with what you produced?

If you feel uncomfortable with your writing and avoid it until the very last minute, you are probably the most common type of student writer.

Developing a writing routine will allow you to become more comfortable with writing and with what you produce. Writing routines involve four parts: getting started, generating ideas, drafting, and revising. Each part of the routine may be separate, or the routine may fluctuate between some of these parts—for example, a writer may write something, crumple the page, try a new approach, crumple the page again, and so on.

Getting started for many writers involves activities that may seem unrelated to writing; activities similar to those previously described. Most writers need "thinking" time to consider what they might write before ever actually putting a word on a page, but sometimes other writers get started by trying to draft from the very beginning. The key to this part of the routine is actually starting. Spend time thinking, writing, or mowing the lawn, but do something!

Another part of a writing routine is the generation of ideas. Before a writer can find a focus and a clear purpose, he or she needs to consider the possibilities of ideas and topics. Many writers use brainstorming, freewriting, or another prewriting technique to generate ideas, but some writers come up with ideas by mulling over the topic before they ever write. Whatever your technique, generating ideas gives you something to write about and stimulates your interest in communicating an idea.

In addition to coming up with ideas, a writer structures ideas and makes decisions about what should be included, what should be left out, and what needs examples or more detail. These decisions generally occur while the writer is drafting. Some writers use many drafts; most writers use at least one draft before writing a final draft. Some writers use time between drafts to solve structural problems and to see which parts are unclear or need to be rewritten.

A final part to any writing routine is revising, but writers do this in a variety of ways. Some writers revise as they draft and cannot move on to the next sentence until the sentence they have written is perfect. Other writers take a more holistic approach and revise for their ideas and clarity and then look at individual sentences, spelling, and grammar.

To design your own writing routine, you will need time and practice. After several writing assignments, though, you will begin to see some kind of routine develop. If your routine leads to D papers, obviously it needs to be changed. If you find that it makes writing easier and more comfortable and that your papers are improving, then you know that your routine is working.

Writing routines are very individual, but to get started you might use the following routine and then make adjustments to suit your own writing style and lifestyle. Your writing routine might begin with any activity you find relaxing. If you begin by staring at a blank piece of paper, you might find doing the dishes, mowing the lawn, or calling a friend more helpful. When you feel ready to write and you have set up a place to write or are sitting in a place where you can write, try an invention technique like brainstorming, freewriting, or one of the other techniques described in Chapter 2 (pages 39–45).

Once you have some ideas, choose a focus for your paragraph, letter, or essay and begin organizing your ideas, keeping your purpose or goal and your target audience (readers) in mind. Once you have written for a while, you may find that your routine needs to include a break. Some students may want to keep writing until they are absolutely finished. Once you have produced a first draft, try putting this draft aside for an hour or a day, depending on your time constraints. Then reread your draft several times; during each reading think about how the purpose could be more clearly identified or accomplished and how you could better appeal to your audience. Write on this first draft, making suggestions to yourself about adding ideas or cutting excess information. Some writers even write every sentence on a 3″ × 5″ card and then organize the sentences into a better order. No matter what you do, make sure that you reread your entire essay and make several changes that improve your paragraph or essay.

Eventually, as you perform different kinds of writing tasks, you will see that one routine may not actually cover every writing situation. For example, an essay that must be written completely in class does not allow the time and comfort level that an out-of-class essay does. However, as you become comfortable with your routine for writing at home or in the library, you can easily adapt it to other types of writing by omitting the steps that are not feasible in class and replacing them with a routine that is. (Chapter 9 discusses techniques for developing an in-class writing routine.) If you are used to thinking about a topic for two or three days before writing anything, obviously you cannot do this in an in-class essay situation, but you can go to class with some ideas and take the first three to five minutes of class to use whichever invention technique works best for you. In other words, your writing routine should never be so rigid that missing one step renders you incapable of writing. Instead, use it as a foundation for writing, a basis for feeling good about writing and knowing that you will produce something that communicates your idea. Remember, each writer is an individual; what works for one will not necessarily work for another. The key is to develop a routine that allows you to produce your best writing in the time that you have available.

# READING AN ESSAY

## Strategy for Reading: Distinguishing Between Major and Minor Points

When we read carefully, we look for the most important and significant ideas and distinguish between those and other less significant ideas. In other words, we read to get the point or main points, but we do not take in all points equally as if they all had equal importance.

If you outlined a well-written essay, for example, you would find that it focuses on an overall idea (thesis), includes ideas that support this overall idea, and perhaps even includes examples that add to the interest of the essay, but are not absolutely vital to the overall point.

When you read for the main point, ask yourself, "What is this writer's point? Why is he or she writing this?" Your answer will likely be the main point. Minor points can be identified as anything that supports the main point. Generally, minor points are divided into supporting details that help the writer establish this main point and minor details that add to the interest but are nonessential.

In the following essay, each paragraph has a main point, and the essay as a whole has a main point. In addition, supporting details are provided to support the writer's point. Read this essay carefully and identify the main points and minor points by labeling them in the margin. When you finish, label the thesis and distinguish between the major and the minor points.

---

### BEFORE YOU READ

1. When is writing easy for you? Under what conditions is it difficult?
2. Have you ever noticed that another writer seemed to write more easily than you? What do you think accounted for the differences between your writing styles?

## The Transaction*

### by William Zinsser

Five or six years ago a school in Connecticut held "a day devoted to the arts," and I was asked if I would come and talk about writing as a vocation. When I arrived I found that a second speaker had been invited—Dr. Brock (as I'll call him), a surgeon who had recently begun to write and had sold some stories to national magazines. He was going to talk about writing as an avocation. That made us a panel, and we sat down to face a crowd of student newspaper editors and reporters, English teachers and parents, all eager to learn the secrets of our glamorous work.      1

Dr. Brock was dressed in a bright red jacket, looking vaguely Bohemian, as authors are supposed to look, and the first question went to him. What was it like to be a writer?      2

He said it was tremendous fun. Coming home from an arduous day at the hospital, he would go straight to his yellow pad and write his tensions away. The words just flowed. It was easy.      3

I then said that writing wasn't easy and it wasn't fun. It was hard and lonely, and the words seldom just flowed.      4

Next Dr. Brock was asked if it was important to rewrite. Absolutely not, he said. "Let it all hang out," and whatever form the sentences take will reflect the writer at his most natural.      5

I then said that rewriting is the essence of writing. I pointed out that professional writers rewrite their sentences repeatedly and then rewrite what they have rewritten. I mentioned that E. B. White and James Thurber were known to rewrite their pieces eight or nine times.      6

"What do you do on days when it isn't going well?" Dr. Brock was asked. He said he just stopped writing and put the work aside for a day when it would go better.      7

*Source:* Zinsser, William. "The Transaction." From *On Writing Well*, 5th ed. by William Zinsser. Copyright © 1995 by William K. Zinsser. Reprinted by permission of Addison Wesley Educational Publishers, Inc.

I then said that the professional writer must establish       8
a daily schedule and stick to it. I said that writing is a craft,
not an art, and that the man who runs away from his craft
because he lacks inspiration is fooling himself. He is also
going broke.

"What if you're feeling depressed or unhappy?" a stu-        9
dent asked. "Won't that affect your writing?"

Probably it will, Dr. Brock replied. Go fishing. Take a      10
walk.

Probably it won't, I said. If your job is to write every     11
day, you learn to do it like any other job.

A student asked if we found it useful to circulate in        12
the literary world. Dr. Brock said that he was greatly enjoy-
ing his new life as a man of letters, and he told several lav-
ish stories of being taken to lunch by his publisher and his
agent at Manhattan restaurants where writers and editors
gather. I said that professional writers are solitary drudges
who seldom see other writers.

"Do you put symbolism in your writing?" a student           13
asked me.

"Not if I can help it," I replied. I have an unbroken        14
record of missing the deeper meaning in any story, play or
movie, and as for dance and mime, I have never had even
a remote notion of what is being conveyed.

"I *love* symbols!" Dr. Brock exclaimed, and he             15
described with gusto the joys of weaving them through his
work.

So the morning went, and it was a revelation to all of      16
us. At the end Dr. Brock told me he was enormously interested in my answers—it had never occurred to him that
writing could be hard. I told him I was just as interested in
*his* answers—it had never occurred to me that writing
could be easy. (Maybe I should take up surgery on the
side.)

As for the students, anyone might think that we left        17
them bewildered. But in fact we probably gave them a
broader glimpse of the writing process than if only one of
us had talked. For of course there isn't any "right" way to
do such intensely personal work. There are all kinds of

writers and all kinds of methods, and any method that helps somebody to say what he wants to say is the right method for him.

Some people write by day, others by night. Some people need silence, others turn on the radio. Some write by hand, some by typewriter, some by talking into a tape recorder. Some people write their first draft in one long burst and then revise; others can't write the second paragraph until they have fiddled endlessly with the first.                                     18

But all of them are vulnerable and all of them are tense. They are driven by a compulsion to put some part of themselves on paper, and yet they don't just write what comes naturally. They sit down to commit an act of literature, and the self who emerges on paper is a far stiffer person than the one who sat down. The problem is to find the real man or woman behind all the tension.                                     19

For ultimately the product that any writer has to sell is not his subject, but who he is. I often find myself reading with interest about a topic that I never thought would interest me—some unusual scientific quest, for instance. What holds me is the enthusiasm of the writer for his field. How was he drawn into it? What emotional baggage did he bring along? How did it change his life? It is not necessary to want to spend a year alone at Walden Pond to become deeply involved with a man who did.                                     20

This is the personal transaction that is at the heart of good nonfiction writing. Out of it come two of the most important qualities that this book will go in search of: humanity and warmth. Good writing has an aliveness that keeps the reader reading from one paragraph to the next, and it's not a question of gimmicks to "personalize" the author. It's a question of using the English language in a way that will achieve the greatest strength and the least clutter.                                     21

Can such principles be taught? Maybe not. But most of them can be learned.                                     22

## Building Your Skills

### Focus on Words

Look up the following words or parts of phrases in a dictionary. Consult the preceding essay and identify the meaning that best fits the way the author uses the word in this essay. Each word or phrase is followed by the number of the paragraph in which it appears.

| | |
|---|---|
| vocation (1) | solitary drudges (12) |
| avocation (1) | symbols (15) |
| vaguely (2) | revelation (16) |
| Bohemian (2) | vulnerable (19) |
| arduous (3) | compulsion (19) |
| essence (6) | personal transaction (21) |
| lavish (12) | gimmicks (21) |

### Focus on the Message

1. Divide a piece of paper in half. Compare the views Zinsser and Dr. Brock give of the writing process. List many specific qualities about their individual processes. How often does Zinsser use minor points and how often does he use supporting details that help him make his point?
2. What is Zinsser's main point? How was the panel discussion Zinsser describes "a revelation" to everyone (para. 16)?
3. In what way are all writers "vulnerable," "tense," and "driven by a compulsion" (para. 19)?
4. Why do you think Zinsser presents such a contrast between himself and Dr. Brock? Does he wish that he could write like Dr. Brock?
5. What is the personal transaction we all receive in writing?

# TECHNIQUES FOR WRITING: PARAGRAPHS AND ESSAYS—RECOGNIZING WRITING CONVENTIONS

Each type of writing has its own set of common practices or conventions that supply the reader with necessary signals for interpreting information and the writer with guidelines for presenting his or her message to the reader. Examples of these conventions include giving an essay a title, indenting the first line of a paragraph, capitalizing the first letter in each sentence. Each of these cues tells the reader that he or she is reading a new paragraph or sentence or changing from one part of the topic to another. A writer who understands and uses these conventions will have a format with which to better communicate his or her ideas. The reader who understands these conventions will read more efficiently and will comprehend more of what he or she reads.

### Effective Paragraphing

The goal of a paragraph, like that of any other writing, is to effectively communicate an idea to an audience. Writing involves organizing information and ideas we want to exchange with our audience into a form that our audience will find accessible. First, we must understand what we want to communicate; then we must identify the structure or organization necessary for presenting this idea. A paragraph is one of these structures. It allows us to organize information and provide the reader with information organized into a manageable block.

A **paragraph** is a unit of several sentences (usually four or more) grouped together to develop a topic identified within the paragraph by a topic sentence. Effective paragraphs have a **topic sentence,** supporting details, and a conclusion. The topic sentence in a paragraph can be placed at the beginning, end, or any other logical place within the paragraph and serves to identify the topic the writer is discussing, as well as to tell the scope or limits of that discussion.

For example, "Students enjoy English" would not be an effective topic sentence because it does not show how thoroughly the writer plans to cover this topic. In addition, it does not evoke much interest from potential readers. A better topic sentence might be "A student who enjoys English is more likely to succeed in an English class than a student who does not." A topic sentence should do the following:

> encourage reader interest,
>
> identify the topic, and
>
> show how the writer plans to develop that topic.

Look at the topic sentence in the paragraph below. How is it developed?

> **A student who enjoys studying English is more likely to succeed in an English class than a student who does not.** Students who enjoy English usually like to write and feel confident about their writing. Often, they feel more at ease when speaking to their instructors and participate more in class. They may bring more enthusiasm and interest both to class and to

their writing assignments. Interested students will find time spent in English class rewarding and stimulating and will probably get better grades than students who just come to class.

Once the topic sentence is written, the topic in the paragraph must be supported or explained, so details and examples are added in supporting sentences that develop the idea presented in the topic sentence. In the above example, the writer explains *why* a student who enjoys English might be more likely to succeed. Supporting sentences should be organized logically, and each should be related to the topic sentence. They should help establish the overall point and persuade the reader.

A paragraph also includes a conclusion, though not one as pronounced as a conclusion in a longer work; it may be a restatement of the topic sentence (although generally a topic sentence is strong enough and does not need restatement) or it may be a transition to a new paragraph. Sometimes, a writer may conclude with a related idea that adds emphasis to the topic covered, as in the example above.

### Distinguishing an Essay from a Paragraph

While a paragraph is sometimes adequate to fulfill an assignment, some assignments require an essay. Above we focused primarily on the paragraph, but sometimes paragraphs are linked together to form an essay. An **essay** is a group of paragraphs that explain, describe, or discuss in detail a topic presented to the reader in a **thesis statement.** A **thesis** can be included in a single statement or sentence or can be split into more than one sentence. The thesis statement for an essay serves the purpose that a topic sentence does for a paragraph. But be careful not to confuse the two. An essay is longer and has several paragraphs, all of which describe, explain, or support the thesis statement. The thesis is crucial to the essay for the following reasons:

A thesis is important because it presents the controlling or main idea in one of the paragraphs of the essay.

A thesis statement identifies and limits to one or two sentences the idea to be discussed in the essay and the detail in which that subject will be discussed; this helps the reader build expectations for what will be presented.

The thesis statement sets the scope of the essay, but unlike a topic sentence, it should be more than a statement of fact. It must state something to be proven, refuted, or demonstrated which identifies an approach for writing (or reading) the essay.

In addition, an essay includes an introduction, a body, and a conclusion. Each part must be related to the thesis statement, must work with the other parts, and must be evaluated according to how well it meets the reader's needs and the writer's purpose. In contrast to a paragraph, an essay provides a more detailed analysis of a topic; a paragraph can only explain or provide information about a topic limited to several sentences.

If you currently write only paragraph-length responses to assignments, work to stretch beyond one paragraph to an essay-length work. One way to do this is to provide an extended related example in a second paragraph that supports your overall idea. Another way is to separate your ideas into logical related paragraphs that work as an introduction, body, and conclusion. However you choose to do this, stretching beyond one-paragraph responses will help you begin to raise your writing to a new, more scholarly level.

## Building Your Skills

### Assignment 1

Divide a piece of paper into two columns and develop a list of conventions for paragraphs and essays. What should all paragraphs include? What should all essays include? Compare the characteristics and write a brief paragraph that discusses what a paragraph includes and what it does. Make sure that your paragraph is a good example of the conventions a paragraph should include.

### Assignment 2

Write an essay that defines the term *essay* for another student. For prewriting, do the exercise in Assignment 1, and for help with structure, write your essay as a set of paragraphs that follow this outline:

| | |
|---|---|
| Paragraph 1 | Define the term *essay*. |
| Paragraph 2 | Discuss the necessary parts of an essay. |
| Paragraph 3 | Discuss the process and work involved in writing an essay. |
| Paragraph 4 | Explain why essay writing is an important skill. |

When you have produced a draft of your essay, cut the paper into four parts and reorganize these sections to form an essay that tells another student how to write a good essay. Make any changes necessary to support this new main point or thesis.

*Assignment 3*

Compare the way you do a particular activity to the way someone you know well performs this same task. For example, compare the way you balance a checkbook, mow the lawn, dress or groom yourself, or travel with the way someone you know does this same thing. Begin by listing your methods and the other person's methods on a piece of paper divided into columns. Then decide on a major point you want to establish (for example, Zinsser shows that people who write well can write very differently) and some supporting details that will allow you to demonstrate your point. Then write a paragraph or essay that compares your method for doing this activity with someone else's.

# READING A STUDENT ESSAY

## Peer Review Strategy: Revising for Structure

When we read another writer's work, we may not realize that we are evaluating his or her writing for the appropriate structure, but as readers we have expectations about how a paragraph or letter should look and how easy or difficult it should be to read. So even though you may not realize it, you already make judgments about the structure of a piece of writing because of the expectations you have as a reader.

In an essay, the structure includes an introduction that gives the reader a purpose for reading, a body that develops an idea, and a conclusion that resolves the issue or draws the essay to a close. An essay includes a thesis, paragraphs that develop the thesis, and a logical connection between all of the paragraphs in the essay. As readers we expect an essay to meet these minimal requirements. In addition, we generally expect that it will make the writer's message or purpose clear. When you read another student's essay to review whether or not he or she is using the appropriate essay format and making his or her message clear, you might use the following questions as a guideline.

To begin, read the entire essay once.

1. What is the thesis? Can you easily identify it?
2. Does the essay include an introduction, a body, and a conclusion? Does it move from point to point easily and clearly? If not, what seems to be missing or unconnected?

3. Look at the paragraphs. Does each paragraph include at least four sentences? Does each include a topic sentence? Does each paragraph clearly develop an idea?
4. Does each paragraph clearly demonstrate an idea related to the thesis of the essay?
5. Overall, how easy or difficult is the essay to read and understand?

Use these questions in your reading of other students' essays, your own essays, and the student essay that follows. Remember that you need to read the essay carefully to evaluate it.

## German Brown

### by Ralph Heaney

The sun's rays were darting intermittently through the dense foliage along the road's edge. It was mid-morning and that special bend in the road was now recognizable. The old brown truck I was driving came to a crawl, and in the midst of my excitement, I found myself halfway out of the truck cab before setting the brake. I gathered the gear from the truck and made my way down the familiar path. 1

Hurriedly moving down the trail toward the habitat of that elusive monster, "Germanis Brownis Gigantis," I sensed excitement in every step. Upon entering the familiar foliage, I felt as if I had entered a new world. My senses appeared to be more acute. Smelling, touching, seeing, and hearing took on a new dimension. I tingled from head to toe. I could hear the guttural noise of the gurgling water. I could smell the scent of pines. I could feel the crumbling of decomposed leaves beneath my feet. I was in awe, walking this trail that was to lead me to the domain of "The Big One." I could also sense my own limitations, for I was but a visitor here. 2

The roar of the rushing water grew more intense. I knew I was nearing my destination. The cold, deep 3 pool was now visible, the pool that harbored "Him." Mistakes could not be afforded now. Keeping quiet and staying out of sight were the ingredients for success. Slowly working my way to the pool's edge, I ever so carefully peered over a granite monolith.

There he was, basking in his emerald green sanctuary. Backing away and still out of his sight, I prepared my tackle for the conquest. Attaching a reddish brown fly to my leader, I gently tossed it upstream above the big pool. I could see the fly slowly float toward the edge of the partially submerged boulder. Would the old "Hook-Jaw" be fooled? I could see the turbulence in the water as he moved towards the fly. His jaw agape, I could actually see him take the lure into his mouth. My heart was in my throat. I set the hook. Fish on!

4

Three weeks and one-hundred and twenty dollars later, "Germanis Brownis Gigantis" became a permanent fixture on the wall of my den: four pounds and twenty inches of pure delight.

5

## Building Your Skills

1. What sensory details does Heaney include to help you understand his story? Do you think someone who does not fish can relate to this story? Why or why not?

_____

_____

_____

_____

_____

_____

_____

_____

_____

_____

2. What is Heaney's main point? What do you think is his reason for writing this essay?

_____

_____

_____

_____

_____

_____

_____

_____

_____

3. How well did Heaney's essay meet with your expectations as a reader? How does the structure of his essay add to or detract from his ability to be clearly and easily understood?

_____

_____

_____

_____

_____

_____

_____

_____

_____

4. As if you were discussing Ralph's paper with him, list three features of his essay that work very well or that really appeal to you as a reader. Then, recommend three changes he could make to improve his essay.

Describe three features that are effective for you as a reader:

a. _____

b. _____

c. _____

Describe three improvements or changes Ralph could make to create a more effective, interesting, or informative essay:

a. _____

b. _____

c. _____

## USING GRAMMAR: RECOGNIZING THE DIFFERENCE BETWEEN INDEPENDENT AND DEPENDENT CLAUSES

Sentences, when we break them down, are simply relationships between sentence parts. These relationships are determined by grammatical conventions (in the case of this text, Standard English grammar) that include rules about appropriate wording and punctuation. Many times, people, identify these conventions as something that "sounds right." One of the important relationships that determine the order, style, and punctuation in a sentence is the use of independent and dependent clauses. An independent clause, as the name implies, stands independently. In other words, an independent clause, like a sentence, can stand alone. They each have a subject and a verb, but a sentence can have more than one subject and verb combination, whereas an independent clause can have only one subject and verb combination. You can write more than one independent clause per sentence, but you could never have more than one sentence within one independent clause. In the following example, notice the two independent clauses; the subjects are printed in bold while the verbs are underlined.

independent clause #1    independent clause #2

**Tommy** <u>went</u> to the store. **He** <u>bought</u> some milk.

Each independent clause has been written here as a separate sentence, but they could be combined to create one sentence with two independent clauses:

independent clause #1      independent clause #2

**Tommy** <u>went</u> to the store, and **he** <u>bought</u> some milk.

We can connect these two independent clauses using a comma and the word *and*. Though the meaning of these examples really is the same, when we read them, we stop longer between sentences in the first example, while in the second, because the independent clauses are connected, we bring the ideas together. Neither of these is more grammatical or more "correct" than the other; a writer can choose whichever fits his or her idea the best.

To test yourself, decide which of the following is an independent clause. Try reading each aloud and stopping at the period to see if you can hear which one is a full sentence and which two are not.

1. When we decided to go for more ice cream.
2. In the dark under the cover of the clouds in the sky.
3. I found the puppy hiding in the closet.

Which one stands out as the complete sentence (or complete independent clause)? If you answered number 3, you are correct. If not, keep practicing. The third is an independent clause and a sentence because it has a subject ("I") and a verb ("found"). The others leave the reader wondering. In each case, the incomplete statements lack the qualities of a sentence or independent clause, but for different reasons.

The first example begins with a dependent word (technically called a subordinating conjunction). This is referred to as a dependent word because when you use this word, the phrase that follows it becomes dependent on an independent clause to create a sentence. Many words that you use every day create dependent clauses. Look at the following list. (This list is also available in the Appendix. You may want to photocopy it to use when you write.)

### Dependent Words (Subordinating Conjunctions)

| | | |
|---|---|---|
| after | before | unless |
| although | how | until |
| as | if | when |
| as if | in order that | whenever |
| as long as | since | where |
| as though | so that | wherever |
| because | that | while |
| | though | |

When you use a dependent word, you create a part of the sentence that explains or shows some kind of relationship. In the following sentence, pay attention to the way the dependent clause adds meaning to the sentence. Also, notice that the sentence can be written with the independent clause first and the dependent clause second.

dependent clause                    independent clause
**Before I left the house,** I locked the front door.

independent clause                    dependent clause
I locked the front door **before I left the house.**

Each sentence uses the dependent clause "before I left the house" to tell when the subject "I" locked the door. Knowing that "before" is a dependent word (by consulting your list or by memory), you can easily see that "before I left the house" needs the independent clause "I locked the front door" to stand alone as a sentence. If you read the phrase "before I left the house," you can easily hear that it is incomplete.

Choose a word from the list of dependent words to fill in the blank in the following sentences:

1. _____ I fed the dog, she was happy.

2. I received the correct change _____ the clerk was angry.

3. _____ I do not have a car, I have to walk to school.

When you use dependent clauses, you need to be sure to include an independent clause. One way to edit your writing to catch any problems is to read your work aloud sentence by sentence. This will help you hear when a group of words needs to be combined with another to create a complete sentence.

The second example, "In the dark under the cover of the clouds in the sky," demonstrates an entirely different kind of phrase. A prepositional phrase is a group of words that begins with a preposition. (This list is also included in the Appendix.)

### Prepositions

| | | | |
|---|---|---|---|
| about | between | in front of | out |
| above | beyond | in spite of | over |
| across | by | inside | regardless of |
| ahead of | down | instead of | through |
| around | during | into | to |
| as | for | like | together |
| at | from | near | under |
| before | in | of | until |
| below | in addition to | off | up |
| beneath | in back of | on | with |
| | | | without |

Typically, these phrases tell how, why, or when, or express relationships similar to a dependent clause. Dependent words form dependent clauses that depend on independent clauses to become part of a sentence. Prepositional phrases also must be added to an independent clause to stand as a complete sentence. They are added most often to describe or identify a direction or time frame, as in the example below. Notice that the prepositions appear in bold print and that an independent clause has been added to make this a sentence.

|prepositional<br>phrase | prepositional<br>phrase | subject verb | prepositional<br>phrase |
|---|---|---|---|

**In** the darkness **of** the night sky, we felt isolated **from** the rest

prepositional phrase
**of** the universe.

The prepositional phrases tell the details of when and where, but without the independent clause that contains both a subject ("we") and a verb ("felt"), this would not be a sentence and would be considered ungrammatical according to Standard English grammar. Prepositional phrases, like dependent clauses, can change position in the sentence and may be written before or after the subject and verb in the sentence. They add variety and meaning to what you say and are already part of your speech patterns. However, when you use prepositional phrases, you must be sure to use an independent clause as well; otherwise, you will produce an ungrammatical construction called a sentence fragment. (Fragments are discussed in detail in Chapter 5.)

In the following paragraph taken from James Trefil's essay "About Sunsets," the independent clauses are printed in bold, the dependent clauses are underlined, and the prepositional phrases appear in italics.

> While we're pondering the color *of the sun at sunset,* **we could equally well ask why the sun appears to be yellow** *at noon.* After all, **we know** *from pictures* taken *by astronauts in space* that the sun as seen *from above the atmosphere* appears to be pure white. **The change** *in color from white in space to yellow on the ground* **must also have something to do** *with the passage of light through the atmosphere.* As it turns out, **one** *of those unexpected connections* I discussed *in the preface of this book* **is this:** when we have figured out why sunsets are beautiful, **we will also have explained why the sky is blue.**

As you can see, this writer chooses to use a variety of dependent clauses and prepositional phrases to augment his independent clauses. As a reader, notice how much detail is included in these parts of his paragraph. Reread his paragraph reading only the parts printed in bold. How much detail is lost when you read his work this way?

Compare the way this author uses clauses and prepositional phrases with your own writing in one of your recent essays. Do you use the same kind of variety of expression? If not, perhaps you would like to incorporate these skills into your writing to increase your competence and versatility.

## Building Your Skills

### Assignment 1

In the following sentences, change each independent clause to a dependent clause and add an additional independent clause. You can use the dependent clause at any point in the sentence, as demonstrated by the example.

*EXAMPLE:*

independent clause
She left work early.

dependent word added to      new independent clause added
independent clause      with subject and verb

<u>Because</u> she left work early, **she** <u>had</u> a peaceful evening.

new independent clause added

with subject and verb      dependent word added to independent clause

**She** <u>had</u> a peaceful evening <u>because</u> she left work early.

1. They rented a small house.

_____

_____

2. Two dogs are sometimes difficult to handle.

_____

_____

3. Lasagna is my favorite food.

_____

_____

4. The president of the United States makes many important decisions.

_____

_____

5. Betsy and Karen go to the movies often.

_____

_____

6. Beverly Richardson is a wonderful teacher.

_____

_____

7. Many students struggle with math and English.

_____

_____

8. Behavioral science is a fascinating area to study.

_____

_____

9. Sailing is an expensive sport.

_____

_____

10. The child could not stand to be away from his mother.

_____

_____

Now, on a piece of paper, write ten sentences of your own using dependent words to create a dependent clause at the beginning of each sentence. When you have finished, move each dependent clause from the beginning to the end of the sentence and make any necessary adjustments to the rest of the sentence.

### Assignment 2

Underline the prepositional phrases in the following sentences.

*EXAMPLE:*

She left the car parked <u>in a dark garage</u>.

1. Across from the theater was a coffee shop.
2. My money is in a local bank.
3. We stayed until dusk.
4. Susie lives between my house and the corner.
5. A big city existed across the river.

6. To get to the party, we had to go over the bridge and beyond the new shopping mall.
7. I want to live a long life with my friends and family.
8. She left after dinner and went to work in the factory after dark.
9. In the alley in the corner, a small kitten was meowing.
10. U2 is releasing a new album in the spring.

Now write ten sentences of your own that use at least two prepositional phrases each. To add variety to your writing, practice using prepositional phrases at the beginning and at the end of your sentences.

### Assignment 3

In the following short paragraph, fill in dependent words to create dependent clauses.

_____ many years, they found each other.

_____ walking around in the supermarket, they bumped

into each other and realized they had been in love from the very begin-

ning. _____ they had dated, separated, and gone their own

ways, each remembered the other and had kept mementos of the relation-

ship they had once had. Now, ten years later, they both felt just the way they

had ten years ago. _____ they left, they had decided to

rekindle an old flame.

Now write a paragraph of your own about an old flame or a new flame. Use dependent and independent clauses in your paragraph, and mark the dependent words and prepositions after you have written the paragraph.

_____

_____

_____

_____

_____

_____

_____

_____

_____

_____

## SEEING THE CONNECTIONS: APPLYING YOUR SKILLS

### *Assignment 1*

If you were an instructor, how would you grade essays? What would you look for? What would make the difference between an A paper and a B paper? Brainstorm by yourself or with a classmate or group about what characteristics an A essay has, a B essay, a C essay, and so forth. Beginning with the characteristics of an essay that would receive an F is probably the easiest way to get started.

**Characteristics for Each Grade**

A _____

_____

_____

_____

B _____

_____

_____

_____

C  _____

_____

_____

_____

D  _____

_____

_____

_____

F  _____

_____

_____

_____

When you have come up with several characteristics for each grade, you have created a grading rubric or guideline. Compare your rubric with another student's or with the rest of your class.

Using your rubric, read "German Brown" by Ralph Heaney and determine the grade this essay would receive based on your rubric, and then determine how you would explain this grade to Ralph if he asked you why you gave it the grade you chose.

As you design a rubric and grade a paper, you can see the same type of process whereby your papers are graded. How do the expectations you had while you were grading differ from your usual expectations while reading another student's essay? Did you focus more on structure, message, grammar, or other characteristics?

### Assignment 2

Brainstorm for five or six minutes about momentous events in your life that have affected you either positively or negatively. Choose a defining moment or event that was either a high or low point in your life. Make two lists: on the first, list the senses that were affected by this experience and the sensory details you remember; on the second, list the causes and effects of this experience.

Write a paragraph or essay that describes this defining moment and explains why it had such an important effect on your life. When you have finished the first draft, compare it with your lists. Are there any sensory details that you could add to make your essay more readable and effective? Then look for causes and effects through the dependent words you have used. Since dependent words often show cause and effect relationships, you will be able to see how much of a connection you are making for your reader.

Write a second draft of your paragraph or essay adding several sensory details and at least three dependent clauses.

### Assignment 3

Read Zinsser's "The Transaction" in this chapter. Write a step-by-step list or outline of the process you follow when you write. This list can include anything you do before actually putting words on paper or during the process.

Write an essay that describes the process you use to write. In either the introduction, the body, or the conclusion, compare your process with the process Zinsser describes in his essay.

After you have written the first draft, consult the list of dependent words in the Appendix. Add at least ten dependent words to independent clauses in your essay. This will make them dependent clauses, so you will then need to link them to an independent clause in one of the ways discussed in the grammar section of this chapter.

Rewrite your essay making any changes that will make your essay more effective and using your newly combined sentences.

# Chapter 4

# Making Sense

In this chapter you will learn

☆ to add to, cut, and reorganize what you write;
☆ to view change as a normal part of the writing process;
☆ to use context clues when you read;
☆ to write an effective introduction;
☆ to revise for first impressions;
☆ to recognize and use four types of sentences.

Take a moment to answer the following questions:

1. How many changes do you generally make to a paragraph or essay before you feel that it is finished? How many times do you reread it?

_____

_____

_____

2. When do you make the most changes to your writing? What kinds of changes do you make most often?

_____

_____

_____

3. How important are introductions to you as a reader? How do you write introductions for your essays?

_____

_____

_____

4. When you read, how do you figure out the meanings of unfamiliar words or concepts?

_____

_____

_____

## ORGANIZING FOR YOUR READER

As you begin using a process when you write—generating ideas, drafting, and rewriting—you may find that you have difficulty deciding which ideas or how many details to include. You may wonder if you have introduced your topic sufficiently or if your reader can follow along with your ideas as he or she reads what you have written. The core of the writing process is really the process of adding to, cutting, or reorganizing what you have written—in other words, changing what you have written to fit your audience and purpose.

Every decision you make in changing a rough draft of an essay or paragraph should be tested by two criteria:

1. How will this help or hinder my reader?
2. How will this clarify my purpose?

Every addition, omission, or change you make should make your essay easier to read or more effective for your reader, as well as clarifying your point in some significant manner. Additions are usually important when you need to give your reader more information or detail to make your point or to help your reader understand your ideas more clearly. Cutting is crucial for taking out too much detail that bogs the reader down or loses your point. Cutting is especially important when you have ideas, sentences, and/or whole paragraphs that do not relate to your main idea. Another important type of change in writing is reordering or reorganizing information. Often this becomes necessary when you have put all of your ideas on paper but you realize that your main idea could be more effectively or clearly presented if your points were organized in a different order or linked together more effectively.

### Ideas for Adding

Even though you may read a draft of an essay or paragraph and think you have included all the necessary facts or details, you may still need to add to what you have written. Remember that your audience has had different life experiences and will have a different perspective, so you need to be as specific as you can to help your reader understand exactly what you want to communicate. Of course, this also means *you* need to identify what you want to communicate. You can add examples for clarification, funny or sad stories to create an emotional reaction or mood, and new sentences or paragraphs to link ideas or to fill in gaps within your paragraph or essay. You can even add a major essay component such as an introduction or a conclusion.

Determining what to add to an essay and where to add it can be difficult. Practice this skill by asking someone else to read your work and tell you one or two things you could add to make your work more effective; if you like their advice, follow their recommendations. Another way to practice making additions to your essay is to put your work aside for a day or two and then read it with a fresh eye. Think to yourself, "What's missing?" or "What could make my work better?" and find at least one thing to add to improve your essay. After you have practiced adding to your writing, you will become more comfortable with incorporating additions naturally into your writing process. They will probably occur during the prewriting, drafting, and rewriting stages, making your writing more enjoyable to read and probably more rewarding for both you and your reader.

### Ideas for Deleting

Deleting should be a part of every writing task, even if what you leave out is only a word or two. A first draft always includes ideas, words, or sentences—sometimes even whole paragraphs—that need to be changed. Every word or sentence you take out of your essay should make your ideas clearer or focus your work overall on a clearer point. For beginning writers this is perhaps one of the skills they are most reluctant to learn. After spending three hours writing, most beginning writers are sensitive about cutting out words and sentences, let alone paragraphs—but an experienced writer will almost always leave out parts of a draft or change words and sentences either while drafting or after a first or second draft is finished.

To make decisions about what, if anything, needs to be deleted or changed within a draft, remember that you need to identify your overall goal in the essay or paragraph, and then identify who will be reading it. Everything in your essay should help you accomplish your goal for your specific audience. Ask yourself the following three questions:

1. Does each paragraph and sentence clearly relate to my point?
2. Are all of the details I provide necessary for my reader to understand my point?
3. Do any of my ideas go off topic?

If you find that you have ideas or details that do not fit with your overall point, you have a decision to make: You can revise your thesis to include these ideas, or you can simply cut them out of your essay. No matter which you choose, do make a change. Once you have revised some of your work, you will become more comfortable with the control you gain by taking this important revision step.

### Ideas for Reorganizing and Connecting
Reorganizing ideas, sentences, and paragraphs involves both cutting and adding. When you read a draft, if you are not pleased with how it presents your overall point or if you have trouble finding your main point, you probably need to spend some time organizing your ideas. One technique for reorganizing is to outline your main point, supporting ideas, examples, and conclusion. Once you have done this, try to move paragraphs or sentences so that you make your overall point more clear.

Identify your thesis (your main idea and the view you want to take about it) and then see how well each part of your essay relates back to your thesis. If you find a sentence or paragraph that does not easily and clearly relate to your thesis, ask these two questions:

1. Would my essay be more effective if I kept this idea, sentence, or paragraph?
2. Do I need to add another sentence or paragraph to link this idea, sentence, or paragraph to my thesis?

If you do not think your essay needs this additional idea, sentence, or paragraph, cut it. If you include additional ideas that take away from your main point, your reader may become lost or confused. In addition, if you have a whole paragraph that really does not relate to your overall point, your reader may become frustrated or bored.

If the idea, sentence, or paragraph seems necessary, but it is not clearly linked to the ideas directly before or after it, consider relocating it to a more appropriate place. For example, in the student essay included in this chapter, the student writer worked through her ideas in several drafts. As she did this, she moved sentences to different locations to more effectively link her ideas together.

In one of the early drafts of the student essay "On the Wings of a New Freedom" (included in this chapter on page 100), the sentences and paragraph structure in paragraphs 4 and 5 were very different from what appears in the final draft. In the earlier version, notice the repetition and use of vague phrases.

> My true thoughts and feelings were finally on paper.
>
> In a short time, I was feeling better, better about myself and life in general. As I allowed my teacher (who had inspired me) to read some of my writing, I realized previously unresolved issues <u>had been dealt with</u>. It seemed that by merely getting my feelings out on paper, they had become <u>easier to deal with</u>. The hardest part was letting go of these feelings. It was through my writing that the healing process had begun.
>
> By writing about those feelings of betrayal from the trust that was broken, I had begun <u>dealing with it</u> without realizing it.

In a later draft, the student writer decided to change the order and content of some of the sentences, and took the essay from an early form that is confusing to read to a finished product that is smooth and much easier to read and understand. Compare this early draft with the final draft included in this chapter.

Reorganizing may seem like a great deal of work, but actually the process of cutting, adding, or reorganizing ideas becomes almost an automatic process for most experienced writers (professional writers, in fact, often consider this the most important part of writing). Practice seeing your writing as if you were a reader and then try adding, cutting, and reorganizing ideas, sentences, and paragraphs to give your writing polish and clarity.

# READING AN ESSAY

## Strategy for Reading: Using Context Clues

Context clues are clues or information within a sentence or paragraph that help you understand the meaning of unfamiliar words or phrases and, in a larger sense, help you understand the meaning of an essay. For example, in the following essay, Peter Elbow defines freewriting and uses the words "coherent" and "interposes" as part of his essay. If you are not familiar with the meaning of words like "coherent" or "interposes," you might feel that you are not getting the meaning of a sentence or even the whole essay.

However, using the context or words and sentences around an unknown word can help you to determine the meaning of a word or phrase and get a better understanding of the essay.

Words are used in a context or with other words and phrases, or with examples that will help you to understand them. Using context clues means being an observant reader and taking time to think. Obviously you could read with a dictionary next to you all of the time, but few people want to stop reading an essay every time they find an unfamiliar word; in fact, looking up words while you are reading can be very distracting and is probably better done after you finish reading an essay. Instead, look at the clues, think, and guess. Most of the time, you will get a fairly good sense of the meaning of the word, and this is a skill that you can improve with practice.

The following examples are taken from Peter Elbow's essay. Before you read his essay, try to guess what the underlined words mean in context and write your definition on the lines after each phrase.

1. "Here is an example of a fairly <u>coherent</u> exercise . . . ."

_____

_____

2. "Almost everybody <u>interposes</u> a massive and complicated series of editings between the time the words start to be born into consciousness and when they finally come off the end of the pencil . . . ."

_____

_____

## BEFORE YOU READ

1. Do you ever have trouble beginning to write? When does this happen to you?
2. How do you usually begin a writing assignment?
3. How much do you worry about grammar and being "correct" when you write?

# Freewriting[*]

by Peter Elbow

The most effective way I know to improve your writing     1
is to do freewriting exercises regularly. At least three times
a week. They are sometimes called "automatic writing,"
"babbling," or "jabbering" exercises. The idea is simply to
write for ten minutes (later on, perhaps fifteen or twenty).
Don't stop for anything. Go quickly without rushing. Never
stop to look back, to cross something out, to wonder how
to spell something, to wonder what word or thought to
use, or to think about what you are doing. If you can't
think of a word or a spelling, just use a squiggle or else
write, "I can't think of it." Just put down something. The
easiest thing is just to put down whatever is in your mind.
If you get stuck it's fine to write "I can't think what to say, I
can't think what to say" as many times as you want; or
repeat the last word you wrote over and over again; or anything else. The only requirement is that you *never* stop.

What happens to a freewriting exercise is important.     2
It must be a piece of writing which, even if someone reads
it, doesn't send any ripples back to you. It is like writing
something and putting it in a bottle in the sea. The
teacherless class helps your writing by providing maximum
feedback. Freewritings help you by providing no feedback
at all. When I assign one, I invite the writer to let me read
it. But also tell him to keep it if he prefers. I read it quickly
and make no comments at all and I do not speak with him
about it. The main thing is that a freewriting must never
be evaluated in any way; in fact there must be no discussion or comment at all.

Here is an example of a fairly coherent exercise     3
(sometimes they are very incoherent, which is fine):

---

[*]*Source:* Elbow, Peter. "Freewriting." From *Writing Without Teachers* by Peter Elbow.
Copyright © 1973 by Peter Elbow. Used by permission of Oxford University Press,
Inc.

I think I'll write what's on my mind, but the only thing on my mind right now is what to write for ten minutes. I've never done this before and I'm not prepared in any way—the sky is cloudy today, how's that? now I'm afraid I won't be able to think of what to write when I get to the end of the sentence—well, here I am at the end of the sentence—here I am again, again, again, again, at least I'm still writing—Now I ask is there some reason to be happy that I'm still writing—ah yes! Here comes the question again—What am I getting out of this? What point is there in it? It's almost obscene to always ask it but I seem to question everything that way and I was gonna say something else pertaining to that but I got so busy writing down the first part that I forgot what I was leading into. This is kind of fun oh don't stop writing—cars and trucks speeding by somewhere out the window, pens clittering across peoples' papers. The sky is still cloudy—is it symbolic that I should be mentioning it? Huh? I dunno. Maybe I should try colors, blue, red, dirty words—wait a minute—no can't do that, orange, yellow, arm tired, green pink violet magenta lavender red brown black green—now that I can't think of any more colors—just about done—relief? maybe.

Freewriting may seem crazy but actually it makes simple sense. Think of the difference between speaking and writing. Writing has the advantage of permitting more editing. But that's its downfall too. Almost everybody interposes a massive and complicated series of editings between the time words start to be born into consciousness and when they finally come off the end of the pencil or typewriter onto the page. This is partly because schooling makes us obsessed with the "mistakes" we make in writing. Many people are constantly thinking about spelling and grammar as they try to write. I am always thinking about the awkwardness, wordiness, and general mushiness of my natural verbal product as I try to write down words.

But it's not just "mistakes" or "bad writing" we edit as we write. We also edit unacceptable thoughts and feelings,

4

as we do in speaking. In writing there is more time to do it so the editing is heavier: when speaking, there's someone right there waiting for a reply and he'll get bored or think we're crazy if we don't come out with *something*. Most of the time in speaking, we settle for the catch-as-catch-can way in which the words tumble out. In writing, however, there's a chance to try to get them right. But the opportunity to get them right is a terrible burden: you can work for two hours trying to get a paragraph "right" and discover it's not right at all. And then give up.

Editing, *in itself,* is not the problem. Editing is usually necessary if we want to end up with something satisfactory. The problem is that editing goes on *at the same time* as producing. The editor is, as it were, constantly looking over the shoulder of the producer and constantly fiddling with what he's doing while he's in the middle of trying to do it. No wonder the producer gets nervous, jumpy, inhibited, and finally can't be coherent. It's an unnecessary burden to try to think of words and also worry at the same time whether they're the right words.  5

The main thing about freewriting is that it is *noediting*. It is an exercise in bringing together the process of producing words and putting them down on the page. Practiced regularly, it undoes the ingrained habit of editing at the same time you are trying to produce. It will make writing less blocked because words will come more easily. You will use up more paper, but chew up fewer pencils.  6

Next time you write, notice how often you stop yourself from writing down something you were going to write down. Or else cross it out after it's written. "Naturally," you say, "it wasn't any good." But think for a moment about the occasions when you spoke well. Seldom was it because you first got the beginning just right. Usually it was a matter of a halting or even garbled beginning, but you kept going and your speech finally became coherent and even powerful. There is a lesson here for writing: trying to get the beginning just right is a formula for failure—and probably a secret tactic to make yourself give up writing. Make some  7 words, whatever they are, and then grab hold of that line and reel in as hard as you can. Afterwards you can throw away lousy beginnings and make new ones. This is the quickest way to get into good writing.

The habit of compulsive, premature editing doesn't    8
just make writing hard. It also makes writing dead. Your voice is damped out by all the interruptions, changes, and hesitations between the consciousness and the page. In your natural way of producing words there is a sound, a texture, a rhythm—a voice—which is the main source of power in your writing. I don't know how it works, but this voice is the force that will make a reader listen to you, the energy that drives the meanings through his thick skull. Maybe you don't *like* your voice; maybe people have made fun of it. But it's the only voice you've got. It's your only source of power. You better get back into it, no matter what you think of it. If you keep writing in it, it may change into something you like better. But if you abandon it, you'll likely never have a voice and never be heard.

Freewritings are vacuums. Gradually you will begin to    9
carry over into your regular writing some of the voice, force, and connectedness that creep into those vacuums.

## Building Your Skills

### *Focus on Words*

Look up the following words or parts of phrases in a dictionary. Consult the preceding essay and identify the meaning that best fits the way the author uses the word in this essay. Each word or phrase is followed by the number of the paragraph in which it appears.

| | |
|---|---|
| ripples (2) | verbal (3) |
| feedback (2) | compulsive (8) |
| coherent (3) | premature (8) |
| incoherent (3) | voice (8) |
| interposes (3) | vacuums (9) |

---

**READING STRATEGY NOTE**

Compare your definitions from context clues with definitions in the dictionary. If your definitions are really far from the meaning, then work on building your skill in this area by making context notes on everything you read.

---

### *Focus on the Message*

1. According to Elbow, why is it important that freewriting provides no feedback or reaction?
2. The way we are schooled in writing produces writing's greatest "downfall" (para. 3), according to Elbow. How does it do this?
3. What does Elbow mean when he writes that we "edit unacceptable thoughts and feelings" (para. 4)? What do you think is his purpose in pointing this out?
4. In what way is "trying to get the beginning just right . . . a formula for failure" (para. 7)? How does freewriting as an exercise change writing as a process?
5. What is "voice"? Can you define it in context? Look it up in the dictionary and then decide what Elbow means when he writes, "Maybe you don't like your voice" (para. 8).

## TECHNIQUES FOR WRITING: CREATING INTEREST—WRITING THE INTRODUCTION

Capturing the reader takes thought. If something shocks you or surprises you, it may indeed do the same for your reader. When you revise or while you are planning the organization of an essay, consider how you can immediately interest your reader in the point you are trying to make. In what ways can you excite your reader or stimulate a memory of a previous experience? An introduction gives your reader a reason to continue reading, as well as providing a guideline for reading. Consider some of the following introduction options, and experiment with a variety of introduction techniques in your writing.

### Beginning with Questions

Questions make your reader start thinking about what you will say or prove—but be careful not to ask questions for which you provide no analysis or conclusion. Writing an essay is like fulfilling a contract with your reader. If you begin with questions, your reader will be expecting answers. If you never offer answers, you break your contract with the reader because you do not live up to your part of the bargain. Occasionally, you may want to ask questions that have no clear or easy answer, such as, "What is the value of human life?" These questions can be effective, but should always be used sparingly.

You can begin an essay with a single question, with multiple questions, or with your thesis statement followed by related questions. You can even write your thesis in the form of a question. For example, if your essay is about gun control, you might begin by asking a question like "Why are many people against gun control?" or "Why would anyone want to support gun control?" Notice that each of these examples would produce a very different essay.

### Beginning with Short Narratives or Anecdotes

Another effective way to draw your reader into your essay is to begin with a funny, sad, or unusual story or joke. Narratives about related experiences can create a mood for your essay, can provide information about how an experience feels, and can make a situation or topic seem like a more realistic possibility or threat. Introductions of this type create a trust between the writer and reader because they establish a writer's credibility and experience in a particular subject area. Be careful, when you write short narratives as introductions, that they do not take over your whole essay. To use this technique as an introduction, you must present a link between the story you tell and the topic or main idea of your essay. Funny anecdotes or jokes can also help stimulate your reader by creating a comfort level or familiarity between you and your reader and by encouraging your reader to feel like reading further.

### Beginning with Statistics

Statistics can inform your reader and can demonstrate how well-informed you are; however, statistics when overused or used without explanation or connection to your thesis can be confusing and annoying to your reader. Used effectively, statistics provide a way to sum up a problem or situation for your reader. They also provide evidence and support for your ideas. Be sure that the statistics you use are reliable. All statistics should come from a trustworthy source—a source that you name and credit with the information you use by telling who conducted the study, where it was published, and any other important information that your reader might need. Be sure, when you use statistics, to link the data to the idea, sentence, or paragraph that follows, so that the statistics do not seem isolated from the rest of your essay. You might even try using questions first in your introduction and then following those questions with statistics. Most of all, statistics can demonstrate your knowledge and research, while informing your reader and increasing his or her concern.

### Beginning with Quotations

A well-chosen quotation can inspire thought and make your reader trust the other information and ideas you provide. Quotations can be serious or funny; they may be chosen for their source or for their historical significance. Using quotations to highlight a point and get your reader's attention is an effective method for beginning an essay. Quotations vary greatly in length; you might begin an essay with just one quoted sentence or you might quote a whole paragraph. No matter what the length of your quote, though, every quote should be followed by a paragraph that clearly establishes its connection to the thesis, and most of the time you should introduce the person who said or wrote what you have quoted. Always make sure that the material you quote will be meaningful to your reader and will help further your point in an important way.

### Beginning with a Shocking Presentation

Shock value can be derived from a variety of sources—stories, statistics, absurd or irreverent questions. Shock value depends on subject matter and presentation. Shocking material should always be in good taste and should be appropriate to the intended audience; otherwise, it may simply disgust readers or keep them from taking the writer seriously. An example of shocking introductory material is usually easy to find in a newspaper. Story headlines or opening lines often use catchy or shocking presentation to grab a reader's attention. Disturbing statistics or emotionally charged stories often appeal to news readers. In the same way, you can begin an essay with an interesting fact or story that creates interest and concern on the part of the reader without offending your audience so much that you lose credibility or the cooperation of your reader.

After you have planned and written the introduction, another important facet to your essay that cannot be overlooked is tying the introduction to your thesis. Whether your introduction includes a story, an example, a list, or questions, it must stimulate your reader's interest and provide a thesis. In Chapter 3, we defined a thesis as a controlling or main idea presented in one of the paragraphs of an essay. The thesis should identify the writer's point and provide a blueprint for the discussion or presentation of the topic in the rest of the essay. Readers develop expectations about what an essay will include based on the introduction and the thesis idea presented. No matter whether your thesis statement is one or more sentences, it is a vital part of the relationship you establish with your reader.

If you cannot find your thesis after writing a draft of an essay, try working with another person. Ask a friend or instructor to read the essay and ask if he or she can find your thesis. If this person finds a thesis, reread your essay to discover whether your thesis is clear enough to direct your reader. If this person cannot find a thesis, ask yourself, "What is my overall idea or point?" "What do I want to communicate?" Then write your answer on a piece of paper; find a place to insert this statement into your essay, preferably somewhere in the first paragraph or two. Make sure that the statement you insert fits with everything else in your essay. If it does, then your essay will be focused. If it does not, then you need either to cut out whatever does not fit with this thesis, or you need to rewrite your thesis to include the other ideas.

## Building Your Skills

### *Assignment 1*

Brainstorm about features of our society that are not what they seem. When is the last time you said, "I can't believe that _____ is really _____!" Write an essay that describes something that seems to be one thing but is really another. For example, if attending college is not what you thought it would be, you could use that as a topic for your essay. Other topics might include being single, getting married, moving out on your own, becoming eligible to vote, and so on. Remember that an essay usually has more than one paragraph, so plan your introduction as a paragraph (four to six sentences), the body as at least one paragraph, and the conclusion as a paragraph.

### *Assignment 2*

Find a shocking or surprising statistic, story, or joke and come up with a topic to write about that correlates with it. Write an introduction that begins with the statistic or story and then presents your thesis. Create a body for the essay that supports or explains your thesis, then conclude with either a comment on the shocking material in your introduction or some other resolution. Revise your essay by evaluating how well each of these parts fits with the others and then rewriting your essay into a smooth, well-written final draft.

### Assignment 3

Look at the essays included in this book, or at essays or articles included in some recent magazines or newspapers. What techniques do these writers use for beginning an essay and for appealing to their readers? Choose a technique you think works well to create interest, and write an essay about a person or organization that has had a lasting effect or left a lasting impression on you. Try to use one of the introductory techniques you observed another writer use. Then rewrite this introduction into two other introductions about the same topic. Choose the introduction you think is the most effective, and write an essay based on the thesis and direction you provide in this introduction.

## READING A STUDENT ESSAY

### Peer Review Strategy: Revising the Introduction

First impressions are as important in writing as they are in job interviews and on dates. We may not mean to be judgmental, but as readers we all make judgments about how interesting or worthwhile a piece of writing will be based on the introduction. Think about the way you read a newspaper or magazine. Do you read every story or article with equal enthusiasm? Probably not. Do you ever skip articles altogether? The first impression—the title, the opening sentence or two, the introductory paragraph—determines the level of enthusiasm the reader feels for the writing and the level of energy he or she will put into reading the work. When papers are being graded, an interesting introduction makes the instructor more likely to give the essay a favorable grade, while a dull, basic introduction may make the difference between a paper receiving an A or a B.

When you revise or read a peer's paper to suggest methods for revision, the introduction is an important place to start. First, the introduction in some way must communicate the overall point to be made or question to be answered. Second, the introduction must set expectations that the rest of the essay will fulfill. Third, the introduction should grab the reader and should present the topic. Look at the following examples and decide which introduction has the most reader appeal.

1. Teen suicide is a big problem.
2. A teenager sits in his room in the dark listening to music, contemplating his own death. He is not ill; he has seemingly every advantage: money, looks, a nice family. After a gunshot, everyone will want to know why he killed himself.
3. Teens should not commit suicide. They should think of all of the life they have ahead of them. They should also think of their loved ones and how this will make them feel. Suicide is an easy way out.
4. What I want to write about is teen suicide. Suicide is bad.

Which essay would you rather read? Why? Essay introductions should be an important part of your revision process. The best time to write or rewrite an introduction is after you have written the essay and know what it will include. In the following student essay, observe the way Goldie Quinn introduces her topic. Does her approach make you want to read further?

## On the Wings of a New Freedom

### by Goldie Quinn

I was fifteen when something happened that would change my life forever. I used to trust anyone. Growing up together in the same house twenty-four hours a day, Charles and I built a trust. I never expected this trust to be broken, but one day, Charles committed an act neither of us could live with. After this experience, I thought that nobody could possibly understand how I was feeling. For this reason, I kept all of my emotions and feelings bottled up inside. As time passed, these feelings began to take their toll.

I experienced many feelings as a result of this incident. Some were new; others were old and familiar. These feelings included guilt, anger, and sadness. The most prominent feeling I experienced, though, was betrayal. An enormous amount of pain came with this new feeling. Because of the pain brought on by this broken trust, I vowed never to trust anyone again. I was under the false impression that if I never trusted anyone or told anyone about my feelings, I could not be hurt again.

Three years after that trust had been broken, I finally allowed one person to pass through the walls that I had built up to keep the feelings in and the hurt out. It was then that my English teacher strongly encouraged me to write. Nobody had ever had any faith in my writing before, but I took her advice and began to write anyway. At first, I only wrote for a few minutes each night and only about whatever I was thinking about at the time. I soon began to write anything and everything that came into my head. I found that by doing this, I was writing for longer and longer periods of time.

3

My true thoughts and feelings began to come out—on paper. In a short time, I began to feel better, better about myself and life in general. It seemed that merely by getting my feelings out on paper, they had become easier to live with. The hardest part was letting go of those feelings. Through writing, my healing process had finally begun.

4

As I allowed my teacher to read some of my writing, I realized the feelings and thoughts I had written on the page were not so different from what other people feel. I began to be able to accept these feelings and to move past these previously unresolved issues. By writing my feelings down, I had already overcome the biggest obstacle: letting my feelings show. I kept these feelings inside out of fear, but once I began writing, the fear seemed to subside, and I was able, then and only then, to recognize and begin to accept what I was feeling. Writing became a way out for me. I used writing to express any and every emotion and feeling. Without writing, I may never have learned how to deal with my feelings. It's ironic that something which I had never believed in before actually opened doors and freed me from my self-imposed prison.

5

## Building Your Skills

1. Evaluate the introduction Quinn uses for her essay. Which words or ideas arouse your interest? Could you suggest any changes that would make the introduction even more appealing?

_____

_____

_____

_____

_____

_____

_____

2. What is Quinn's main point? Does she introduce this main point in the intro-duction? When did you first recognize her main point?

_____

_____

_____

_____

_____

_____

_____

3. Outline the main topic of each paragraph in Quinn's essay. How does this structure enhance or detract from her point? Why do you think she chooses the organization presented here?

_____

_____

_____

_____

_____

_____

_____

_____

_____

_____

4. As if you were discussing Goldie's paper with her, list three features of her essay that work very well or that really appeal to you as a reader. Then, recommend three changes she could make to improve her essay.
   Describe three features that are effective for you as a reader:

   a. _____

   b. _____

   c. _____

   Describe three improvements or changes Goldie could make to create a more effective, interesting, or informative essay:

   a. _____

   b. _____

   c. _____

# USING GRAMMAR: SENTENCE TYPES—
# OPPORTUNITIES FOR EXPRESSION

Knowing the four basic sentence types created by independent clauses and dependent clauses can help you more easily identify reasons and ways to punctuate your writing, as well as making the addition of more sentence variety an easier and more well-defined task. Look at any example of professional writing (a newspaper, a magazine, a novel), and you will find that rarely do writers use the same sentence structure over and over again. If they did, most readers would quickly become bored or frustrated by the monotony. By learning about the different types of sentences, you can learn to use them in your own writing, although you probably already know how to use at least two sentence types in your writing and certainly you use all of them in your speech.

## Simple Sentences

The following is an example of a simple sentence, which can be defined as a group of words having one subject and verb combination. Notice in the following sentence that the word *mechanic* is the subject (the *who* or *what* that the sentence is about), while *repaired* is the verb (the action or state of being in the sentence). A simple sentence can also have a second subject or a second verb, as in the examples below. Each simple sentence is a single independent clause; it can have more than one subject or verb, but it must be a single independent clause.

subject     verb

The mechanic repaired my car.

subject     subject     verb

The mechanic and his helper repaired my car.

subject     verb     verb

The mechanic checked and repaired my car.

## Compound Sentences

A compound sentence uses two or more independent clauses or two subject and verb combinations connected either by a comma and a coordinating conjunction (words like *and, but, so,* etc.) or a semicolon. In the example below, each independent clause can stand alone as a sentence, or it can be combined with the word *and* (or another coordinating conjunction) as a compound sentence.

one independent clause          one independent clause

subject      verb                subject   verb

The mechanic checked the engine, <u>and</u> he repaired my car.

Compound sentences connect ideas of equal importance. They provide a link between sentence parts, but they show a different type of relationship than does a complex sentence, which has only one part that can stand alone.

## Complex Sentences

When we use a dependent clause with an independent clause, we produce another type of sentence. The complex sentence combines a dependent clause with an independent clause—though the dependent clause can appear either before or after the independent clause. By combining dependent and independent clauses, we can produce new types of relationships, such as showing that one event occurred because of another.

one dependent clause            one independent clause

dependent word                   subject   verb

<u>After</u> the mechanic checked the engine, he repaired my car.

one independent clause          one dependent clause

subject      verb       dependent word

The mechanic repaired my car <u>after</u> he checked the engine.

In the above sentences, notice that the word "after" creates a dependent clause (a group of words beginning with a dependent word, also known as a subordinating conjunction). Notice that when the dependent clause occurs before the independent clause, it is followed by a comma.

## Compound-Complex Sentences

Another type of sentence that combines independent and dependent clauses is the compound-complex sentence. This type of sentence consists of a dependent clause and two independent clauses. Look at the variety of ways these sentence parts can be combined in the following compound-complex sentences:

dependent clause               one independent clause

dependent word                   subject      verb

<u>While</u> I waited, the mechanic repaired my car,

second independent clause

subject   verb

and he checked the engine.

one independent clause          dependent clause

subject        verb              dependent word

The mechanic repaired my car <u>while</u> I waited,

second independent clause

subject   verb

and he checked the engine.

one independent clause                    second independent clause

subject          verb                    subject   verb

The mechanic repaired my car, and he checked the engine

dependent clause

dependent word

<u>while</u> I waited.

Recognizing sentence types and learning to use new types can add variety and precision to your writing. Different types of sentences create different types of relationships between the ideas that you are trying to communicate. The sentence "I went to the store, and I came home" creates a different relationship than "After I went to the store, I came home." Each is grammatically correct and communicates the sequence of events, but the second sentence emphasizes the time and which event came first much more than the first sentence does. Learning to use different types of sentences will help you communicate exactly what you want to say to your reader. In addition, learning sentence types will help you learn to write and punctuate sentences in a variety of ways.

## Building Your Skills

### Assignment 1

Identify the type of sentence (simple, compound, complex, or compound-complex) below using the lists of subordinating and coordinating conjunctions in the Appendix.

_____ 1. Quirsha and Bobby had a date, but she was late.

_____ 2. The raft floated down the river after bumping into rocks and trees aimlessly.

_____ 3. Because I know you, I will let you attend, and I will sell you tickets at half price.

_____  4. My family loves traveling; we all have a great time together.

_____  5. The dog ran away, and then he came back.

_____  6. After she swam all day, her skin was red, and her eyes were bloodshot.

_____  7. Even though he lied, I forgave him.

_____  8. We waited in line although it was very cold.

_____  9. Whenever I wish I had a fancy car, I realize that I can't afford fancy payments or fancy friends.

_____  10. Ideas were tossed around the room until finally we all agreed.

## Assignment 2

Write five sentences with only one independent clause per sentence. Change each sentence from a simple sentence to a compound sentence, from a compound to a complex, and finally, from a complex to a compound-complex. Evaluate the way the meaning changes as you add to or take away from the original sentence.

## Assignment 3

Read the following paragraph. After you have read it once, go back and try to identify which type each sentence is. Some sentences may be difficult to identify because they are not as straightforward as the above examples. However, you should practice seeing grammar as it is actually used, not just as it appears in examples in a book. Identify as many sentence types as you can and ask a tutor or your instructor for assistance if you have a great deal of difficulty. Ask yourself the following questions: How does this student vary the types of sentences she uses? How effective is her paragraph? How does her sentence structure add to her effectiveness overall?

### THE SUCCESSFUL VERSUS THE UNSUCCESSFUL STUDENT

Students can be divided into two very distinct types. Some students are successful in school. Some are not. The differences in these types are easily identifiable. The successful student is always on time, usually early. The successful student studies hard. He or she is always in class and always prepared. Furthermore, this student invariably has done the reading and taken notes, and he or she comes prepared for class discussion. The unsuccessful student, on the other hand, often arrives to class late or unprepared. Reading assignments may or may not be important enough for this student to actually read. In fact, the unsuccessful student can be found sleeping or talking through class on occasion, if this student comes to class at all. The differences in these students' behavior account for the differences in their success. Being successful in school is a matter of being present, working hard, and being prepared.

## SEEING THE CONNECTIONS: APPLYING YOUR SKILLS

### Assignment 1

Find a recent essay you have written and make a photocopy of it. Cut the essay into pieces: the title, the separate paragraphs, and any drawings or diagrams.

On a separate piece of paper, write one or two sentences identifying your purpose and audience for this essay. Then use the pieces like parts of a puzzle and find a new introduction and a new order for the paragraphs. Add or delete whatever is necessary to make this new organization work for the new purpose and audience you have identified. Write the new draft as an essay.

Have an unsuspecting reader read both essays and choose the one he or she likes best. Ask this reader to explain his or her choice, and then decide whether or not you agree.

### Assignment 2

Take a recent essay that you have written and look at the way you move from detail to detail or paragraph to paragraph. What was your purpose in this essay? Who was your intended audience? Outline the essay's main points and supporting details. Look at the way you organized your points. Is this the most effective order? Rewrite the essay reorganizing where necessary and adding to or deleting from your paragraphs to connect the ideas better for your reader. Make at least five major cuts, additions, or changes in organization.

*Assignment 3*

Read the essays by Peter Elbow and Goldie Quinn in this chapter.

Think about a time you were angry or someone hurt your feelings or your pride. Freewrite for five minutes about this issue or incident. Time yourself with a timer or have someone else time your writing, and do not stop writing for the whole five minutes. Organize your ideas about this incident and describe in a letter to the person who made you angry or hurt your feelings, or to someone else, how this event has affected you, how you finally resolved your feelings, or why your feelings are still unresolved. Be as honest and truthful as you can be.

When you are finished, put the letter or essay away for a few minutes or hours, then come back to it and identify the types of sentences you have used. Write *simple, compound, complex,* or *compound-complex* next to each sentence and then count the number of each type. Then change five of those sentences to whatever sentence type you used the least. How does sentence variety affect your message and the readability of your essay?

## Chapter 5

# *Developing Your Ideas*

In this chapter you will learn

☆ to recognize and use different organization patterns;
☆ to expand single paragraphs to longer essay-length works;
☆ to analyze what you read for figurative and connotative meaning;
☆ to develop your ideas and recognize reader-based and writer-based writing;
☆ to use different types of punctuation to write more clearly;
☆ to avoid punctuation mistakes that create fragments, run-ons, and comma splices.

Take a moment to answer the following questions:

1. How do you determine when a paragraph or essay includes enough detail?

_____

_____

_____

2. What are the most important features of a paragraph?

_____

_____

_____

3. What are the most important features of an essay?

_____

_____

_____

4. Do you feel more comfortable writing paragraphs or writing one- to two-page essays? Explain your answer.

_____

_____

_____

# EXPANDING PARAGRAPHS INTO ESSAYS

Chapter 3 presents the ways paragraphs and essays differ, but sometimes stretching what you have to say into essay form can be difficult. Do you ever feel at the end of a paragraph that you've written all you can about that topic? This problem can occur for several reasons: maybe your topic is too limited. Perhaps you have not thought through your topic adequately. In this situation, go back to prewriting. Refer to the notes, brainstorming, or freewriting you have created, and expand your topic if it's too limited, or think through the kinds of details your reader will need that perhaps you have not considered in your paragraph. (See Chapter 2, pages 39–45.) If you have enough information, but you need to know how to put your ideas into paragraph or essay form, the following guidelines will help.

### The Benefits of Organizing Information
Paragraphs and essays are organized to emphasize an idea and make the subject matter interesting and informative for the reader. Organization in paragraphs is somewhat different from that in essays, though organization in each has the same purpose—better understanding for the reader and better communication for the writer.

#### Paragraphs
Paragraphs usually focus on a specific topic and give specific information about that topic. The organization can take one of several forms. The following diagrams represent several possible organizational styles for para-

graphs. None is more correct than any other; the best style for an individual paragraph depends completely on the audience and the writer's purpose.

### Style One

Topic Sentence First

This diagram represents the most common organizational pattern for a paragraph—the line at the top represents the topic sentence, the middle depicts the examples that support or explain that topic sentence, and the point at the bottom indicates the conclusion. When would this paragraph style be most appropriate? What would it emphasize? This paragraph format focuses the reader's attention on the topic sentence and provides examples or explanations that convince or persuade the reader.

### Style Two

Topic Sentence Last

This type of paragraph begins with an example, usually a story or anecdote. It proceeds from the story to a point or topic sentence that prepares the reader for the idea in the topic sentence. The topic sentence then comes at the end of the paragraph and sums up the idea provided in the example. Here the example is the primary focus and the topic sentence can have a great deal of impact.

Compare the first two styles as shown in the paragraphs below. How are they different?

When my father died, everything in my life changed. He provided me with love, money for college, and the security of knowing I would always have a place to live.

My father has always given me love, money for college, and the security of knowing I would always have a place to live. When he died, everything in my life changed.

Notice that the placement of the topic sentence—at the beginning or at the end—affects the impact of the statement and what the paragraphs accomplish. The first paragraph emphasizes the writer's loss; whereas, the second surprises the reader with this loss after commending the father.

### Style Three

Topic Sentence in the Middle

This type of paragraph begins with an example or anecdote that piques the reader's interest and leads into the topic sentence, which appears somewhere in the middle of the paragraph. After the topic sentence, supporting details fill out the paragraph, and a concluding sentence or two ties the examples and topic together. This format is particularly good when a writer is discussing a topic with which the reader is unfamiliar or when a writer is attempting to persuade. It allows the writer to catch the reader's interest before taking a stand in the topic sentence. These paragraphs also tend to be a bit longer and more developed than some of the others.

### Style Four

Topic Sentence and Restatement

This type of paragraph, though it looks very different, is really quite similar to Style One. The lines at the top and bottom represent the topic sentence. Sometimes the topic sentence is stated partially in the first sentence and finished in the last sentence, after pertinent details or examples have been given. Sometimes it is restated in a different way at the end of the paragraph. The supporting details are contained in the middle of the paragraph, elaborating the topic and leading to the concluding sentence that completes the topic. Note that restatement in this case does not simply mean that you change the words around; the concluding sentence may draw on ideas from the earlier topic sentence, but it adds something significant beyond that sentence. Compare the following paragraphs with each other and with the paragraphs above. How does the message and emphasis change in these?

I remember spending many afternoons talking with my father. I used to play golf and tennis with him. When my father died, everything in my life changed. He provided me with love, money for college, and the security of knowing I would always have a place to live.

The death of my father made me see how important people can be in our lives without our realizing their importance. My father has always given me love, money for college, and the security of knowing I would always have a place to live. When he died, everything in my life changed.

The placement of the topic sentence is especially important when you write longer essays. Encountering a variety of paragraph styles can heighten the reading experience for your audience. As you read, noticing the placement of the topic sentence can also give you clues to the meaning and help you find the main point and supporting details. To remember these styles, you might draw these diagrams on an index card and label the parts. Once you have practiced looking for topic sentences and paragraph structure, this will become a useful habit while reading and writing.

### Essays

An essay, like a paragraph, can be organized by a variety of methods, but it must include a thesis statement (a sentence or two that tells what the essay will be about and how much of the topic will be covered), a body, and a conclusion. The following chart compares the way paragraphs and essays differ in structure:

| Paragraph | Essay |
|---|---|
| topic sentence ⟶ | thesis statement |
| examples, supporting details ⟶ | body paragraphs |
| concluding sentence ⟶ | concluding paragraph |

The structural elements in a paragraph are expanded in an essay so that the topic sentence becomes a thesis statement that introduces the concepts to be covered and the scope of discussion to take place in the whole essay. Instead of a few supporting sentences, the essay format uses individual paragraphs to develop individual supporting details or examples. Finally, the concluding sentence in a paragraph is expanded in an essay, becoming a concluding paragraph or two that present final comments or resolution.

   Learning to expand what you have to say does not mean using filler or trivial information to make your essay seem longer. Instead it means developing what you have to say. We will learn more about development later in this chapter, but another technique that will help you stretch what you have to say is outlining your ideas to see where you can add information to clarify your point and better inform and interest your reader. Remember that in the earlier paragraph examples the focus was on the loss of the student's father. In an essay, the student would make this the basis for her thesis statement and would then make each detail a topic for a paragraph. Her outline might look like this:

**Thesis:**   When my father died, everything in my life changed.

**Supporting Paragraphs** (show how my life changed):

Loving relationship, played sports, spent hours talking

Money for college

Security, place to live

**Conclusion:**   Tell story about how I have begun to accept my father's death.

Notice the detail and process in this outline. The thesis statement is the focus of the opening paragraph, as well as of the essay; each point that follows represents an idea that makes a topic sentence for a body paragraph with supporting details; the conclusion would sum up the student's thoughts and communicate her final acceptance of this event. An essay expands your opportunities to communicate an idea by allowing you to develop it more fully and in greater detail.

# READING AN ESSAY

## Strategy for Reading: Getting Beyond the Obvious

As readers, we often must interpret words, phrases, and ideas beyond their literal meaning. For example, if we read, "She had a hot car," we might interpret this to mean either that her car was overheated or that it was very nice-looking. Although writers have a responsibility to communicate their message clearly, sometimes they use figurative words, connotation, or other forms of writing for effect or comparison. These methods require interpretation and thought. They are not an attempt to confuse the reader; rather, they bring humor, interest, and variety to writing.

To go beyond the obvious content of what you read, you must read carefully and consider the meaning or the point. You must observe the context of the words, the way they are being used, whether or not the writer seems serious or sarcastic. Essays sometimes use words, phrases, and ideas in ways that force you to go beyond their literal meaning. Just as explaining a joke usually ruins the joke, these devices are only funny or interesting if they are not over-explained. Learning to see this other level in an essay is a valuable reading skill that readers can develop through practice.

Several types of words create meaning that must be analyzed and interpreted. Figurative language is the use of a word in a way that is different from its literal meaning. For example, if someone says of a person that "He flew the coop," literally this would mean that the person took flight, but figuratively the phrase means that the person left.

Define the following figurative phrases:

1. kicked the bucket _____

2. fair-weather friend _____

3. woke up on the wrong side of the bed _____

In each phrase, the word does not mean what it literally says. The writer assumes that the reader knows this phrase. Many times figurative language is more subtle, though. For example, an author who describes a person as an angel is probably not being literal.

Most language that we use to communicate a clear idea is denotative. If someone asks you for a chair, the word *chair* does not require interpretation. He or she asks for a chair and you understand that the person wants a chair. Denotative language means exactly what it says and uses words in a clear way. Connotation, on the other hand, requires interpretation; in fact, when we read words that have connotations, we often must interpret exactly what a writer means. If a person says, "Terry is a feminist," the speaker may mean to describe Terry's political or personal beliefs, or the speaker may be implying something negative or positive about Terry's character or beliefs. If the speaker is a feminist, then probably he or she is simply presenting a shared characteristic. However, if the speaker is anti-feminist, he or she may be implying something negative about Terry. Thus, connotations are meanings associated with a word or phrase that may or may not be communicated depending on the speaker/writer and the listener/reader. We interpret connotations based on the context of what is being said or written and what we know about the subject. In written works, we use the clues provided in sentences and paragraphs surrounding the phrase. Look at the following examples, and then try to interpret the possible connotations or what each sentence seems to imply about the subject:

1. He can't walk by a mirror without glancing at himself.

_____

_____

2. The politician was seen arriving at a hotel with a woman.

_____

_____

3. She is obviously a blonde.

---

---

Sometimes interpreting meaning that is not obvious requires more than just a careful observation of the words and phrases. In the essay that follows, titled "Notes on Punctuation," observe not only Thomas's use of language, but his use of punctuation. Why does he use punctuation marks in a way that makes it seem as though he cannot type and hits the keys too many times? Try to go beyond what he literally says to derive the meaning of this essay and the techniques he is using to communicate this message.

---

### BEFORE YOU READ

1. How effectively do you feel you use punctuation? Are there any types of punctuation you avoid using because you are unsure about how to use them properly?
2. Write a one- or two-sentence definition of the word *punctuation*. After you have created your own definition, look up the word in a dictionary so that you can see another definition. How close are the two definitions?

---

### Notes on Punctuation\*

by Lewis Thomas

There are no precise rules about punctuation (Fowler[1] lays out some general advice (as best he can under the complex circumstances of English prose (he points out, for example, that we possess only four stops (the comma, the

1

\**Source:* Thomas, Lewis. "Notes on Punctuation." From *The Medusa and the Snail* by Lewis Thomas. Copyright ©1979 by Lewis Thomas. Used by permission of Viking Penguin, a division of Penguin Books USA, Inc.

[1] H. W. Fowler, author of *Modern English Usage* (1926, revised 1965 by Sir Ernest Gowers), a standard reference work.

semicolon, the colon and the period (the question mark
and exclamation point are not, strictly speaking, stops; they
are indicators of tone (oddly enough, the Greeks
employed the semicolon for their question mark (it produces a strange sensation to read a Greek sentence which
is a straightforward question: Why weepest thou; (instead
of Why weepest thou? (and, of course, there are parentheses (which are surely a kind of punctuation making this
whole much more complicated by having to count up the
left-handed parentheses in order to be sure of closing with
the right number (but if the parentheses were left out,
with nothing to work with but the stops, we would have
considerably more flexibility in the deploying of layers of
meaning than if we tried to separate all the clauses by
physical barriers (and in the latter case, while we might
have more precision and exactitude for our meaning, we
would lose the essential flavor of language, which is its
wonderful ambiguity)))))))))))).

    The commas are the most useful and usable of all the
stops. It is highly important to put them in place as you go
along. If you try to come back after doing a paragraph and
stick them in the various spots that tempt you you will discover that they tend to swarm like minnows into all sorts of
crevices whose existence you hadn't realized and before
you know it the whole long sentence becomes immobilized
and lashed up squirming in commas. Better to use them
sparingly, and with affection, precisely when the need for
each one arises, nicely, by itself.

    I have grown fond of semicolons in recent years. The
semicolon tells you that there is still some question about
the preceding full sentence; something needs to be added;
it reminds you sometimes of the Greek usage. It is almost
always a greater pleasure to come across a semicolon than
a period. The period tells you that that is that; if you didn't
get all the meaning you wanted or expected, anyway you
got all the writer intended to parcel out and now you have
to move along. But with a semicolon there you get a pleasant little feeling of expectancy; there is more to come;
read on; it will get clearer.

2

3

Colons are a lot less attractive, for several reasons: 4
firstly, they give you the feeling of being rather ordered
around, or at least having your nose pointed in a direction
you might not be inclined to take if left to yourself, and,
secondly, you suspect you're in for one of those sentences
that will be labeling the points to be made: firstly, secondly
and so forth, with the implication that you haven't sense
enough to keep track of a sequence of notions without
having them numbered. Also, many writers use this system
loosely and incompletely, starting out with number one
and number two as though counting off on their fingers
but then going on and on without the succession of labels
you've been led to expect, leaving you floundering about
searching for the ninethly or seventeenthly that ought to
be there but isn't.

Exclamation points are the most irritating of all. 5
Look! they say, look at what I just said! How amazing is my
thought! It is like being forced to watch someone else's
small child jumping up and down crazily in the center of
the living room shouting to attract attention. If a sentence
really has something of importance to say, something quite
remarkable, it doesn't need a mark to point it out. And if
it is really, after all, a banal sentence needing more zing,
the exclamation point simply emphasizes its banality!

Quotation marks should be used honestly and spar- 6
ingly, when there is a genuine quotation at hand, and it is
necessary to be very rigorous about the words enclosed by
the marks. If something is to be quoted, the exact words
must be used. If part of it must be left out because of
space limitations, it is good manners to insert three dots to
indicate the omission, but it is unethical to do this if it
means connecting two thoughts which the original author
did not intend to have tied together. Above all, quotation
marks should not be used for ideas that you'd like to dis-
own, things in the air so to speak. Nor should they be put
in place around clichés; if you want to use a cliché you
must take full responsibility for it yourself and not try to
job it off on anon., or on society. The most objectionable
misuse of quotation marks, but one which illustrates the

dangers of misuse in ordinary prose, is seen in advertising, especially in advertisements for small restaurants, for example "just around the corner," or "a good place to eat." No single, identifiable, citable person ever really said, for the record, "just around the corner," much less "a good place to eat," least likely of all for restaurants of the type that use this type of prose.

The dash is a handy device, informal and essentially    7
playful, telling you that you're about to take off on a different tack but still in some way connected with the present course—only you have to remember that the dash is there, and either put a second dash at the end of the notion to let the reader know that he's back on course, or else end the sentence, as here, with a period.

The greatest danger in punctuation is for poetry.    8
Here it is necessary to be as economical and parsimonious with commas and periods as with the words themselves, and any marks that seem to carry their own subtle meanings, like dashes and little rows of periods, even semicolons and question marks, should be left out altogether rather than inserted to clog up the thing with ambiguity. A single exclamation point in a poem, no matter what else the poem has to say, is enough to destroy the whole work.

The things I like best in T. S. Eliot's poetry, especially in    9
the *Four Quartets,* are the semicolons. You cannot hear them, but they are there, laying out the connections between the images and the ideas. Sometimes you get a glimpse of a semicolon coming, a few lines farther on, and it is like climbing a steep path through woods and seeing a wooden bench just at a bend in the road ahead, a place where you can expect to sit for a moment, catching your breath.

## Building Your Skills

### *Focus on Words*

Look up the following words or parts of phrases in a dictionary. Consult the preceding essay and identify the meaning that best fits the way the author uses the word in this essay. Each word or phrase is followed by the number of the paragraph in which it appears.

| | |
|---|---|
| precise (1) | immobilized (2) |
| indicators (1) | notions (4) |
| tone (1) | succession (4) |
| deploying (1) | floundering (4) |
| exactitude (1) | banality (5) |
| ambiguity (1) | omission (6) |
| minnows (2) | clichés (6) |
| crevices (2) | parsimonious (8) |

### Focus on the Message

1. What does Thomas mean when he writes "we possess only four stops" (para. 1)? How does Thomas describe commas, semicolons, colons, exclamation points, quotation marks, and dashes? What are the advantages and disadvantages of using each?

2. Find several places where Thomas uses figurative language and connotation. How do these phrases or words add to the meaning of his essay or support his point? (Hint: para. 6 uses the words "it is good manners to insert three dots to indicate the omission." Is this likely to appear in a book of good manners?)

3. Scan the paragraphs in Thomas's essay. Where does he use unconventional or unusual punctuation? What point is he trying to make about the way in which punctuation affects meaning?

4. How does Thomas incorporate humor or sarcasm into this essay? Does he sound serious throughout the whole essay, or does he sometimes sound playful? How does his use of figurative and connotative language add to this technique?

5. How does Thomas organize his essay? Underline the topic sentence of each paragraph. How much does he vary the placement of topic sentences throughout his essay? Write an outline demonstrating the structure of his essay, including the thesis, the major points, and the concluding point. Why do you think he chooses this order?

## TECHNIQUES FOR WRITING: THE WELL-DEVELOPED PARAGRAPH, THE WELL-DEVELOPED ESSAY

Understanding development is an important part of learning to write effectively. We refer to a piece of writing as developed when the writer has thought through his or her topic carefully, has supplied the reader with enough information and background on the topic, and has provided enough ideas or examples to make ideas or concepts clear for the reader.

Earlier in this chapter, we discussed the structure of paragraphs and essays in a general way, but development in each can depend on the subject, the type of assignment, and most important, on the audience. Subjects that are familiar to most people will naturally require less development than an obscure or less widely known topic. The characteristics of the target audience also can determine how much to develop or discuss a topic. A historical analysis of the Civil War would need much more development if it were being written for students who had little knowledge about this event than if it were being written for a group of history professors.

Development also varies depending on the type of assignment or writing task. Compare the development necessary in a letter written to a friend about an event in your life to the development needed for the same letter to your instructor. A friend who knows you very well is less likely to need as much information and detail as your instructor. When you analyze your own work to discover if you have developed your topic enough, ask yourself the following questions:

1. Do all of my ideas seem related and important to my thesis statement?
2. Have I included details that will help my reader read and relate to my point or experiences?
3. Have I connected ideas for my reader so that he or she will see the relationships or causes and effects I am trying to establish?
4. Can I add information to keep any part of my essay from being misunderstood?
5. Can I add any information to make my essay more interesting or readable?

When you have answered these questions and made any necessary changes, the next step is to let someone you trust (perhaps a fellow writing student) read your written work and answer these questions with you.

Compare the level of development in the following paragraphs:

PARAGRAPH *A*

She has always been there for me. She is someone I can always count on. My sister is a very special person. I really love her and think a lot of her. Most people value their sisters, but I really value mine.

PARAGRAPH *B*

One of the people I respect and love the most is my sister, Vicki. My sister is not an ordinary person, at least not in my opinion. Whenever I have doubted myself, she has encouraged me and bolstered me with her faith in my abilities. She can take a moment that seems like the worst time in my life and make it seem easy to overcome. She is truly someone I can always count on.

In paragraph A, we know very little about why the writer values her sister, but in paragraph B, the ideas are developed with examples and important details. Development in a paragraph leads to greater clarity (clearer meaning) in the paragraph, as well as to easier reading. When you read, you may not specifically think of these terms, but you are certainly looking for development in what you read. If writing is not developed, it may leave you confused, bored, or simply dissatisfied. When you see this as a writer, it can give you incentive to work to provide clarity and development in everything you write. Remember that reading for development in your own writing takes place mostly during the revision stage, not while you are trying to formulate ideas or reasons to write.

### Reader-Based Versus Writer-Based Writing

Development can be viewed in another way. When a writer develops an idea fully, he or she most often produces reader-based writing. Reader-based writing is writing that identifies and works to communicate with an audience (the reader). It acknowledges that a reader will be trying to understand the message, and thus it provides adequate information, organizes ideas in a logical manner, and incorporates grammar and wording that make the writing easier to read. In addition, it purposely captures the reader's interest and presents the subject matter clearly for the reader rather than making the reader work to figure out what the writer is trying to say. Every writing task requires that you identify your audience; when you are not writing just for yourself, you need to write specifically for your audience; in other words, you must supply all the information your audience will need, make connections between the ideas you present, and provide an interesting, thoughtful point. When a writer does not supply necessary information or uses unclear wording, confusing grammar, or concepts that are not clearly explained, he or she is typically writing for himself or herself, usually without even realizing it.

### *My Bad Vacation*

My vacation this summer was a disaster. We left to come home and the car caught on fire. I really did not have fun. In fact, I will remember this as my worst vacation ever.

Does this paragraph speak to you as a reader?

Is the writing reader-based or writer-based?

The short passage above is a good example of writer-based writing. The writer probably understands his own point, but he has not provided enough detail for his readers. In a personal journal this type of writing would be perfectly appropriate, but any writing that will be read by someone else should not be writer-based. What necessary information is missing from the paragraph? Where did the writer go on his vacation? Why didn't he have fun? Was the whole vacation a disaster or just the trip home? As readers, we have expectations about what an essay about a disastrous vacation will include. When a writer leaves out important information, we feel confused or we simply lack interest in what has been written. Readers have a variety of expectations, which makes knowing your audience a valuable skill. Along with expecting a certain amount of information, readers also expect a particular form of grammar, a clear and familiar format for the ideas, and a recognizable communication style. While you are reading essays, you are building your own expectations as a reader, and when you write, you are using your own expectations as the guidelines for writing reader-based prose. When you write, you must gather enough information, organize it, and write about it so that a reader can easily understand your point. When you do this, you are supplying your readers with writing designed just for them.

## Building Your Skills

### Assignment 1

Reread one of the last paragraphs or essays you wrote. Write an outline that illustrates the order of your points and what you actually say (not what you meant to say) in your paragraph or essay. Does the paragraph or essay use reader-based or writer-based writing? What features lead you to believe this? Rewrite your paragraph or essay developing a particular point more fully. If this point is not included in your original thesis, rewrite your thesis so that it includes your new point. If you decide that your essay is written for you instead of for your reader, make changes so that it provides what is needed for a reader-based essay (a thesis, details, developed ideas, connections between ideas, and a conclusion).

### Assignment 2

Brainstorm to get ideas for a paragraph or essay about your life growing up. Choose a topic from your brainstorm, and make a list of the points you would need to include to fully develop your topic in an essay. Which points would be most effective if described in full detail? Which could be grouped to make a point about your topic? Write a developed essay that describes a particular experience or set of related experiences that reflect an important element in your upbringing. Reread your essay and mark sentences that include details with a highlighting pen. Are there any places with little or no highlighting? If so, rewrite your essay adding details to appeal to your reader.

### Assignment 3

**Step 1:** Write a paragraph describing the ideal _____. (Fill in the blank with the word of your choice: day, car, man, woman, date, etc.) Be sure to supply your reader with all important details about this ideal person or thing.

**Step 2:** Outline your paragraph, identifying the topic sentence and the major points. Then, convert this paragraph outline to an outline for a whole essay. Convert your topic sentence to a thesis statement for a whole essay that becomes part of the essay's introduction. Convert each major point to a topic sentence for a paragraph. Convert the concluding idea to a topic sentence for the conclusion. Write an essay using your outline and developing your ideas to meet the level of detail necessary in an essay.

**Step 3:** Compare the structure and development of your paragraph with your essay. Which do you think is a more interesting or effective piece of writing?

## READING A STUDENT ESSAY

### Peer Review Strategy: Revising for Development

When you read a friend's paper or your own for revision, one approach is to read for development. This technique is particularly good when an essay is shorter than you think it should be or when you have a core idea, but you are not sure you have taken it far enough.

When you read an essay for development, look for structure first: introduction, a body that supports and gives a detailed discussion of the main point, and a conclusion that leaves you as a reader satisfied. If any of these parts is missing, begin the rewriting process by filling in the missing introduction, conclusion, or supporting details.

Once you have evaluated the basic structure, the second focus is on logical development or on the progression of ideas. Ideas in an essay should build on one another as if the writer were using building blocks. If a block or a connection between ideas is missing, the essay will be structurally weak and confusing to read. Train your eyes to notice the progression of ideas or how each idea leads (or does not lead) to the next as you read other people's essays and your own. If you find a leap in logic or a missing link or idea, add or connect the idea that is needed to continue the progression of ideas.

As you read the following student essay, pay close attention to the main point, the overall structure, and the movement from one idea to the next. Label and underline the essay's thesis, the topic sentences, and the details that lead the reader from one idea to the next. Then decide whether this is written using reader-based or writer-based writing.

### Transportation, Not!

#### by Tom Hester

Motor vehicles are not what they seem. They are used for transportation, but that is not the main reason people buy them. People buy motor vehicles to show off, to look good, to add to their collections, and for many other reasons. [1]

When motor vehicles were first introduced to the public, the option to use other types of transportation was more feasible than it is now. Of course, at that time, there were only a couple of different types of motor vehicles to choose from. This led certain segments of our society to request that motor vehicle manufacturers make vehicles more suited to the different economic classes in our society. We now have motor vehicles to meet almost any budget. [2]

Today, no matter what your income level, motor vehicle transportation is a necessity. This is especially true for people living in large cities or rural areas who must travel long distances. Even though motor vehicles have become a necessity, this has not stopped them from becoming status symbols. Most people look at the type of vehicle a person drives and stereotype that person based on that vehicle. A person driving a Lexus [3] may be stereotyped as wealthy, while a person driving a VW van may be stereotyped as poor. This is not the only way to stereotype cars and their drivers, but it is the most common way.

Personal preference often is the reason for choosing a vehicle, yet we think that a Corvette driver is different from the driver of a low rider—all based on a stereotype. The stereotyping of individuals based upon the type of vehicle a person drives is, in most cases, inaccurate. It is safer to assume that a person is driving a certain type of vehicle because he or she likes it or it was affordable.

4

When buying a vehicle, we expect it to provide us with transportation as a given. People would not buy vehicles if they could not be used for transportation. There are, of course, exceptions, such as vehicles that are purchased for museums or private collections. Some vehicles are also used as race cars or for hobby shows. In these exceptions, the motor vehicles are transported by trailer and are typically not used for transportation at all.

5

The motor vehicle has a number of uses besides transportation. A vehicle known as an RV can be used as a home on wheels. The poor and homeless also sometimes use their vehicles as homes, if they are lucky enough to have vehicles. The motor vehicle has also been credited with changing the sexual habits of people for several generations. And a vehicle can be used as a getaway in a robbery, although this is not a recommended use.

6

The motor vehicle is a boon and a burden to society, but mostly a burden. It boosts the economy by sales and related manufacturing business. In fact, the motor vehicle industry employs one in six Americans and makes up nearly 20% of the gross national product. The burdens of the motor vehicles though include increased traffic congestion and pollution, the ever-

7

increasing prices for fossil fuels, and the increasing
costs of buying and maintaining a vehicle.

    While the motor vehicle has remained a source of          8
transportation, it has evolved into something more
than a sum of its parts. The motor vehicle has become
an extension of our personal image, a way to tell the
world a little about ourselves without any personal
contact. The motor vehicle also gives us the illusion of
total freedom and the ability to go wherever we wish.
It asks nothing in return except for fuel, brakes, tires,
oil, transmission fluid, water, and the occasional tune-
up. The costs sometimes seem to outweigh the benefits,
but until something better comes along, we'll just keep
on trucking and driving.

## Building Your Skills

1.  Describe or outline the overall structure of Hester's essay. What is his thesis?
    How well does each paragraph develop or support that thesis?

    _____

    _____

    _____

    _____

    _____

    _____

    _____

    _____

    _____

2. Which points are developed the most in Hester's essay? Which could be developed more fully?

_____

_____

_____

_____

_____

_____

_____

_____

3. Who do you think is Hester's primary audience? Would you describe this essay as mostly reader-based or writer-based writing? Why?

_____

_____

_____

_____

_____

_____

_____

_____

4. As if you were discussing Tom's paper with him, list three features of his essay that work very well or that really appeal to you as a reader. Then, recommend three changes he could make to improve his essay.

Describe three features that are effective for you as a reader:

a. _____

b. _____

c. _____

Describe three improvements or changes Tom could make to create a more effective, interesting, or informative essay:

a. _____

b. _____

c. _____

## USING GRAMMAR: PUNCTUATING SENTENCES FOR CLARITY

Effective and grammatical sentences include a subject, a verb, and a clear point. In our discussion in Chapter 3, we defined independent and dependent clauses. Knowing these sentence parts can make learning punctuation an easier task. An independent clause, like a sentence, has a subject and a verb, but remember that a sentence may have more than one independent clause. Furthermore, recall that the dependent clauses we discussed earlier begin with dependent words (consult the list in the Appendix). As you will see, sentences can be punctuated in many ways; how you choose to punctuate them is part of your style as a writer and can affect the clarity and effectiveness of your work overall. In addition, punctuation is vital to making your ideas clear and accessible to your reader. The following is a presentation of the many options available for punctuating your sentences.

❏ **Punctuate a single independent clause by placing a period, question mark, or exclamation point at the end.**

*EXAMPLE:*

The fire raged through the night.

❏ **Punctuate two independent clauses in one sentence by doing any one of the following:**

❏ **Place a comma and a coordinating conjunction between the two independent clauses (consult the Appendix for a list of coordinating conjunctions).**

*EXAMPLE:*

The fire raged through the night, **but** the firefighters worked to get it under control.

❏ **Place a semicolon between the two independent clauses (do not capitalize the first letter following the semicolon).**

*EXAMPLE:*

> The fire raged through the night; the firefighters worked to get it under control.

❏ **Place a semicolon, a conjunctive adverb, and a comma between the two independent clauses (see the list of conjunctive adverbs in the Appendix).**

*EXAMPLE:*

> The fire raged through the night; **still,** the firefighters worked to get it under control.

### Fragments, Run-ons, and Comma Splices

When students have trouble with fragments, run-ons, and comma splices, it is usually because they misunderstand either the structure of a sentence or the use of particular marks of punctuation. The following guidelines will help you understand what each of these problems is and how to change each problem sentence to a grammatical sentence. If you repeatedly have problems with one or all of these, you might try copying the solutions listed below onto a notecard and keeping it with you when you revise your writing.

#### Fragments

A **fragment** occurs when a group of words begins with a dependent word (subordinating conjunction) and is not followed by an independent clause. In the first example below, the group of words beginning with the word *because* is not a sentence because it starts with a dependent word and does not include an independent clause before the period. When the writer places a comma instead of a period after *film,* the group of words becomes grammatical and no longer includes a fragment.

*EXAMPLE:*

> Because I don't like the star in that film. I won't be going to that movie.
> Because I don't like the star in that film, I won't be going to that movie.

A **fragment** can also occur when a group of words does not contain a subject or a verb. For example, the next group of words does not have a subject or a verb; we don't know what happened or who or what the sentence is about.

In the dark, around the corner of a mysterious building.

Usually these types of fragments occur because the writer has put a period before the actual end of the sentence, but sometimes as you write quickly, you may leave out an important word or part of a sentence, so be careful to read individual sentences in your paper to check for groups of words written as sentences that are incomplete.

### Run-ons or Fused Sentences

**Run-on sentences** occur when two complete statements or independent clauses are fused together without the necessary punctuation. Notice that the following sentence could be divided between "night" and "the" to form two sentences.

*EXAMPLE:*

> The fire raged through the **night the** firefighters worked to get it under control.

It is a run-on because the two independent clauses—"the fire raged through the night" and "the firefighters worked to get it under control"— are fused or run together without any punctuation. To edit a run-on sentence and make it grammatical, use one of the following methods. Because each method is equally grammatical, you should learn to use all of them.

❏ **Add a dependent word to one of the independent clauses, making one independent clause into a dependent clause. (Add a comma after the dependent clause when it comes first.)**

*EXAMPLE:*

> **Though** the firefighters worked to get the fire under control, it raged through the night.

❏ **Place a period between the two independent clauses and capitalize the first word of the second independent clause.**

*EXAMPLE:*

> The fire raged through the night. The firefighters worked to get it under control.

❏ **Connect the two independent clauses using a semicolon.**

> *EXAMPLE:*
>
>> The fire raged through the night; the firefighters worked to get it under control.

❏ **Connect the two independent clauses using a semicolon, a conjunctive adverb, and a comma.** (See Appendix for list.)

> *EXAMPLE:*
>
>> The fire raged through the night; **however,** the firefighters worked to get it under control.

❏ **Connect the two independent clauses using a comma and a coordinating conjunction.** (See Appendix for list.)

> *EXAMPLE:*
>
>> The fire raged through the night, **but** the firefighters worked to get it under control.

### Comma Splices

A **comma splice** is a run-on that uses a comma between independent clauses.

> *EXAMPLE:*
>
>> The fire raged through the night, the firefighters worked to get it under control.

When you combine two independent clauses, remember that you need more than just a comma. You also need a coordinating conjunction. Comma splices are common to first drafts. If you read and observe your commas carefully, you can easily detect them. When you do find a comma splice, you can simply add a coordinating conjunction, or you can make changes to the sentence as directed in the preceding section on run-ons.

Each of these sentence problems—the fragment, the run-on, and the comma splice—can be detected and easily corrected with a clear understanding of punctuation. Furthermore, the more you practice and understand these punctuation marks, the greater the variety you can include in your writing.

## Building Your Skills

### Assignment 1

Add punctuation to make the following sentences grammatical. Remember, you have several choices, so practice different methods.

1. The old man stood silently in line he was not sure what to say.

2. Learning to use a computer can be difficult computers make other parts of our lives easier.

3. Even though she seemed unhappy about the results. She never voiced her opinion.

4. Traveling can be fun, it can also be very expensive.

5. The economy seemed shaky many investors were reluctant to risk losing their money.

6. After losing all of his money. One investor became very agitated.

7. After spending a relaxing weekend at home, Maria went back to work she was tired by 10:30.

8. Many people are concerned about the changing values of modern society some would like to see big changes in this value system.

9. You probably are not well-informed. Unless you read newspapers regularly.

10. Learning grammar rules seems very challenging, it's really not that difficult.

### Assignment 2

With another student, make up a list of ten to fifteen sentences containing fragments, run-ons, and comma splices. Then rewrite the sentences individually, using appropriate punctuation to correct each sentence. When you are both finished, compare the ways you changed the sentences, making sure that each of the new sentences is grammatical.

### Assignment 3

On a 3″ × 5″ or larger notecard, summarize Lewis Thomas's advice in "Notes on Punctuation" for using the punctuation marks he discusses. Review a recent piece of your own writing. How do you use these marks of punctuation? Are there some you purposely avoid? Rewrite your essay, punctuating according to Thomas's recommendations and using all of the punctuation marks he discusses. Evaluate how these changes affect your overall message. How do they affect your style?

## SEEING THE CONNECTIONS: APPLYING YOUR SKILLS

### Assignment 1

Find examples of each of the paragraph styles discussed earlier in this chapter. Cut one example of each type from magazines or newspapers. Create a diagram sheet or poster that includes the diagram shape for each style, a sample paragraph, and labels illustrating the parts of the paragraphs in whatever order they appear.

### Assignment 2

In Tom Hester's essay "Transportation, Not!" he uses sarcasm and subtle humor. What could you write about that is funny? Make a list of topics that lend themselves to satire—for example, parenting, marriage, cooking, fixing up the house, dealing with in-laws. Write whatever comes to mind. Then freewrite for five to ten minutes about one of these topics. You might recall a specific event, such as painting the kitchen, and tell details about the dripping paint, the painted dog, and so on. Purposely try to see the humor in the situation.

Write an essay that discusses the funny side of a situation or that looks sarcastically at something that is normally serious. When you finish your first draft, let someone else read your essay. Have this person tell you what is funny and what is not. Also make sure that you have supplied a clear point. Rewrite your essay to produce a final draft that includes humor and a clear purpose, as well as a variety of the punctuation discussed in this chapter.

### Assignment 3

Read Thomas's "Notes on Punctuation" in this chapter. Follow the Before You Read directions and list your definition and a dictionary definition for punctuation. Brainstorm to discover other associations you have with punctuation.

Write an essay that discusses the advantages and disadvantages of using punctuation. How is it useful? In what ways does it present problems? Use at least two examples as you explain your point—one to show the advantages, the second to illustrate the disadvantages.

Rewrite your first draft making sure that the advantages and disadvantages are linked effectively in your essay; then use each of the following types of punctuation at least once:

| | |
|---|---|
| parentheses   ( ) | quotation marks   "   " |
| commas   , | dashes   — |
| semicolons   ; | exclamation points   ! |
| colons   : | |

# Chapter 6

# Making Connections for Your Reader

In this chapter you will learn

☆ to distinguish between rhetorical strategies and use them when you write;
☆ to identify organizational strategies when you read;
☆ to use transitions in your writing;
☆ to revise for transitions and the connections between ideas;
☆ to distinguish between regular and irregular verbs;
☆ to use verbs in the appropriate tense.

Take a moment to answer the following questions:

1. What creates structure in an essay?

_____

_____

_____

2. As a reader, how important do you think structure is? In what ways does an essay's structure affect you while you are reading?

_____

_____

_____

3. How do you connect ideas when you write? What methods do you use most often?

_____

_____

_____

4. How does essay structure relate to purpose and audience?

_____

_____

_____

## CREATING STRUCTURE: PATTERNS FOR ORGANIZING YOUR IDEAS

When we identify a piece of writing as an essay, we actually mean that we recognize it as an essay because it includes structural elements that distinguish it as an essay. **Structure** is defined in an essay as the elements that lead the reader through the essay and point out the main ideas, the supporting ideas, and any relationships between ideas. Without structure, an essay really could not exist, just as without structure a house could not exist. The structure of a house allows the builder or designer to include fancy windows or add special features in the kitchen or living room, and in a similar way, the structure of an essay supports or provides a foundation for a persuasive thesis, for shocking, funny, or surprising examples, or for any other kind of creative use of words and phrases. We even identify different types of essays based on the structure the writer uses to communicate the message or main idea. At its most basic level, structure in an essay can be described as an introduction, a body, and a conclusion, but obviously an essay includes other elements to build a structural foundation. Writers use patterns and techniques such as transitional phrases and paragraphs to promote the logical progression of ideas. They may use subtitles to create structure and to allow for easy reading. A well-written essay should be well organized and reasonably easy to read and understand. It will most likely be structured for the reader's convenience and ease of reading. When a piece of writing is not structured well, reading can be extremely difficult and confusing.

The introduction, body, and conclusion are essential parts of any essay that help the reader to find the overall point, the discussion of that point, and some sort of resolution to that point. But other techniques and patterns occur within this overall structure that help the reader follow the point through an essay. These patterns assist the writer by providing different strategies for communicating ideas with diverse emphases and approaches. They help readers build expectations for what they are reading, as well as helping them to identify when a writer is proving a point, telling a story, or comparing two things. Patterns such as these are called **rhetorical modes** or strategies.

Nine rhetorical modes are typically used in essays in a variety of combinations. In other words, most essays use a combination of modes. For example, a writer may argue a point about a problem in society, use examples from society to back up his or her point of view, and then identify major effects that are occurring in society as a result of this problem; all of these strategies work together to communicate an overall message. Typically we call the strongest element or strategy the dominant rhetorical mode. In the example above, if the focus of the essay was arguing the significance of the societal problem, we would call the essay an argumentation or persuasive essay. The other modes we could then discuss as supporting the dominant mode.

## The Rhetorical Modes

### Description

Description, when it is used as the primary mode of communication in an essay, uses language to produce a detailed, picturesque view of the topic of the essay. In a descriptive essay, a writer must provide details that appeal to the senses of the reader. Typically description must also include a reason to read that engages the reader in the description for a purpose. If the description is shocking or particularly appealing, this reason may not be openly stated, but rather implied. If the description centers on a person, often it will present admirable qualities or features that make this person noteworthy and thus interesting to read about.

> The house smelled like Christmas. Coming from the kitchen were the aromas of ham, turkey, roast, and the rest of a glorious meal. I could also smell the crackling fire in the living room where I stood. Upon entering the family room, I was met with a collection of perfumes and colognes, combined with the smell of our youngest family member, a baby. Christmas came and went and took its aromas away with it.

### Narration

Narration, simply defined, is storytelling. In essays, narratives are typically personal stories that recount the details of an event. Sometimes narratives tell a story about someone or something else not related to a personal experience. Narration is almost always paired with careful description, but description in an essay can occur without narration. As a rhetorical strategy, narration requires the writer to present parts of a story in an easy-to-read order and with enough detail to satisfy the reader. When narratives lack order or detail, readers will probably find them boring or confusing.

> I remember the holidays I used to spend at home. On Christmas especially the house always made me feel special, different. Our family problems were left on the doorstep and exchanged for laughter and the wonderful aromas that filled the kitchen. As kids, we played with toys casually, sneaking over to shake a package each time no one was looking. I remember the security and comfort of this day. Although much of our family had not even seen each other all year long, the fights and conflicts that produced rifts between the family on any other day were ignored on this special day of the year. I remember this day and this tradition as some of the most important events in my life, and now that I am older, I wish that for just one day I could go back to the way things used to be.

### Illustration/Example

Illustration, also known as example, is the controlling or dominant rhetorical mode in an essay when the essay focuses on a primary example of the author's topic or when the author focuses on illustrating several examples as the thesis or main point of the essay. An example or illustration essay is usually structured so that explaining and supporting the interpretation of the example is the main focus of the essay. Therefore, if the reader understands the example and the support the author has used to illustrate the relationship between the example and the topic, then the reader will certainly find the essay credible and, most likely, convincing.

> The effectiveness of discipline in children is greatly increased when parents or other care-providing adults are consistent. For a closer look at discipline and consistency, let's examine the relationship between a mother named Irene and her two-year-old daughter, Daphne. Often when Irene says "No" to Daphne, her daughter smiles and laughs as a way of talking her mother into whatever she wants. If they go to the grocery store, Daphne is able to get Irene to buy something for her, even after Irene has repeatedly told her no, by persisting with complaints or cute behaviors. Irene cannot understand why Daphne bothers her so much for the things that she wants, but as we can see from this example, Daphne's behavior is learned. If she complains or looks cute for long enough, she will accomplish her goal.

Because her persistence has paid off in the past, she has learned that her mother will consistently give in.

### Process Analysis

As the name seems to indicate, process analysis involves analyzing a process. Two major features of this mode are the use of clear directions or steps and the necessity for providing a purpose for reading. Process analysis can also be combined with other modes so that the analysis of what happens in a process may be linked to an argument for or against that process. When a writer analyzes a process, he or she must clearly explain how to do something or how something is done. For example, to explain how to make fried chicken or how to fix a flat tire, or even how a trial is conducted, a writer would use process analysis. These topics would also require the writer to give us reasons for wanting to read and learn about these processes.

Writing an effective essay involves many steps. First, choose a topic by brainstorming, and then decide on a thesis or main idea that you want to communicate. Second, organize information about your topic. If you are describing a personal experience, you might think through the events that took place, or if it's another kind of essay, you could outline your major ideas. Third, begin to write a first draft. Try to get your ideas on paper; then think about how to rewrite them. Once you have a first draft, reread the whole thing and begin to add to the ideas that need more detail and take out anything that does not help to support or establish your main idea or thesis. Next, have a friend or tutor read the draft and suggest possible changes. And finally, make changes that clarify your message, rewrite your essay, and turn it in. Once you have turned in the paper, celebrate!

### Classification

Classification, like process analysis, requires careful attention by the writer to establishing purpose—the writer must provide a reason for classifying items into groups. An essay that uses classification as its dominant rhetorical mode could, for example, classify jobs by considering those that have the greatest effect on the health of the nation, or might discuss types of students and how each type performs in school. Just classifying is not enough; an essay must express the reason for classifying and how the information gained from this classification is useful. In addition, though all essays require transitions, classification requires that thoughtful links or connections be established between categories or groups. Be careful, when using this mode, not to list categories or identify them without really discussing them.

Violence is a major issue in our society. While many people view violence as unacceptable, some types of violence are commonly accepted and participated in within our society. The violence involved in war, self-defense, movies, and sports are all types of violence that a majority of people in society seem to support, either actively or passively. Violent crimes, domestic violence, and sexual violence are obviously less acceptable types of violence to most, although certainly they are accepted and practiced by some. When we use the word violence, too often we lump all types into one, but it is more helpful in preventing unacceptable types of violence if we acknowledge or discuss the types we see as acceptable.

**Comparison/Contrast**

Comparison/contrast is a rhetorical mode with which most students are very familiar; however, it can still be a challenge to use. Two forms of comparison are possible. Using A to represent the first item to be compared and B to represent the second item or the item we are comparing with A, we can discuss the two forms.

| SUCCESSIVE COMPARISON | ALTERNATING COMPARISON |
|---|---|
| A | A |
| B | B |
| | A |
| | B |
| Features of A are discussed fully and then compared with B. | Features of A and B are compared and contrasted by discussing one then the other, using a back-and-forth technique. |

A comparison can be made so that all points about the first item to be compared are discussed first and then all the comparisons to the second item follow, or a comparison can be made by comparing aspects of the first item with aspects of the second in an alternating pattern. The alternating pattern is represented in the example below.

In my family, it has always been customary for us to respect others' property. We were taught to touch only our own things and never to become rowdy or loud in another person's home. But many times when I see children in stores or when friends bring children to my house, they seem to feel as if my things belong to them. I never presume that others need to prepare for me or my children, or that it is acceptable for us to "make ourselves completely at home." My friend, Jane, feels that when she comes to my house to visit, I should put everything in my home on a shelf out of the reach of her three-year-old. But I believe that she should teach her three-year-old to leave other people's things alone rather than redecorating my home. Though I know people have different ideas about manners and raising children, I think every person should learn to respect other people's property.

### Definition

Sometimes to truly understand a concept, we must clearly define it. Although that sounds easy, try defining a disease or a philosophical concept and what you soon learn is how difficult this can be in practice. Definition requires clear, succinct discussion of a concept or object to tell what its major features are. If a writer defines love, he or she must define it so that his or her readers will clearly understand and relate to the definition. In addition, definition challenges the writer to give a reason for defining this idea or object—that is, why defining it is important or significant to readers. Two obvious connections to this mode would be comparison and argumentation. When a writer defines something unfamiliar, he or she must compare it with things we already know. Typically when a writer defines, he or she argues for or defends that definition as well, so though this mode may be dominant in an essay, it almost always requires a combination using either comparison, argumentation, or both.

Poetry can be defined in many ways. Poetry means something different to every reader. One possible definition of poetry is a collection of words that not only touches the heart, but cuts through the soul. Poetry has the power to force the reader to think about issues and ideas that perhaps the reader would rather not. Poetry forces us to think! It makes us see reality. Poetry barges in, finds what we thought was hidden, and forces us to wear it like a new jacket.

### Cause/Effect

Discussing causes and effects requires the writer to explore relationships between actions and the results of those actions. Though both causes and effects may be discussed in the same essay, typically they do not receive equal time. An essay that concentrates on the causes will undoubtedly consider the effects as well, but the writer will normally attempt to focus on the reasons why what he or she suggests as causes really are causes. A focus on effects necessitates some discussion of causes as well, but this type of essay will focus on what resulted from a particular problem. Obviously, examples are likely to be part of a cause/effect essay.

To illustrate this rhetorical strategy, think about writing an essay on teenage pregnancy. If we focus on the causes of teenage pregnancy, we might write about causes within the family, societal attitudes, or teens ignoring warnings about becoming pregnant. If we focus on the effects of teenage pregnancy, we would create a completely different essay; we might discuss the problems created for teens who become pregnant or who father a child; we might outline the various school programs that have been created to help pregnant teens continue their education. No matter what effects we chose to focus on, though, we would produce a much different essay.

In addition to choosing whether to focus on cause or effect, this strategy makes it especially important that the writer clearly understand his or her audience. Thinking from the perspective of a person who is in the midst of the problem or issue might prevent the writer from making assumptions or careless statements about such a person. Offending your audience obviously produces an ineffective essay. In cause/effect essays this is of particular concern because we often generalize when we discuss the causes or effects of a problem. Be sensitive to your potential readers, and present touchy subjects carefully.

> Teenage pregnancy has drastic and long-lasting effects on young women. When a teenager becomes pregnant, she is faced with a whole new set of decisions, priorities, and responsibilities. Depending on the choices she makes, her life will change in many ways. If she aborts the child, she must face the guilt and lack of acceptance by others. She may struggle with these feelings, and others will view her differently for the rest of her life. If she keeps the baby, she will have to decide whether to stay in school or not, and she will have to make plans for supporting the child. If the father is responsible, he too will have to make plans. If the teen gives the child away in an adoption, she likely will carry guilt and worry about the child throughout her life. In fact, she may feel very depressed after the birth of the child and after the adoption is final. No matter what kind of decisions a young mother makes, she faces a long road of guilt or frustration ahead. Perhaps the best help anyone can offer is love and support for a teen mother.

### Argument/Persuasion

Over two thousand years ago, philosophers like Aristotle believed that all communication was essentially persuasive in intent. If we weren't trying to persuade someone to see our view, to believe our claim, or to understand something about our personality or life, why would we write at all? But in discussing the structure of an essay, we describe an essay as argumentative when it promotes a particular point of view about a topic about which people may have a variety of opinions. When we argue, we do not always use logic and reason. In fact, many arguments are based on emotional response. As a strategy in an essay, argument can be challenging for a number of reasons.

Argument requires

> understanding and clearly stating your point of view,
>
> narrowing your topic to one aspect of an issue,
>
> using evidence to support your view,
>
> thinking open-mindedly about the issue to clearly understand why people agree and disagree about it, and
>
> showing how the evidence offered is connected to the overall point.

Argument often requires different techniques when we are writing than when we face an audience and tell them our view through speech. While people can ask questions and show disapproval or agreement during a discussion, written arguments do not receive this immediate feedback. In fact, writers must project to some extent what effect their written argument will have on their audience. A reader who disagrees with a point of view is going to judge an essay more harshly, and the writer should foresee this and provide the best evidence possible. A reader who is unfamiliar with the topic about which a writer is arguing is likely to need extra information. A good argumentative essay will persuade an audience to think about the view presented, even if it does not totally change their minds. Trying to convince readers who disagree may backfire on the writer if he or she does not show the audience enough respect and tolerance. Few people want to read an essay if they feel they are being insulted or attacked.

In addition to using researched evidence or personal experience, argumentative essays use appeals. Three of the most important appeals are the logical, the emotional, and the ethical. When a writer appeals to logic, he or she appeals to the reader's capacity for rational, reasonable thought. Outlining the reasons for installing a stoplight on a busy street might involve citing the increase in traffic, the number of accidents, and the relatively low cost when compared with the costs from accidents. Reasons such as these appeal to the reader's sense of what seems rational. This appeal is also typically based in fact or something that can be proven or supported by fact.

The emotional appeal is probably the most commonly used and perhaps, on some primal level, the most persuasive. Most people respond to emotional stimuli such as the need to prevent the death of innocent people, the need to protect children, and so on. An emotional appeal in the previous argument would use traffic fatalities or the danger presented to neighborhood children as a way of motivating readers to want a stoplight erected. Even though the appeal or approach is different, the argument is really the same: we need a stoplight.

The ethical appeal works on another level than the other two by tapping into our sense of morals, our sense of what *should* be. An ethical appeal in the stoplight argument might begin by describing the money taxpayers spend each year on snack foods or some other apparently useless item, and then might demonstrate ways that money would be better spent on a stoplight that protects motorists and neighborhood children.

Look for the thesis or argument in the following example of an argumentative paragraph. Try to find the support the writer uses and look for any appeals to emotion, logic, or ethics.

> Passenger-side airbags have been advertised as a safety feature on many new vehicles. However, these airbags are not very safe for children. In fact, children under twelve years of age should never sit in a passenger seat that has airbags. This is especially dangerous for infants. When an infant is placed in the correct rear-facing position and the airbag deploys, the infant's face is thrown into the passenger seat or head rest, which can cause near fatal or fatal injuries to the child. Manufacturers who advertise airbags as a safety feature are ignoring the substantial threat they pose to young children. Furthermore, the original testing of airbags on man-sized dummies shows a lack of foresight and sensitivity on the part of researchers and manufacturers. Not only should changes be made in airbags, but the way tests are conducted for new "safety" products should be overhauled as well.

The rhetorical strategies do not determine the whole structure of an essay, but they do influence both the structure of the essay and the way the author's message is presented to the audience. In addition to choosing the rhetorical strategies a writer thinks will best communicate his or her idea, a writer must think carefully about whether his or her choices are appropriate for the target audience. All of these decisions, when we look at them out of context, may seem very difficult, but understanding that strategies are at work in essays can help us both as writers planning for effective communication and as readers trying to understand a writer's approach and point of view. Study the following essay and the other essays in this book for practice identifying the strategies that make them effective for you as a reader. Consciously reading for structure will help you develop your reading skills and a greater sensitivity to the techniques a writer is using to influence or persuade you.

# READING AN ESSAY

## Strategy for Reading: Identifying Organizational Strategies for Better Reading

The rhetorical strategies used in an essay serve as a structural base or blue-print for readers. When we read an argumentative essay, we expect that it will pursue and argue a point effectively. How does a writer argue a point? He or she provides the reader with examples, evidence, and reasons to believe his or her view. Each mode or strategy discussed at the beginning of this chapter builds reader expectations and serves the writer's purpose. Look at the following list and describe the expectations you would have for each mode.

### Description

_____

_____

_____

### Narration

_____

_____

_____

### Illustration/Example

_____

_____

_____

### Process Analysis

_____

_____

_____

### Classification

_____

_____

_____

**Comparison/Contrast**

_____

_____

_____

**Definition**

_____

_____

_____

**Cause/Effect**

_____

_____

_____

**Argument/Persuasion**

_____

_____

_____

When we read a narrative we expect a clear story; when we read definition, we expect the writer to present a clear definition of a concept worth defining. As you read the following essay by Malcolm X, make notes next to each paragraph indicating the rhetorical strategy or strategies used. When you finish, decide which is the dominant mode.

---

### BEFORE YOU READ

1. What do you know about Malcolm X?
2. What motivates you to read or write? Do you want to become educated? Why or why not?
3. How do you feel about reading and writing in front of other people? Do you feel comfortable writing to others? How do you feel about reading aloud?

# A Homemade Education*

## by Malcolm X

It was because of my letters that I happened to stumble upon starting to acquire some kind of homemade education. [1]

I became increasingly frustrated at not being able to express what I wanted to convey in letters that I wrote, especially those to Mr. Elijah Muhammad. In the street, I had been the most articulate hustler out there—I had commanded attention when I said something. But now, trying to write simple English, I not only wasn't articulate, I wasn't even functional. How would I sound writing in slang, the way I would *say* it, something such as, "Look, daddy, let me pull your coat about a cat, Elijah Muhammad—" [2]

Many who today hear me somewhere in person, or on television, or those who read something I've said, will think I went to school far beyond the eighth grade. This impression is due entirely to my prison studies. [3]

It had really begun back in Charlestown Prison, when Bimbi first made me feel envy of his stock of knowledge. Bimbi had always taken charge of any conversation he was in, and I had tried to emulate him. But every book I picked up had few sentences which didn't contain anywhere from one to nearly all of the words that might as well have been in Chinese. When I just skipped those words, of course, I really ended up with little idea of what the book said. So I had come to the Norfolk Prison Colony still going through only book-reading motions. Pretty soon, I would have quit even these motions unless I had received the motivation that I did. [4]

I saw that the best thing I could do was get hold of a dictionary—to study to learn some words. I was lucky enough to reason also that I should try to improve my pen- [5]

*Source:* Malcolm X. "A Homemade Education." From *The Autobiography of Malcolm X* by Malcolm X, with the assistance of Alex Haley. Copyright © 1964 by Alex Haley and Malcolm X. Copyright © 1965 by Alex Haley and Betty Shabazz. Reprinted by permission of Random House, Inc.

manship. It was sad. I couldn't even write in a straight line. It was both ideas together that moved me to request a dictionary along with some tablets and pencils from the Norfolk Prison Colony school.

I spent two days just riffling uncertainly through the dictionary's pages. I'd never realized so many words existed! I didn't know *which* words I needed to learn. Finally, just to start some kind of action, I began copying.

6

In my slow, painstaking, ragged handwriting, I copied into my tablet everything printed on that first page, down to the punctuation marks.

7

I believe it took me a day. Then, aloud, I read back, to myself, everything I'd written on the tablet. Over and over, aloud, to myself, I read my own handwriting.

8

I woke up the next morning, thinking about those words—immensely proud to realize that not only had I written so much at one time, but I'd written words that I never knew were in the world. Moreover, with a little effort, I also could remember what many of these words meant. I reviewed the words whose meanings I didn't remember. Funny thing, from the dictionary first page right now, that "aardvark" springs to my mind. The dictionary had a picture of it, a long-tailed, long-eared, burrowing African mammal, which lives off termites caught by sticking out its tongue as an anteater does for ants.

9

I was so fascinated that I went on—I copied the dictionary's next page. And the same experience came when I studied that. With every succeeding page, I also learned of people and places and events from history. Actually the dictionary is like a miniature encyclopedia. Finally the dictionary's A section had filled a whole tablet—and I went on into the B's. That was the way I started copying what eventually became the entire dictionary. It went a lot faster after so much practice helped me to pick up handwriting speed. Between what I wrote in my tablet, and writing letters, during the rest of my time in prison I would guess I wrote a million words.

10

I suppose it was inevitable that as my word-base broadened, I could for the first time pick up a book and read

11

and now begin to understand what the book was saying. Anyone who has read a great deal can imagine the new world that opened. Let me tell you something: from then until I left that prison, in every free moment I had, if I was not reading in the library, I was reading on my bunk. You couldn't have gotten me out of books with a wedge. Between Mr. Muhammad's teachings, my correspondence, my visitors—usually Ella and Reginald—and my reading of books, months passed without my even thinking about being imprisoned. In fact, up to then, I had never been so truly free in my life.

## Building Your Skills

### Focus on Words

Look up the following words or parts of phrases in a dictionary. Consult the preceding essay and identify the meaning that best fits the way the author uses the word in this essay. Each word or phrase is followed by the number of the paragraph in which it appears.

articulate (2)       immensely (9)
slang (2)            inevitable (11)
emulate (4)          word-base (11)
riffling (6)

### Focus on the Message

1. Why did Malcolm X begin to educate himself? What feelings or ideas motivated him?
2. Why does Malcolm X write that people who read what he has written will think he "went to school far beyond the eighth grade" (para. 3)? What does he want his readers to recognize from this comment?
3. Why did Malcolm X pretend to read by going through "book-reading motions" (para. 4)? Have you ever done anything similar?
4. Why does copying the first page of the dictionary make Malcolm X feel so excited?
5. How could Malcolm X become "free" while he was in prison?

READING STRATEGY NOTE

Which rhetorical mode in Malcolm X's essay seems to be dominant? Why? How did it build your expectations as a reader?

## TECHNIQUES FOR WRITING: USING TRANSITIONS

Besides having an introduction, body, and conclusion, and using rhetorical
modes that complement each other, essays also must include transitions.
Transitions are phrases, whole sentences, or even whole paragraphs that
link one idea to the next. Rather than jumping abruptly from point to
point, a writer must carefully present his or her view by linking ideas for
the reader. Transitions tie ideas together, show differences, identify agreement or disagreement, and indicate relationships between ideas. Simply
put, transitions connect the writer's ideas to make his or her message clear.

The easiest way to define transitions is to say that they are phrases,
sentences, or paragraphs that tie one idea to another. This process of linking ideas requires the writer to look for connections that need to be made
and to write a word, sentence, or paragraph that will make a readable,
interesting, and worthwhile bridge between the two ideas. Transitions
should always add to the quality of the writing and enrich an essay. Readers
easily detect an essay that is missing transitions because they must labor to
connect the ideas presented. In fact, the easiest way to catch a missing transition in your own writing is to let someone else read your writing. When a
reader says, "I don't understand how this causes that" or "I'm not sure how
these ideas are related," most likely the necessary transitions are missing.

No exhaustive list of transitional techniques exists, but fortunately
once a writer understands the concept of providing transitions, he or she
can begin to develop his or her own style of linking ideas together. Transitions can be made with phrases, sentences, or paragraphs; they are at work
in any effectively written essay.

### Using Words and Phrases for Transitions

Transitional words or phrases are words that link one idea to the next
within one or two sentences. These are very important because they show
relationships, such as when an event took place, the causes for a situation,

the effects of a decision, or a comparison between two items. Many of the phrases we use for transition can be related to the rhetorical strategies discussed earlier in this chapter. The following lists illustrate the variety of transitional words a writer can employ.

> **To show time or sequence:**   after, before, when, while, whenever, since, during, first, second, third
>
> **To show cause and effect:**   because, consequently, therefore, thus, hence, since, then, as a result
>
> **To show agreement:**   likewise, moreover, and, in fact, furthermore, also, accordingly, in addition
>
> **To show disagreement:**   instead, but, though, even though, although, however, nevertheless, on the other hand, still

**When** we use these transitional phrases, we try to establish a connection or link between two ideas or thoughts. **In fact,** these phrases are an essential part of most writing. **Though** the phrases and words that provide transitions **within** this paragraph have been printed in bold to make them easier to see, most readers recognize the relationships these words indicate, **even if** they do not notice them as transitional phrases.

All readers, speakers, and writers recognize and use transitions, but learning to use transitions often enough and whenever they are appropriate is an important skill for speakers and writers; learning to understand what transitions mean and to identify them in a paragraph or essay is important for readers. Much of the meaning in a sentence or paragraph can be derived by understanding transitions. To practice using and noticing transitional phrases, look for them in your own writing, listen for them when you speak, and when you read, pay attention to how writers use transitions. To become more proficient at using transitional phrases, make a list of phrases to keep with you when you write. Refer to the list often as you are trying to connect ideas. One important part of using transitions, though, is placing them where they will clarify, not confuse meaning.

For example, a writer would not want to write the following sentence:

> **After** we left the bank, **but before** we went to the **other** store **across** town, I lost my wallet.

This sentence is confusing because it uses too many references to time and place. The transitions make it very difficult to follow. It could easily be rewritten more clearly:

> I had gone to the bank and was heading to the store when I
> realized I had lost my wallet.
> After going to the bank, I lost my wallet somewhere on my way
> to the store.

Notice that each of these sentences keeps the sequence of events clear and both focus on losing the wallet more than the other ideas. Too many transitional words or phrases or words in an illogical order are just as confusing as no transitions at all. Not all transitional phrases work in all situations.

Just as the prior example violates a sense of time and sequence, the following examples also pose a problem. See if you can detect why the transitional phrase is not appropriate.

> 1. Although she loves him, she married him Saturday.
> 2. My car would not start because I had to go to class.

Which words provide transitions? Do they violate your sense of what the sentence should say? Each transitional word is odd because it does not demonstrate the appropriate or expected relationship within the sentence. Try to replace the transitional words in these sentences with other transitional words that seem to fit better (look at the words listed above for possibilities).

> 1. _____ she loves him, she married him Saturday.
> 2. My car would not start _____ I had to go to class.

### Using Sentences for Transitions

Transitions are not always limited to words or phrases; sometimes, they can be whole sentences or paragraphs. Writers sometimes employ a sentence to tie together two ideas. For example, the paragraph below demonstrates a sentence that links two seemingly unrelated sentences together.

> Understanding what motivates a person in an argument can be very difficult. Many people become frustrated and simply give up. But giving up can be even more frustrating than patiently searching for the reason or underlying purpose for an argument. Although most people argue for a reason, the real reason is rarely actually stated and usually goes unmentioned time and time again.

Does this paragraph move from one topic to another or does it consistently discuss the focus of the topic sentence? The first sentence indicates that the paragraph will discuss motivations for arguments, but is that what it discusses at the end of the paragraph? How and where does the point or topic of the paragraph shift? Do you detect a shift in the sentence "But giving up can be even more frustrating than patiently searching for the reason or underlying purpose for an argument"? Notice the way that it leads us into the conclusion that most people have an unstated reason for arguing. The transitional sentence links the motivation in the first sentence with the way people argue in the last sentence.

### Using Paragraphs for Transitions

Providing an adequate transition can also require a whole paragraph. In an essay that is several pages long, paragraphs that link one aspect of the discussion to another help to make the essay easier to understand. Paragraph-length transitions identify ways that one part of an essay is related to another. They appear in the body of an essay and help the reader to connect ideas that develop the thesis or main idea. As a writer, be careful not to use short, choppy transitions, though. Sometimes when writers are first trying to employ transitional paragraphs they write one- or two-sentence paragraphs and end up with single sentences spread throughout their essays. This technique goes against the very purpose of the transition, which is to make the essay run smoothly from point to point. If transitions stand out too much they tend to detract from the point rather than adding to the reader's overall understanding.

## Building Your Skills

### *Assignment 1*

Choose one of the following topics and write three separate paragraphs, emphasizing a different rhetorical strategy in each paragraph. For example, use narration by telling a personal experience about this topic; use cause/effect to explain the causes or effects of this topic; and then use definition to define and explain this topic so that others will clearly understand it.

| | |
|---|---|
| teenage pregnancy | gambling |
| alcoholism | voting |
| attending college | watching television |
| making a new discovery | raising children |
| learning to write well | buying a car or house |

*Assignment 2*

Do a brainstorm, cluster, or freewriting about people you believe are heroes in our society. Then answer the following questions:

1. Do we need heroes? Why or why not?
2. What do our heroes tell us about our culture, society, lifestyle?
3. How do you define the word "hero"?

Write an essay using one of the following options:

**Option 1:**   Compare a hero of the past to a current hero. What qualities do these heroes share? In what ways are they different? Explore the connections between these heroes and society.

**Option 2:**   Describe the downfall of a recent hero. What changed this hero's status? How does this change reflect our society?

*Assignment 3*

Brainstorm about many of the topics people argue about—controversial topics like environmental policies, gun laws, or public policies and issues such as smoking in public. Choose a limited issue from one of these larger topics. For example, a discussion of gun laws can include arguments about which guns should be prohibited, whether any kind of gun should be prohibited, who should be able to carry a gun, and so on.

Once you have chosen a topic that you can argue, write three paragraphs. Write the first argumentative paragraph using an emotional appeal; try to persuade your reader by using reasons that will help your reader become emotionally involved in the topic.

In your second paragraph, try to persuade your reader with an ethical approach about the same topic. Remember to advocate a particular response or viewpoint based on what the reader should do or what an ethical person would do in relation to the topic you have chosen.

In your third paragraph, present a logical appeal—a well-reasoned, thoughtful argument that will make your reader recognize the logic and reasoning behind your view. Typically, logical appeals focus on clear reasons and evidence to argue a point, so use these techniques to help your reader understand your point of view.

Rewrite the three original paragraphs into an essay. To create an essay using these various appeals, you will need to use transitions and clearly link one point to the next. You will no doubt need to cut some parts of paragraphs out, as well as adding sentences and perhaps full paragraphs to provide the appropriate transitions and connections between your ideas. Once you have linked the individual parts, read the essay as a whole to make sure that it moves clearly and easily from one topic to the next. A better technique may be to let another student read your essay to test whether you make your point clear and whether you move from point to point in a way that is easy to read and understand.

# READING A STUDENT ESSAY

## Peer Review Strategy: Revising for Transitions

An essay that has transitions is easy to read; in fact, unless a transition is missing, most readers will probably not even realize that transitions are present at all. On the other hand, when an essay is missing transitions, it makes the reader work to decipher the writer's point. If two ideas are not connected for the reader, he or she must take the time to connect the ideas and then analyze why this is important to the essay topic. Consider the following sentences:

He left. She was unhappy.

These two sentences may be connected, but they might just as easily be about two people who do not even know each other. If we add a word and change the punctuation, though, the relationship can easily be clarified:

She was unhappy because he left.
He left because she was unhappy.

Notice the differences in meaning you can achieve through changing the placement of a few words.

Transitions are also a vital part of the revision process, because they allow you to intensify or clarify your meaning with the addition of one word, one or two sentences, or even a paragraph. The first step, however, is to read an essay and decide whether the essay makes connections between ideas for the reader or whether transitions could create an essay that is easier to read and more meaningful—in other words, a reader-based essay.

One way to read for connections is holistically—by reading the whole essay and judging whether or not each paragraph and sentence leads clearly and easily from one idea to the next. Another good way, especially if you have not read essays for transitions before, is to underline or circle transitional words, phrases, sentences, or paragraphs and then observe, first, how well they connect the ideas and second, whether there are any large areas of the essay where you have not underlined or circled anything.

If you decide that an area needs a transition, identify the two points that need to be connected and use either a word from the lists in this chapter, a sentence that leads from one idea to the next, or a paragraph that brings the two concepts together smoothly.

As you read the following essay, circle or underline the transitional words, phrases, sentences, or paragraphs in the space provided. Also, identify the thesis and primary audience for the essay. Observe whether any areas are missing transitions or seem to leave out connections between ideas.

The Hero Dilemma

by Christine Heaney

When mass murderer Jeffrey Dahmer was himself        1
murdered in a Wisconsin prison, the reaction by the public was varied and quite interesting, especially towards the chief suspect Christopher Scarver. (Mr. Scarver, a 25 year old inmate of the same institution as Dahmer, is also a convicted murderer. His earliest release date is 2042.) When approached for a comment during televised news reports, several individuals responded with the observation that Mr. Scarver was a "hero" for his alleged actions. Such a statement leads one to wonder just what qualities are expected of a hero. Does one action on the part of a person, criminal behaviors notwithstanding, or a life of continuing practice of discipline and fortitude constitute a hero? Is a hero by any other name still a hero?

In a very unscientific survey of a number of peo-      2
ple, none agreed on the subject. The response was wide
and far-flung. Some could not give an answer; others
stumbled in thought before responding. One man
stated, after a moment, that Chuck Yeager was his
hero. Yeager, he clarified, as a test pilot in the 1950s,
routinely put his life on the line for his country's
space exploration program. The respondent also stated
that Yeager's mother had been one of his grade school
teachers and was influential in his attitude regarding
her son. Still, he felt Yeager was an appropriate choice
given the pilot's sense of dedication and duty.

When questioned, one young man stated decidedly      3
that he did not believe in heroes. He felt that the concept of the hero was a myth. This young man main-
tained that the hero would have to be a super-human
of unrealistic characteristics that one could not sustain. He said that he did not believe in anyone else;
he believed in himself and that this self-reliance
would carry him through life. It could be that the
ideal of a hero is somewhere in between the two
answers.

In today's culture, such responses do not appear 4
unusual. But it seems that the image of the hero may
reflect one's own view of the world. In a society that
places emphasis on monetary and material wealth as
well as power in the marketplace, hero traits fluctuate.
And given the mindset of pop culture, hero worship of
sports figures, business moguls, and entertainment
stars rises. Added to this may be politicians and religious leaders. All are humans with the very real
human trait of being able to fall flat on their face.
Today's hero may not be so tomorrow.

This comes back to the question if a hero is made 5
in a single act or a commitment to a life of aspirations
and values. Throughout history, questions such as
these have been examined in literature and theater of
the day. If one reviews today's offerings of the written
word and the visual presentations of films and television, the representation of the hero does appear, as it
does routinely on the evening news as in the case of
Mr. Scarver. Earlier in the century, Ernest Hemming-
way and James Joyce explored the hero in their writings. It might be said that Alice Walker did the same

with her character Celie in <u>The Color Purple</u>. Poet

Maya Angelou often addresses the "heroes and

s-heroes" that affect her life; those individuals that

continue to inspire and teach. And every summer,

action hero movies abound.

Surely, explorations of lives invested in struggle 6

and perseverance reveal the heroic models. But the

player who runs faster or wins the game is also seen

by many as the hero (at least of the day). Or at times,

it is the underdog who prevails in his or her attempt

to beat the system that gets the heroic label. Many

secretly cheered him on when hijacker D.B. Cooper

jumped from a plane in flight with a suitcase full of

cash never to be heard from again. The answer to the

question may be in wanting to emulate the feats of

another: win the race, get the girl, amass the money,

or kill the bad guy.

The issue begs clarity: What is a hero? One might 7

argue that heroic qualities are debatable. A hero might

be brave, valiant, fearless, courageous, a champion, but

is virtue also a requirement? Mythological, historical,

and religious figures of the past such as Superman,

Robin Hood, George Washington, King David, and
Solomon all possessed heroic traits, but they were
known for their principled and moral values as well.
Exemplary, righteous, and untarnished lives set the
standard of these heroes and others that readily come
to mind.

Contemporary heroes share few of these charac-                    8
teristics. Indeed, to live up to exalted standards in
today's world would take super-human efforts and
deny the reality of human flaws. But can one really
assume that humans are capable of living up to heroic
standards of great expectations? Events over the last
few decades have revealed numerous sport stars,
politicians, and religious leaders' falls from grace.
Super star sport heroes, able to contract inflated com-
mercial endorsements, are idolized by many of today's
youth while charges of tax evasion, drug use, criminal
activities, and deplorable behaviors on and off the
playing field makes it difficult to admire them. Politicians have been caught in corruption, fraud, and
unethical campaign practices. Several religious leaders
have been involved in criminal and sex scandals. The

scrutiny of the investigatory mass media makes it difficult to hide the flaws. Heroes of the past may not have fared any better with their lives so closely observed and reported. One can imagine the National Inquirer's headlines exposing the daily behaviors of King David, George Washington, or Robin Hood. Heroic efforts can prove difficult to sustain.

This brings us back to the question of heroic standards once again. It remains a good question. But is it possible that the difficulty that many find in defining a hero or identifying with one is that the concept is hard to comprehend? People must find their own standards and values for their heroes and their own way of worshipping them.

9

The dilemma leads one to believe that a hero may really be a mythical legend not based in reality.

10

## Building Your Skills

1. How many words, phrases, sentences, or paragraphs did you underline or circle? How do these transitions affect your ability to read Heaney's essay?

_____

_____

_____

_____

_____

_____

_____

_____

_____

2. What are Heaney's major points? How does she tie them to her minor points? Who do you think is her primary audience?

_____

_____

_____

_____

_____

_____

_____

_____

_____

3. What rhetorical modes does Heaney use? Which one is the dominant rhetorical strategy? What expectations does this create for you as a reader?

_____

_____

_____

_____

_____

_____

_____

_____

_____

4. As if you were discussing Christine's paper with her, list three features of her essay that work very well or that really appeal to you as a reader. Then, recommend three changes she could make to improve her essay.

Describe three features that are effective for you as a reader:

a. _____

b. _____

c. _____

Describe three improvements or changes Christine could make to create a more effective, interesting, or informative essay:

a. _____

b. _____

c. _____

# USING GRAMMAR: IDENTIFYING VERBS
# AND VERB TENSE

Verbs are important to communication because they indicate an action or state of existence and the time in which either takes place. Without a verb we cannot have a sentence. Observe the following groups of words:

> Alex after a long shift at the refinery.
> The man in the dark around the corner of that building.

In both sentences, you probably can sense that something is missing. If you guessed that the verb is missing, you were right. Now, look at the sentences again, but this time fill in the blank with something that makes sense.

> Alex, after a long shift at the refinery, _____.
> The man in the dark around the corner of that building
>
> _____.

What did you use to fill in the blank? Does it show an action? Does it show that something is in existence? Does it give a sense of the time this action took place? Any answers that do these things will probably be verbs.

When we write, we use verbs according to mutually understood patterns that our audience knows and uses. In speaking, we may be more conversational in our use of verbs; we may speak in fragments and employ less formal patterns of language. In writing, however, leaving out the verb or using verbs in a confusing way can frustrate and annoy readers, causing them to lose interest. Look at the following paragraph, for example:

> When I <u>am</u> a little girl, I <u>tried</u> to teach my cousin to read. He <u>studies</u> very hard, but he <u>do not know</u> how to read until he <u>turning</u> eight years old.

Do you find this paragraph confusing? Do you find that you must review words to get the message? Notice the underlined words. Change the underlined words so that the paragraph makes sense to you. After you do this, try to identify what you have changed. The underlined words in this passage are verbs and almost every one of them gives the reader a different sense of time. When you rewrote the paragraph did the time change? Look at one way to rewrite this paragraph:

> When I <u>was</u> a little girl, I <u>tried</u> to teach my cousin to read. He <u>studied</u> very hard, but he <u>did</u> not <u>know</u> how to read until he <u>turned</u> eight years old.

In the second example, when did the speaker teach her cousin? How do we know this information? We can tell that this activity took place in the past. We know this from the verbs, and more specifically from the way that these verbs end: most end with *-ed*. We recognize that *was* and *tried* are verbs that indicate that something has already taken place, but we probably do not have to think this through consciously. We recognize and understand patterns that we have been exposed to in reading, writing, and speech. In fact, if you grew up speaking English, you probably have learned most of these patterns through what you have read and heard all of your life. Sometimes people do not pick up these patterns, though.

If you did not recognize and understand this pattern, it may be that you have not learned this particular pattern or that English is not your first language and the verb forms are still something that you are learning. If you have not done much reading, Standard English grammatical patterns like verb tense may be unfamiliar to you. Whatever the reason for your difficulty, reading and knowing where to look up verb forms can help any writer learn to use Standard English verbs in the appropriate forms in writing. The benefit of learning this information is that you can understand a greater variety of reading materials more easily, and you can write more effectively and for a wider audience.

Verbs affect us as readers and writers in many ways. We learn very important information from them: what happens, what exists, the time of the action, the sequence of events or actions. A crucial part of using verbs is choosing the appropriate tense. The tense of a verb is the time reference that is derived from the way the verb ends or is written.

      **subject   verb**                  **verb**

The man **parked** his car and **took** the bus.

For example, in the sentence example above, the verbs "parked" and "took" are both past tense because they refer to an action that has already taken place. In present tense, we would write,

      **subject  verb**                 **verb**

The man **parks** his car and **takes** the bus.

This means the man is doing this activity at this time. If the man were going to do these actions in the future, we would write subject    verb                              verb

The man **will park** his car and **will take** the bus.

Tense in regular verbs follows patterns; the verb *walk* is a good example:

| | |
|---|---|
| **present** | walk or walks |
| **past** | walked |
| **future** | will walk |

Each time we change the tense of the verb, we add something new:

an *-s* is added in present tense for verbs used with *he, she, it,* or other third-person references;

an *-ed* ending is added in past tense;

the word *will* is added in future tense.

Standard English actually has other tenses, but these are the basic three all writers should be able to identify. Most of the time we do not look at tense apart from what we are reading or writing; in fact, the tense of verbs is so obvious to readers and writers most of the time that they understand the tense without ever consciously noting the tense of the verbs. Imagine reading this note from a loved one or family member:

> I will be back at 5:00. Then we will go to the movie.

What information is given about the time when events will take place? What is the message? The writer says "I will be back," so we know that the writer is leaving and in the future will be returning. We also know that after that—again, in the future—the writer and someone else will be going to see a movie. If this seems like easy information to understand, then you already have a good sense of verb tense.

We can divide verbs into two classes: **regular verbs** follow consistent, regular patterns for changing tense, while **irregular verbs** do not follow consistent patterns to change tense and actually vary widely in the changes they go through when changing tense. The following is a chart that shows how regular verbs change to accommodate different tenses. Regular verbs, in fact, are so named because they follow the "regular" or normal pattern for changing to indicate tense.

|               | Singular (only one) | Plural (more than one) |
|---------------|---------------------|------------------------|
| *First Person*  | I walk.             | We walk.               |
| *Second Person* | You walk.           | You walk.              |
| *Third Person*  | He, She, It **walks**. | They walk.          |

Notice that regular verbs retain the same form in present tense, except when we use them with a third person subject such as *he, she, it,* or even a person's name. In the chart, notice *walks* has an added -*s* because it describes the action of a third person singular subject. To indicate past tense, we add -*ed* to regular verbs. Another past tense form of a verb can be made using helping verbs or additional verbs that show an action or state that has already taken place; these past tense forms are called past participles, and they are always used with a helping verb. With regular verbs, the past participle is the same as the simple past tense form. In the case of *walk* the past participle then would be *walked,* or in sentence form "I have walked." To indicate an action that will take place in the future, we add the word *will* to the base or infinitive form of the verb. The **infinitive** form of a verb is the most basic form of the word and is typically used with the word *to* as in *to live, to die, to be, to skip, to play.* Every verb has an infinitive form, and usually speakers of English can ask themselves what form of the verb goes with *to* and quickly identify the infinitive. Try substituting one word in the phrase below.

I love to _____.

Words like *dance, study, play,* and *exercise* could all be used in this sentence, and each of them is an infinitive form of a verb. Notice that each of them uses the three patterns identified for regular verbs as well.

| I dance.       | We danced.     | They will dance.   |
|----------------|----------------|--------------------|
| They study.    | She studied.   | I will study.      |
| **He plays.**  | They played.   | She will play.     |
| We exercise.   | She exercised. | You will exercise. |

Notice that "He plays" adds *-s* to *play* because the subject "he" is third-person singular, but otherwise every use of these verbs is the same except for tense. Regular verb patterns can easily be learned and adapted into your writing.

Unlike the clear, easy-to-learn forms of regular verbs, irregular verbs lack consistent patterns. Many of the patterns reflect the histories of the verbs and the changes in spelling and pronunciation that have occurred over time. Although these forms are harder to learn, most handbooks have a full listing of the forms that irregular verbs use in Standard English. The key is knowing what form of the verb to use and when.

The irregular verbs listed in the Appendix of this book take a variety of forms as they change tense. Like the regular verbs, the irregular verbs have appropriate forms for present, past, and future tense, but while the regular verbs have set, easy-to-follow patterns, irregular forms follow a variety of patterns, and often writers have simply memorized the appropriate forms. Many writers, however, find forms of at least a few irregular verbs problematic. If you find that your verb forms are often marked as problems on papers or if you are not sure about what tense or form of a verb to use in what situation, the best way to become proficient is to study the list provided in the Appendix or to refer to a dictionary for the present, past tense, and other forms of the verb.

Let's look at how a list like this might help you determine what verb form to use in a given situation. We will use what is arguably the most difficult irregular verb for students learning English or those who use non-standard forms in their speech. First, when we look at verb forms, we start with the infinitive. The infinitive form of a verb is the most basic form of the verb before it undergoes changes for tense. In the case of the following verb, the infinitive is *to be*. In the following chart, observe the many forms of this verb.

| Subject | Singular (only one) present/past | Plural (more than one) present/past |
|---------|----------------------------------|-------------------------------------|
| *First Person*  | I am/was.              | We are/were.    |
| *Second Person* | You are/were.         | You are/were.   |
| *Third Person*  | He, She, It is/was.   | They are/were.  |

Notice that the present tense form of this verb is not made simply by adding an -s to the verb when the subject is third person. In fact, the forms are spelled quite differently. In the past tense, instead of simply adding -ed, again the forms are different.

Use the Appendix to look up present and past tense forms of irregular verbs. Remember that any verb that does not add -s for third-person plural in present tense or -ed to make the past tense is an irregular verb. The other columns on the irregular verb list present the infinitive and past participle forms used to make tenses besides present and past. We can make future tense by adding *will* to the infinitive form of any verb (regular or irregular), as in "He *will be* late," or "She *will think* the problem through." Past participle forms of a verb are made by adding -ed to regular verbs and a variety of endings or changes to irregular verbs. We use the past participle form of a verb with helping verbs to make a variety of tenses. We combine past participles with *have, has,* or *had* to create new forms of verbs that have somewhat different meanings from the simple present and past tenses we have discussed.

Look at the following examples:

He **has walked** to the store.
He **walked** to the store.
He **will be walking** to the store.


She **fights** fires.
She **has been fighting** fires.
She **has fought** fires.


Do these sentences express the same meaning? Each set of three uses the same subject and the same action, and yet clearly, each sentence, because it is written in a different tense, expresses a different meaning. The first set uses the regular verb *walked*. The first and third sentences add meaning and tense by adding helping verbs that change the main verb. "Has walked" to the store means the activity is already done and gives the impression that the person receiving this message is unsure of whether the subject, "He," has already walked to the store or not. Similarly, the third sentence adds meaning with helping verbs: Instead of simply saying "he will walk to the store," by saying "He will be walking" the speaker seems unsure about when in the future he will walk to the store. It is less definite then "He will walk." Though you may want to memorize the many verb forms, that is not very practical. Again, most of the forms of verbs you will learn to use effectively you will learn through speaking, reading, and applying them in your own writing.

To test your knowledge of verb tense, fill in the blanks in the following paragraph to see how well you can use the tenses for common verbs. When you finish, compare the forms you chose with another student's choices.

> Well-chosen and meaningful verbs _____ important to communicating a message very clearly. This crucial decision _____ automatic in many cases, but writers _____ carefully _____ their drafts for meaningless, bland, or overly general verbs. The best method for choosing verbs well _____ to consult a thesaurus. In this book, you _____ a list of words and _____ a word that expresses your exact meaning. Most writers, however, _____ about this choice in drafts after their first draft. Placing too much emphasis on finding the exact words in a first draft _____ you completely unable to write, so _____ not _____ too involved with this process until you actually have some part of your essay written.

In practice the task of choosing the appropriate verb or detecting when the verb is inappropriate or nonstandard is not as easy as this presentation may make it seem. In fact, because much of how we use verbs is determined by the way we have heard and seen them used, learning to use standard forms can be challenging. If we have learned forms that are nonstandard (as virtually everyone has at some time), we must learn to detect these nonstandard forms in our writing and replace them with the standard form as a way of maintaining communication in our essays that reaches a general audience who is accustomed to standardized forms. If you have difficulty using Standard English verb forms, you might try regularly consulting a list of the irregular verbs and their varied forms for changing tense. A list is provided in the Appendix. This list, though it is not exhaustive, will give you many forms and can be supplemented with reference books such as a dictionary and a grammar handbook. Another important source of grammar improvement and general learning about language is reading. The more you function as an audience member, the more you understand as a writer what your audience needs. This is as true for grammar as for any other skills you acquire through reading.

## Building Your Skills

### Assignment 1

In the following paragraphs, fill in an appropriate verb form so that the paragraph makes sense and the same tense is used throughout.

**Paragraph 1:**  After she _____ for college, her parents were sad for a few days. They _____ her so much that they had _____ a trip to see her the following weekend. When they _____ their daughter on the phone to tell her, she was not very enthusiastic, so they _____ it was best for them to stay home.

**Paragraph 2:**  Mandy couldn't wait to see her friend John. It _____ so long since they had seen each other. She _____ he would remember how much fun their last date _____. She _____ the same music just to remind him. In fact, she was even _____ the same dress.

**Paragraph 3:**  David is doing well in his new job. He _____ being a mechanic for a machine shop. He _____ fairly good money and _____ good hours. He _____ that he _____ even be the manager someday. I _____ thrilled that his job _____ such a positive feature of his life.

## Assignment 2

Marcy wrote an essay and found after reading it that it did not reflect what she wanted to say because it did not illustrate how long ago the event she was describing had happened. In the following essay, change the verbs after the first two sentences so that they are consistent with the new tense Marcy has established. When you are finished, reread the paragraph and make a note about how this revision changes Marcy's message.

When I **was** seventeen, I **went** to visit my Aunt Martha in Hawaii. I **did** not

**realize** at the time what an effect this experience **would have** on my life. I am

riding on the airplane and I am so excited. I have waited for three months to

arrive in Hawaii, and when I do, my aunt greets me with several leis made of

purple orchids. Upon my arrival, I know that I will be going to fancy restau-

rants and shops that I dream of. I also can tell that my aunt wants to take me to

some historical sites and old churches. We will have a fabulous time!

### Assignment 3

In the following excerpts, the verbs have been printed in bold. Change
the tense of the verbs to past or future, and substitute more meaningful or
interesting verbs wherever necessary. As you work, make whatever other
changes are necessary to accommodate the way you change the verbs.

Buying a home **is** not very enjoyable. The realtor, title company, and

bank financing the loan **try** to be helpful but the process **is** still tedious and

demanding at best. First a home must **be found.** Then you **need** to make a

bid through your realtor. If the owners **accept** your bid, you must **try** to get

a loan. Once you **have filled** out the many pages of a loan application, you

**need** to wait, and wait, and wait. Respect **is** due to all homeowners for

enduring this process.

## SEEING THE CONNECTIONS: APPLYING YOUR SKILLS

### Assignment 1

Brainstorm about your personal talents and accomplishments. What
do you do well? Identify a task that you perform well or a talent you have,
and list the skills or set of steps necessary for this task or accomplishment.

Write a process analysis essay that describes to an inexperienced person how to perform this task or learn this skill.

When you have a finished draft of your essay, cut the essay into sections, with each section focusing on or explaining an idea or point. For example, if your essay included the following two sentences, you would cut these into two sections, because one sentence deals with one step, and the second sentence deals with another.

> Spread the bread thickly with peanut butter. Spread on the jelly next.

When you have cut your essay into individual points or sections, lay them out on a table in the order in which you think they belong. Identify which parts include transitions. Rewrite your essay using each part, but add a transitional word to any parts that do not already have one, and add several sentences to your essay that connect your ideas better or add greater interest or detail.

Put both essays away for at least twenty-four hours and then reread them. Compare your essays and decide which one would be most helpful to an inexperienced reader. In addition, look for changes that should be made so that your essay is consistent in verb tense and punctuated correctly.

### Assignment 2

Read Christine Heaney's essay included in this chapter. Then identify someone you really admire or look up to. Brainstorm about the qualities this person has that makes him or her admirable. Then write a freewriting for five to ten minutes that describes this person and why he or she is so admirable. Look at your freewriting closely and decide which rhetorical modes you use in it. What is the dominant mode?

Identify the most notable feature about this person and write a first draft that follows the structure below.

| | |
|---|---|
| Introduction | How important are heroes? What significance should they have in our lives? |
| Body paragraph #1 | How is the person you admire special? What do you admire about this person? |
| Body paragraph #2 | Describe a time or experience where you observed this admirable characteristic. In other words, provide an example. |
| Conclusion | What overall effect does this person have on your life or the lives of others? |

Once you have finished, label the rhetorical modes you used and answer the following:

How does each rhetorical mode add to the quality and effectiveness of your essay? How did you use transitions to lead your reader from one mode to the next? How many types of sentences have you used (i.e., simple, compound, complex, and compound-complex)?

Rewrite your essay, adding transitions wherever necessary and changing some of your sentences so that you use more variety while still retaining your point.

### Assignment 3

Read the essay "A Homemade Education" by Malcolm X in this chapter. Look at the educational process he describes, and circle the verbs he uses to portray his actions.

Brainstorm or freewrite about a time when you felt inferior or limited by the lack of a particular ability. Make a list of feelings and reactions you had to this difficult time. Write an essay that describes the process you used or underwent to overcome or accept this limitation or disability. How has this process affected your life?

Circle or highlight all of the verbs in your first draft. Rewrite at least half of these verbs substituting stronger, more interesting, or more concise verbs in their place. Rewrite your essay using your verb substitutions and then compare your final draft to your first draft. What differences can you detect based on the use of more carefully chosen verbs? Which draft do you like best?

# Chapter 7

# Emphasizing Your Point

In this chapter you will learn

- ☆ to measure an essay's unity, coherence, and clarity;
- ☆ to identify and evaluate fact, opinion, and bias;
- ☆ to write effective conclusions using a variety of methods;
- ☆ to recognize and use Standard English subject–verb agreement;
- ☆ to recognize and use Standard English pronoun agreement;
- ☆ to recognize and use consistent references to person.

Take a moment to answer the following questions:

1. How do you determine when you have effectively made your point in an essay? How do you know when you have made your point when you speak?

_____

_____

_____

2. When you read, how do you know when you have understood the point?

_____

_____

_____

3. How are facts different from opinions?

_____

_____

_____

4. What is a bias? Are people usually aware of their own biases? How do you think biases affect reading and writing?

_____

_____

_____

## ACHIEVING UNITY, COHERENCE, AND CLARITY

We determine how good the structure of an essay is by using three measures of an essay's effectiveness: unity, coherence, and clarity. Not surprisingly, these are the same features that allow a reader to easily read an essay, understand its point or thesis, and see how well the writer's views are supported. Each of these words describes a goal every essay should meet, but each term identifies a different but related quality in an effective essay. An essay is effective when the reader can easily understand the main idea of the essay and how all of the parts of the essay relate to and support that idea. However, what is clear to one audience may not be clear to another. Vocabulary, the placement of paragraphs, the organization of ideas, the detail with which ideas are presented, the sentence structure, and the use of conventional punctuation and grammar can all determine how clear a piece of writing is.

### Unity

Unity is achieved in an essay or paragraph when the writer includes only ideas that have a clear relationship to the central point or thesis and no parts stand out or seem to take the attention of the reader from the overall goal or meaning of the work. A unified piece of writing gains its harmony from unified subject matter—in other words, everything in a paragraph or essay develops the topic or thesis in an important way. Writing lacks unity when it goes off topic, includes unrelated or unclear examples, or provides excess information that could be left out without the paragraph or essay losing any of its effectiveness.

Unity derives from all facets of the essay working together. When you look for unity in your own or other people's essays, identify the thesis, the topic sentences, and the basic essay structure to see that each of these parts contributes to the unifying idea or thesis. Evaluate whether the sentences, examples, explanations, and ideas are clearly necessary and important to effectively presenting the thesis (or topic sentence in the case of a paragraph). Although this can be challenging in your own essays, it is fairly easy to identify unity problems when you read someone else's writing. The reason problems in unity are difficult for the writer to detect, but easy for the reader, is that typically we leave out ideas that seem obvious to us, and we sometimes in our enthusiasm for our topic want to include everything we know about the topic whether or not it is important or relevant. Readers, who have different experiences and viewpoints, will quickly identify missing parts of an essay or added, unnecessary information because they are looking for the point, and they may not share the writer's experiences or enthusiasm. A unified essay or paragraph is focused on one point and emphasizes this main idea throughout, whereas a paragraph or essay lacking unity presents the reader with the dilemma of sifting through all of the information provided to determine the focus. Many readers resent being given this overload of information because it is confusing and difficult to decipher. The confusion, disorientation, and general feeling of being let down is an unmistakable reaction to a lack of unity in a piece of writing.

Look at the following paragraphs. Can you detect any problems with unity as you read them? After each, make a comment about whether or not each paragraph is unified, and mark any places in the paragraphs that break the unity of the whole work.

Mary and Candace wanted to visit Mexico, but they had a limited budget. Mary was a photographer while Candace was a freelance writer. Even though they had very little money, they knew that they could create a magazine article worthy of the finest travel magazine. Mary had taken many photographs that had been displayed in a Los Angeles art gallery. They decided to submit a letter describing their idea to a magazine to see if the magazine would sponsor their trip for the exclusive rights to the story and photos.

Most sports enthusiasts have favorite teams. In fact, when asked, the average sports fan can tell another person exactly why his or her team is better than the other teams. I like the San Francisco 49ers, and I like to watch all of their games. Liking one team over another usually has more to do with where a person lives than it does with what the team actually does. In fact, die-hard fans remain faithful despite many losing seasons and still find reasons that their team is "the best."

In each of these paragraphs, one sentence takes away from the unity of the paragraph by bringing up an idea or thought that is not clearly related to the rest of the paragraph. In the first paragraph, the sentence "Mary had taken many photographs that had been displayed in a Los Angeles art gallery" is out of place because it gives added detail, and although it could be related to the topic, the writer never tells us how this detail is related to the trip to Mexico. In the second paragraph, the sentence "I like the San Francisco 49ers, and I like to watch all of their games" is similar. Unlike the other sentences, this sentence describes the writer's favorite team rather than sports fans in general. This takes away from the paragraph's focus and thus its unity.

## Coherence

Coherence is very closely related to unity and it certainly promotes unity. When we describe an essay as coherent, we mean that it moves from one idea to the next without confusing or losing the reader. Coherence is generally accomplished by arranging ideas logically, making clear connections between ideas, and making sure that no gaps exist between parts of the essay. The thesis should not stand apart from the rest of the essay, but instead should be integrated into the essay. A coherent essay will lead the reader from the introduction and thesis into a discussion in the body that follows a clear and established progression of ideas, and then to a conclusion that develops the idea to a feeling of completeness. Once again, coherence can be relative to the audience reading the essay. If someone with limited experience with the subject matter reads an essay, he or she may think the essay lacks coherence or a logical order because of an inability to see connections between ideas that other, more experienced readers might find obvious.

Read the short essay excerpt below and try to determine whether or not it presents ideas coherently.

On that December 20th morning, it was cold and damp. We left for our vacation never knowing what was about to happen. As we rode in the car speaking only occasionally, we all watched the road because of the traffic

and weather conditions. Then all of a sudden _____

_____.

How do you expect this paragraph to end? What elements lead you to believe it will end in this way? Notice that all of the description seems to be leading to a single event. This builds the reader's expectations by presenting ideas in a logical, related way. Even though we do not know what will happen, we expect something to happen because of phrases like "never knowing what was about to happen" and "because of the traffic and weather conditions." Coherence is created when the writer leads us from one point to the next, connecting each point along the way. Compare the technique used to create coherence in the following paragraph with the preceding one. Does it use the same techniques to provide coherence?

The first day of college after ten years of homemaking was a frightening experience. I couldn't help feeling a bit out of place. First, even though I worked very hard at home, I did not know what kind of work or the amount of work to expect from school. Second, I was intimidated by the other students and feared that I might look too old or unprepared in classes full of young students. Instead of a room of very young faces, I was met with a room full of people of different ages and backgrounds. Despite my fears, I managed to make it through my first day of classes. I was so relieved, and I have been happy with my decision ever since.

Notice in this example paragraph that the coherence is derived by following the sequence of events (i.e., first, second, and so on). If these steps were presented out of order or without a logical connection, they would confuse or frustrate the reader. Look at an earlier version of the same paragraph and try to pinpoint the ways that it lacks coherence.

*First Draft:*

> Coming back to school after ten years of homemaking can be a frightening experience. Even though I worked very hard at home, I did not know what kind of work or the amount of work to expect from school. I did not actually understand the process of registering for classes and applying for financial aid. There were many lines and people and I really did not know who I should discuss registering with. I was intimidated by the other students and feared that I might look too old or unprepared in classes full of young students. For all of my fears, I managed to go to my classes the first day. I have been pleased ever since.

What is missing in this paragraph that the revised paragraph has connected and made clear? Notice that the first draft presents a variety of ideas without leading clearly from one to the next. Try to determine which sentences need to be changed. Now look at the revised version to see how the changes this writer chose improved her work. In the revised version, the topic of overcoming the feeling of being out of place is consistent throughout the whole paragraph. Unlike the first draft, where the writer discusses registration, the revised version maintains its coherence by keeping its focus on the unexpected qualities and struggles this student encountered on the first day of classes.

## Clarity

Clarity, another test of the quality of an essay, is derived from both unity and coherence, but it also has other sources. Aside from clear structure and moving smoothly from one idea to the next, clarity most often results from clear, concise wording and sentence structure. Look at the following sentences:

> When I think about him, I feel special. He is so nice.

How specific is this description? How clearly can you understand how this writer feels about "him"? In what way do these sentences lack clarity? The words *special* and *nice* are vague and meaningless. What do *special* and *nice* really mean? Is he kind-hearted, generous, good-looking, well-mannered, all of these qualities? As you can see, just one or two words can take away from the clarity of a sentence or paragraph.

How, then, can a writer be sure if he or she is writing clearly, when one word can make a whole paragraph seem confusing or meaningless? The answer is to choose words carefully and to write sentences for their maximum effectiveness. Unfortunately, many times students want to achieve clarity in the first draft. This rarely happens, even for professional writers. Achieving clarity in writing requires a process that consists of writing an initial draft, reading, and revising to include more descriptive words, clear grammar, and coherence and unity. One way to think about clarity is to look at it as a path. An essay is clear and the major point is emphasized if a reader has no difficulty following the writer's path. If the reader gets sidetracked, gets lost, or takes too many detours, the essay has highlighted too many unimportant ideas, has not used words and sentences that clearly express meaning, or may not have a central focus at all. As with all of the important decisions in the writing process (and unity, coherence, and clarity are certainly no exception), knowing your purpose and identifying your audience determine what you write, what you keep, and what you change.

# READING AN ESSAY

## Strategy for Reading: Facts, Opinions, and Biases

Each of us is bombarded daily with facts and opinions, interacting with the preconceived ideas that we hold, as well as the beliefs people have about us. Careful readers distinguish between facts, opinions, and biases because they do not want to be misinformed or persuaded by someone with ulterior motives. As readers, we should always evaluate the worthiness and accuracy of ideas presented to us. As writers, we should do our best to present ideas truthfully and accurately.

When writers try to convince or persuade us, they use a combination of facts, opinions, and shared biases. When we agree with the writer, we are likely to evaluate the evidence he or she offers as factual, worthwhile, and accurate. When we disagree, we often question even the facts presented, or at least the interpretation of those facts. But facts, opinions, and biases are notable for their differences and how these affect readers.

A fact, unlike an opinion or bias, can be proven beyond a doubt. For example, if we read that California has two of the most populous cities in the nation, we know we can decide whether this is a fact by comparing the populations of San Francisco and Los Angeles with those of other cities in other states. If we read that Los Angeles is the best city to visit, can we prove that as a fact? No, that is an opinion. We can support or defend an opinion, but we can never actually prove it. It may seem like a fact to us, but it is not a fact. Instead it is a viewpoint. A bias is a bit more insidious or less recognizable. People can have biases for or against something or someone.

A bias is a deeply held belief of which we may be totally unaware or that has an influence on our thinking and decision making that we may not realize. Teachers often have a bias in favor of education. Students may have a bias toward education and may think generally that schools are positive places, or they may have a bias against schools and teachers, believing that mostly negative experiences occur in schools. In reading and writing, biases become an important consideration because they can sometimes lead us to draw faulty conclusions and to miss the point.

Most of us write believing that we are addressing an audience that agrees with us; we read believing that only writers who use ideas we agree with are accurate or worth reading. Are either of these beliefs true? Problems in writing and reading occur when we assume that everyone shares or should share the same biases and beliefs that we have. As an example of bias, let's look at a minor bias that hurts no one, for the most part. How do you feel about cats? Are cats cuddly, wonderful creatures, or are they useless pets? Should they sleep on the bed? Live indoors? Stay outside all of the time? Everyone has beliefs about cats. What possible biases might readers/writers have? Cats are unclean or evil? Cats are annoying and useless? If a person who believes cats are useless reads a story about a cat or an essay that uses a cat anecdote for an example, how will this bias affect his or her reading?

Label the following examples as fact, opinion, or bias by circling one choice. Then explain your classification.

1. Dallas is located in Texas.          fact      opinion      bias

   Reason_____

2. Joan is pretty, but she's like most pretty women.          fact      opinion      bias

   Reason_____

3. Jack Kennedy was a great president.          fact      opinion      bias

   Reason_____

As you read the following essay by Alleen Pace Nilsen, pay attention to the definitions, descriptions, and other ideas that she presents. Annotate the margins as you read, noting when she uses facts, opinions, or biases. Also note how you feel as you read her essay. Do you agree or disagree with any parts of her essay? Try to avoid letting biases, opinions, and your own feelings about Nilsen's topic get in the way of a thorough reading and understanding of this essay.

---

### BEFORE YOU READ

1. What is the purpose of a dictionary? In what ways is the information contained in a dictionary influenced by people?
2. Brainstorm for a moment about the words you can think of to describe women in our society. After you have 10 or 15, try to think of an equivalent term used to describe men.

---

## Sexism in English: A 1990s Update[*]

### by Alleen Pace Nilsen

Twenty years ago I embarked on a study of the sexism inherent in American English. I had just returned to Ann Arbor, Michigan, after living for two years (1967–69) in Kabul, Afghanistan, where I had begun to look critically at the role society assigned to women. The Afghan version of the *chaderi* prescribed for Moslem women was particularly confining. Few women attended the American–built Kabul University where my husband was teaching linguistics because there were no women's dormitories, which meant that the only females who could attend were those whose families happened to live in the capital city. Afghan jokes and folklore were blatantly sexist, for example this proverb, "If you see an old man, sit down and take a lesson; if you see an old woman, throw a stone."

But it wasn't only the native culture that made me question women's roles; it was also the American community. Nearly six hundred Americans lived in Kabul, mostly supported by U.S. taxpayers. The single women were career secretaries, schoolteachers, or nurses. The three women who had jobs comparable to the American men's jobs were textbook editors with the assignment of developing reading

[*]*Source:* Nilsen, Alleen Pace. "Sexism in English: A 1990s Update." Reprinted by permission of the author.

books in Dari (Afghan Persian) for young children. They
worked at the Ministry of Education, a large building in the
center of the city. There were no women's restrooms, so
during their two-year assignment whenever they needed to
go to the bathroom they had to walk across the street and
down the block to the Kabul Hotel.

The rest of the American women were like myself—      3
wives and mothers whose husbands were either career
diplomats, employees of USAID [United States Agency for
International Development], or college professors who had
been recruited to work on various contract teams including an education team from Teachers College, Columbia
University, and an agricultural team from the University of
Wyoming. These were the women who were most influential in changing my way of thinking. We were suddenly
bereft of our traditional roles; some of us became alcoholics; others got very good at bridge, while others
searched desperately for ways to contribute either to our
families or to the Afghans. The local economy provided
few jobs for women and certainly none for foreigners; we
were isolated from former friends and the social goals we
had grown up with. Most of us had three servants (they
worked for $1.00 a day) because the cook refused to wash
dishes and the dishwasher refused to water the lawn or
sweep the sidewalks—it was their form of unionization.
Occasionally, someone would try to get along without servants, but it was impossible because the houses were huge
and we didn't have the mechanical aids we had at home.
Drinking water had to be brought from the deep well at
the American Embassy, and kerosene and wood stoves had
to be stocked and lit. The servants were all males, the highest–paid one being the cook, who could usually speak
some English. Our days revolved around supervising these
servants. One woman's husband got so tired of hearing her
complain about such annoyances as the *bacha* (the house-
keeper) stealing kerosene and needles and batteries, and
about the cook putting chili powder instead of paprika on
the deviled eggs, and about the gardener subcontracting
his work and expecting her to pay all his friends, that he

scheduled an hour a week for listening to complaints. The rest of the time he wanted to keep his mind clear to focus on his important work with his Afghan counterparts and with the president of the university and the Minister of Education. What he was doing in this country was going to make a difference! In the great eternal scheme of things, of what possible importance would be his wife's trivial troubles with the servants?

These were the thoughts in my mind when we finished our contract and returned in the fall of 1969 to the University of Michigan in Ann Arbor. I was surprised to find that many other women were also questioning the expectations that they had grown up with. In the spring of 1970, a women's conference was announced. I hired a babysitter and attended, but I returned home more troubled than ever. Now that I knew housework was worth only a dollar a day, I couldn't take it seriously, but I wasn't angry in the same way these women were. Their militancy frightened me. Since I wasn't ready for a revolution, I decided I would have my own feminist movement. I would study the English language and see what it could tell me about sexism. I started reading a desk dictionary and making notecards on every entry that seemed to tell something about male and female. I soon had a dog–eared dictionary, along with a collection of notecards filling two shoe boxes.

Ironically, I started reading the dictionary because I wanted to avoid getting involved in social issues, but what happened was that my notecards brought me right back to looking at society. Language and society are as intertwined as a chicken and an egg. The language that a culture uses is telltale evidence of the values and beliefs of that culture. And because there is a lag in how fast a language changes—new words can easily be introduced, but it takes a long time for old words and usages to disappear—a careful look at English will reveal the attitudes that our ancestors held and that we as a culture are therefore predisposed to hold. My notecards revealed three main points. Friends have offered the opinion that I didn't need to read the dictionary to learn such obvious facts. Nevertheless, it

4

5

was interesting to have linguistic evidence of sociological observations.

### Women Are Sexy; Men Are Successful

First, in American culture a woman is valued for the attractiveness and sexiness of her body, while a man is valued for his physical strength and accomplishments. A woman is sexy. A man is successful.     6

A persuasive piece of evidence supporting this view is the eponyms—words that have come from someone's name—found in English. I had a two–and–a–half–inch stack of cards taken from men's names, but less than a half-inch stack from women's names, and most of those came from Greek mythology. In the words that came into American English since we separated from Britain, there are many eponyms based on the names of famous American men: *bartlett pear, boysenberry, diesel engine, franklin stove, ferris wheel, gatling gun, mason jar, sideburns, sousaphone, schick test,* and *winchester rifle.* The only common eponyms taken from American women's names are *Alice blue* (after Alice Roosevelt Longworth), *bloomers* (after Amelia Jenks Bloomer), and *Mae West jacket* (after the buxom actress). Two out of the three feminine eponyms relate closely to a woman's physical anatomy, while the masculine eponyms (except for *sideburns,* after General Burnside) have nothing to do with the namesake's body, but instead honor the man for an accomplishment of some kind.     7

Although in Greek mythology women played a bigger role than they did in the biblical stories of the Judeo–Christian cultures and so the names of goddesses are accepted parts of the language in such place names as Pomona from the goddess of fruit and Athens from Athena and in such common words as *cereal* from Ceres, *psychology* from Psyche, and *arachnoid* from Arachne, the same tendency to think of women in relation to sexuality is seen in the eponyms *aphrodisiac* from Aphrodite, the Greek name for the goddess of love and beauty, and *venereal disease,* from Venus, the Roman name for Aphrodite.     8

Another interesting word from Greek mythology is 9
*Amazon.* According to Greek folk etymology, the *a* means
"without" as in *atypical* or *amoral,* while *mazon* comes from
*mazos,* meaning *breast* as still seen in *mastectomy.* In the
Greek legend, Amazon women cut off their right breasts so
they could better shoot their bows. Apparently, the story-
tellers had a feeling that for women to play the active,
"masculine" role that the Amazons adopted for themselves,
they had to trade in part of their femininity.

This preoccupation with women's breasts is not lim- 10
ited to ancient stories. As a volunteer for the University of
Wisconsin's *Dictionary of American Regional English* (DARE),
I read a western trapper's diary from the 1830s. I was to
make notes of any unusual usages or language patterns. My
most interesting finding was that he referred to a range of
mountains as *The Teats,* a metaphor based on the similarity
between the shapes of the mountains and women's breasts.
Because today we use the French wording, *The Grand
Tetons,* the metaphor isn't as obvious, but I wrote to map-
makers and found the following listings: *Nippletop* and *Little
Nipple Top* near Mt. Marcy in the Adirondacks, *Nipple
Mountain* in Archuleta County, Colorado, *Nipple Peak* in
Coke County, Texas, *Nipple Butte* in Pennington, South
Dakota, *Squaw Peak* in Placer County, California (and many
other locations), *Maiden's Peak* and *Squaw Tit* (they're the
same mountain) in the Cascade Range in Oregon, *Mary's
Nipple,* near Salt Lake City, Utah, and *Jane Russell Peaks*
near Stark, New Hampshire.

Except for the movie star Jane Russell, the women 11
being referred to are anonymous—it's only a sexual part of
their body that is mentioned. When topographical features
are named after men, it's probably not going to be to draw
attention to a sexual part of their bodies but instead to
honor individuals for an accomplishment. For example, no
one thinks of a part of the male body when hearing a reference to Pike's Peak, Colorado, or Jackson Hole, Wyoming.

Going back to what I learned from my dictionary 12
cards, I was surprised to realize how many pairs of words

we have in which the feminine word has acquired sexual connotations while the masculine word retains a serious businesslike aura. For example, a *callboy* is the person who calls actors when it is time for them to go on stage, but a *callgirl* is a prostitute. Compare *sir* and *madam*. *Sir* is a term of respect while *madam* has acquired the specialized meaning of a brothel manager. Something similar has happened to *master* and *mistress*. Would you rather have a painting by an *old master* or an *old mistress*?

It's because the word *woman* had sexual connotations, as in "She's his woman," that people began avoiding its use, hence such terminology as *ladies room, lady of the house*, and *girls' school* or *school for young ladies*. Feminists, who ask that people use the term *woman* rather than *girl* or *lady*, are rejecting the idea that *woman* is primarily a sexual term. They have been at least partially successful in that today *woman* is commonly used to communicate gender without intending implications about sexuality.                                     13

I found two hundred pairs of words with masculine and feminine forms, e.g., *heir–heiress, hero–heroine, steward–stewardess, usher–usherette*, etc. In nearly all such pairs, the masculine word is considered the base, with some kind of a feminine suffix being added. The masculine form is the one from which compounds are made, e.g., from *king–queen* comes kingdom but not *queendom*, from *sportsman–sportslady* comes *sportsmanship* but not *sportsladyship*. There is one—and only one—semantic area in which the masculine word is not the base or more powerful word. This is in the area dealing with sex and marriage. When someone refers to a *virgin*, a listener will probably think of a female unless the speaker specifies *male* or uses a masculine pronoun. The same is true for *prostitute*.                                     14

In relation to marriage, there is much linguistic evidence showing that weddings are more important to women than to men. A woman cherishes the wedding and is considered a bride for a whole year, but a man is referred to as a groom only on the day of the wedding. The word *bride* appears in *bridal attendant, bridal gown, bridesmaid, bridal shower*, and even *bridegroom*. *Groom* comes                                     15 from the Middle English *grom,* meaning "man," and in this sense is seldom used outside of a wedding. With most pairs of male/female words, people habitually put the masculine word first—*Mr. and Mrs., his and hers, boys and girls, men and women, kings and queens, brothers and sisters, guys and dolls,* and *host and hostess*—but it is the *bride and groom* who are talked about, not the *groom and bride.*

The importance of marriage to a woman is also shown         16
by the fact that when a marriage ends in death, the woman gets the title of *widow.* A man gets the derived title of *widower.* This term is not used in other phrases or contexts, but *widow* is seen in *widowhood, widow's peak,* and *widow's walk.* A *widow* in a card game is an extra hand of cards, while in typesetting it is an extra line of type.

How changing cultural ideas bring changes to lan-          17
guage is clearly visible in this semantic area. The feminist movement has caused the differences between the sexes to be downplayed, and since I did my dictionary study two decades ago, the word *singles* has largely replaced such sex–specific and value–laden terms as *bachelor, old maid, spinster, divorcee, widow,* and *widower.* And in 1970 I wrote that when a man is called a *professional* he is thought to be a doctor or lawyer, but when people hear a woman referred to as a *professional* they are likely to think of a prostitute. That's not as true today because so many women have become doctors and lawyers that it's no longer incongruous to think of women in those professional roles.

Another change that has taken place is in wedding          18
announcements. They used to be sent out from the bride's parents and did not even give the name of the groom's parents. Today, most couples choose to list either all or none of the parents' names. Also it is now much more likely that both the bride and groom's picture will be in the newspaper, while a decade ago only the bride's picture was published on the "Women's" or the "Society" page. Even the traditional wording of the wedding ceremony is being changed. Many officials now pronounce the couple "husband and wife" instead of the old "man and wife," and

they ask the bride if she promises "to love, honor, and cherish," instead of "to love, honor, and obey."

### Women Are Passive; Men Are Active

The wording of the wedding ceremony also relates to the second point that my cards showed, which is that women are expected to play a passive or weak role while men play an active or strong role. In the traditional ceremony, the official asks, "Who gives the bride away?" and the father answers, "I do." Some fathers answer, "Her mother and I do," but that doesn't solve the problem inherent in the question. The idea that a bride is something to be handed over from one man to another bothers people because it goes back to the days when a man's servants, his children, and his wife were all considered to be his property. They were known by his name because they belonged to him and he was responsible for their actions and their debts.                                          19

The grammar used in talking or writing about weddings as well as other sexual relationships shows the expectation of men playing the active role. Men *wed* women while women *become* brides of men. A man *possesses* a woman; he *deflowers* her; he *performs*; he *scores*; he *takes away* her virginity. Although a woman can *seduce* a man, she cannot offer him her virginity. When talking about virginity, the only way to make the woman the actor in the sentence is to say that "She lost her virginity," but people lose things by accident rather than by purposeful actions, and so she's only the grammatical, not the real–life, actor.                                          20

The reason that women tried to bring the term *Ms.* into the language to replace *Miss* and *Mrs.* relates to this point. Married women resented being identified only under their husband's names. For example, when Susan Glascoe did something newsworthy, she would be identified in the newspaper only as Mrs. John Glascoe. The dictionary cards showed what appeared to be an attitude on the part of editors that it was almost indecent to let a respectable woman's name march unaccompanied across the pages of a dictionary. Women were listed with male                                          21 names whether or not the male contributed to the woman's reason for being in the dictionary or in his own right was as famous as the woman. For example, Charlotte Brontë was identified as Mrs. Arthur B. Nicholls, Amelia Earhart as Mrs. George Palmer Putnam, Helen Hayes as Mrs. Charles MacArthur, Jenny Lind as Mme. Otto Goldschmit, Cornelia Otis Skinner as the daughter of Otis Skinner, Harriet Beecher Stowe as the sister of Henry Ward Beecher, and Edith Sitwell as the sister of Osbert and Sacheverell. A very small number of women got into the dictionary without the benefit of a masculine escort. They were rebels and crusaders: temperance leaders Frances Elizabeth Caroline Willard and Carry Nation, women's rights leaders Carrie Chapman Catt and Elizabeth Cady Stanton, birth control educator Margaret Sanger, religious leader Mary Baker Eddy, and slaves Harriet Tubman and Phyllis Wheatley.

Etiquette books used to teach that if a woman had *Mrs.* in front of her name then the husband's name should follow because *Mrs.* is an abbreviated form of *Mistress* and a woman couldn't be a mistress of herself. As with many arguments about "correct" language usage, this isn't very logical because *Miss* is also an abbreviation of *Mistress.* Feminists hoped to simplify matters by introducing *Ms.* as an alternative to both *Mrs.* and *Miss,* but what happened is that *Ms.* largely replaced *Miss* to become a catch–all business title for women. Many married women still prefer the title *Mrs.,* and some resent being addressed with the term *Ms.* As one frustrated newspaper reporter complained, "Before I can write about a woman, I have to know not only her marital status but also her political philosophy." The result of such complications may contribute to the demise of titles, which are already being ignored by many computer programmers who find it more efficient to simply use names; for example, in a business letter: "Dear Joan Garcia," instead of "Dear Mrs. Joan Garcia," "Dear Ms. Garcia," or "Dear Mrs. Louis Garcia." 22

The titles given to royalty provide an example of how males can be disadvantaged by the assumption that they 23

are always to play the more powerful role. In British royalty, when a male holds a title, his wife is automatically
given the feminine equivalent. But the reverse is not true.
For example, a *count* is a high political officer, with a *count-
ess* being his wife. The same is true for a *duke* and a *duchess*
and a *king* and a *queen*. But when a female holds the royal
title, the man she marries does not automatically acquire
the matching title. For example, Queen Elizabeth's husband has the title of *prince* rather than *king*, but if Prince
Charles would have become king while he was still married
to Lady or Princess Diana, she would have been known as
the queen. The reasoning appears to be that since masculine words are stronger, they are reserved for true heirs
and withheld from males coming into the royal family by
marriage. If Prince Philip were called *King Philip*, it would
be much easier for British subjects to forget where the true
power lies.

The names that people give their children show the          24
hopes and dreams they have for them, and when we look
at the differences between male and female names in a
culture we can see the cumulative expectations of that culture. In our culture girls often have names taken from
small, aesthetically pleasing items, e.g., *Ruby*, *Jewel*, and
*Pearl*. *Esther* and *Stella* mean "star," *Ada* means "ornament,"
and *Vanessa* means "butterfly." Boys are more likely to be
given names with meanings of power and strength, e.g.,
*Neil* means "champion," *Martin* is from Mars, the god of
war, *Raymond* means "wise protection," *Harold* means "chief
of the army," *Ira* means "vigilant," *Rex* means "king," and
*Richard* means "strong king."

We see similar differences in food metaphors. Food is a          25
passive substance just sitting there waiting to be eaten. Many
people have recognized this and so no longer feel comfortable describing women as "delectable morsels." However,
when I was a teenager, it was considered a compliment to
refer to a girl (we didn't call anyone a *woman* until she was
middle-aged) as a *cute tomato*, a *peach*, a *dish*, a *cookie*, *sugar*, or
*sweetiepie*. When being affectionate, women will occasionally
call a man *honey* or *sweetie*, but in general, food metaphors

are used much less often with men than with women. If a man is called a *fruit,* his masculinity is being questioned. But it's perfectly acceptable to use a food metaphor if the food is heavier and more substantive than that used for women. For example, pin–up pictures of women have long been known as *cheesecake,* but when Burt Reynolds posed for a nude centerfold, the picture was immediately dubbed *beefcake,* c.f., *a hunk of meat.* That such sexual references to men have come into the general language is another reflection of how society is beginning to lessen the differences between their attitudes toward men and women.

Something similar to the *fruit* metaphor happens with references to plants. We insult a man by calling him a *pansy,* but it wasn't considered particularly insulting to talk about a girl being a *wallflower,* a *clinging vine,* or a *shrinking violet,* or to give girls such names as *Ivy, Rose, Lily, Iris, Daisy, Camellia, Heather,* and *Flora.* A plant metaphor can be used with a man if the plant is big and strong, for example Andrew Jackson's nickname of *Old Hickory.* Also, the phrases *blooming idiots* and *budding geniuses* can be used with either sex, but notice how they are based on the most active thing a plant can do, which is to bloom or bud.

26

Animal metaphors also illustrate the different expectations for males and females. Men are referred to as *studs, bucks,* and *wolves* while women are referred to with such metaphors as *kitten, bunny, beaver, bird, chick,* and *lamb.* In the 1950s we said that boys went *tomcatting,* but today it's just *catting around* and both boys and girls do it. When the term *foxy,* meaning that someone was sexy, first became popular, it was used only for girls, but now someone of either sex can be described as a *fox.* Some animal metaphors that are used predominantly with men have negative connotations based on the size and/or strength of the animals, e.g., *beast, bull–headed, jackass, rat, loan shark,* and *vulture.* Negative metaphors used with women are based on smaller animals, e.g., *social butterfly, mousy, catty,* and *vixen.* The feminine terms connote action, but not the same kind of large-scale action as with the masculine terms.

27

### Women Are Connected with Negative Connotations, Men with Positive Connotations

The final point that my notecards illustrated was how many positive connotations are associated with the concept of masculine, while there are either trivial or negative connotations connected with the corresponding feminine concept. An example from the animal metaphors makes a good illustration. The word *shrew,* taken from the name of a small but especially vicious animal, was defined in my dictionary as "an ill-tempered scolding woman," but the word *shrewd,* taken from the same root, was defined as "marked by clever, discerning awareness" and was illustrated with the phrase "a shrewd businessman."

28

Early in life, children are conditioned to the superiority of the masculine role. As child psychologists point out, little girls have much more freedom to experiment with sex roles than do little boys. If a girl acts like a *tomboy,* most parents have mixed feelings, being at least partially proud. But if their little boy acts like a *sissy* (derived from *sister*), they call a psychologist. It's perfectly acceptable for a little girl to sleep in the crib that was purchased for her brother, to wear his hand–me–down jeans and shirts, and to ride the bicycle that he has outgrown. But few parents would put a boy baby in a white and gold crib decorated with frills and lace, and virtually no parents would have their little boy wear his sister's hand–me–down dresses, nor would they have their son ride a girl's pink bicycle with a flower–bedecked basket. The proper names given to girls and boys show this same attitude. Girls can have "boy" names—*Cris, Craig, Jo, Kelly, Shawn, Teri, Toni,* and *Sam*—but it doesn't work the other way around. A couple of generations ago, *Beverly, Frances, Hazel, Marion,* and *Shirley* were common boys' names. As parents gave these names to more and more girls, they fell into disuse for males, and some older men who have these names prefer to go by their initials or by such abbreviated forms as *Haze* or *Shirl.*

29

When a little girl is told to *be a lady,* she is being told to sit with her knees together and to be quiet and dainty. But when a little boy is told to *be a man,* he is being told to

30

be noble, strong, and virtuous—to have all the qualities that the speaker looks on as desirable. The concept of manliness has such positive connotations that it used to be a compliment to call someone a *he–man,* to say that he was doubly a man. Today many people are more ambivalent about this term and respond to it much as they do to the word *macho.* But calling someone a *manly man* or a *virile man* is nearly always meant as a compliment. *Virile* comes from the Indo–European *vir* meaning "man," which is also the basis of *virtuous.* Contrast the positive connotations of both *virile* and *virtuous* with the negative connotations of *hysterical.* The Greeks took this latter word from their name for *uterus* (as still seen in *hysterectomy*). They thought that women were the only ones who experienced uncontrolled emotional outbursts and so the condition must have something do to with a part of the body that only women have.

Differences between positive male and negative  **31**
female connotations can be seen in several pairs of words which differ denotatively only in the matter of sex. *Bachelor* as compared to *spinster* or *old maid* has such positive connotations that women try to adopt them by using the term *bachelor–girl* or *bachelorette.* *Old maid* is so negative that it's the basis for metaphors: pretentious and fussy old men are called *old maids,* as are the leftover kernels of unpopped popcorn and the last card in a popular children's game.

*Patron* and *matron* (Middle English for *father* and  **32**
*mother*) have such different levels of prestige that women try to borrow the more positive masculine connotations with the word *patroness,* literally "female father." Such a peculiar term came about because of the high prestige attached to *patron* in such phrases as a *patron of the arts* or *a patron saint. Matron* is more apt to be used in talking about a woman in charge of a jail or a public restroom.

When men are doing jobs that women often do, we ap-  **33**
parently try to pay the men extra by giving them fancy titles; for example, a male cook is more likely to be called a *chef,* while a male seamstress will get the title of *tailor.* The armed forces have a special problem in that they recruit under such slogans as "The Marine Corps Builds Men!"

and "Join the Army! Become a Man." Once the recruits are enlisted, they find themselves doing much of the work that has been traditionally thought of as "women's work." The solution to getting the work done and not insulting anyone's masculinity was to change the titles as shown below:

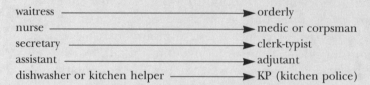

waitress ────────────────────▶ orderly

nurse ───────────────────────▶ medic or corpsman

secretary ───────────────────▶ clerk-typist

assistant ───────────────────▶ adjutant

dishwasher or kitchen helper ────▶ KP (kitchen police)

Compare *brave* and *squaw.* Early settlers in America     34
truly admired Indian men and hence named them with a word that carried connotations of youth, vigor, and courage. But they used the Algonquin's name for "woman," and over the years it developed almost opposite connotations to those of *brave. Wizard* and *witch* contrast almost as much. The masculine *wizard* implies skill and wisdom combined with magic, while the feminine *witch* implies evil intentions combined with magic. Part of the unattractiveness of both *witch* and *squaw* is that they have been used so often to refer to old women, something with which our culture is particularly uncomfortable, just as the Afghans were. Imagine my surprise when I ran across the phrases *grandfatherly advice* and *old wives' tales* and realized that the underlying implication is the same as the Afghan proverb about old men being worth listening to while old women talk only foolishness.

Other terms which show how negatively we view old     35
women as compared to young women are *old nag* as compared to *filly, old crow* or *old bat* as compared to *bird,* and being *catty* as compared to being *kittenish.* There is no matching set of metaphors for men. The chicken metaphor tells the whole story of a woman's life. In her youth she is a *chick.* Then she marries and begins *feathering her nest.* Soon she begins feeling *cooped up,* so she goes to *hen parties* where she *cackles* with her friends. Then she has her *brood,* begins to *henpeck* her husband, and finally turns into *an old biddy.*

I embarked on my study of the dictionary not with                36
the intention of prescribing language change but simply to
see what the language would tell me about sexism. Nevertheless I have been both surprised and pleased as I've
watched the changes that have occurred over the past two
decades. I'm one of those linguists who believes that new
language customs will cause a new generation of speakers
to grow up with different expectations. This is why I'm
happy about people's efforts to use inclusive language, to
say *he or she* or *they* when speaking about individuals whose
names they do not know. I'm glad that leading publishers
have developed guidelines to help writers use language
that is fair to both sexes, and I'm glad that most newspapers and magazines list women by their own names instead
of only by their husbands' names and that educated and
thoughtful people no longer begin their business letters
with "Dear Sir" or "Gentlemen," but instead use a memo
form or begin with such salutations as "Dear Colleagues,"
"Dear Reader," or "Dear Committee Members." I'm also
glad that such words as *poetess, authoress, conductress,* and
*aviatrix* now sound quaint and old–fashioned and that
*chairman* is giving way to *chair* or *head, mailman* to *mail car-
rier, clergyman* to *clergy,* and *stewardess* to *flight attendant.* I
was also pleased when the National Oceanic and Atmos-
pheric Administration bowed to feminist complaints and in
the late '70s began to alternate men's and women's names
for hurricanes. However, I wasn't so pleased to discover
that the change did not immediately erase sexist thoughts
from everyone's mind as shown by a headline about Hurricane David in a 1979 New York tabloid, "David Rapes Virgin Islands." More recently a similar metaphor appeared in
a headline in the *Arizona Republic* about Hurricane Charlie:
"Charlie Quits Carolinas, Flirts with Virginia."

What these incidents show is that sexism is not some-         37
thing existing independently in American English or in the
particular dictionary that I happened to read. Rather, it
exists in people's minds. Language is like an x–ray in providing visible evidence of invisible thought. The best thing
about people being interested in and discussing sexist lan-

guage is that as they make conscious decisions about what pronouns they will use, what jokes they will tell or laugh at, how they will write their names, or how they will begin their letters, they are forced to think about the underlying issue of sexism. This is good, because as a problem that begins in people's assumptions and expectations, it's a problem that will be solved only when a great many people have given it a great deal of thought.

## Building Your Skills

### Focus on Words

Look up the following words or parts of phrases in a dictionary. Consult the preceding essay and identify the meaning that best fits the way the author uses the word in this essay. Each word or phrase is followed by the number of the paragraph in which it appears.

| | |
|---|---|
| embarked (1) | gender (13) |
| inherent (1) | suffix (14) |
| chaderi (1) | sex-specific (17) |
| linguistics (1) | value-laden (17) |
| blatantly (1) | incongruous (17) |
| militancy (4) | metaphors (25) |
| feminist (4) | predominantly (27) |
| predisposed (5) | proverb (34) |
| eponyms (7) | prescribing (36) |
| sexual connotations (12) | |

### Focus on the Message

1. On what did Nilsen's "feminist movement" focus (para. 4)? What did she discover as she conducted her study?
2. What does Nilsen mean when she writes "because there is a lag in how fast a language changes—new words can easily be introduced, but it takes a long time for old words and usages to disappear—a careful look at English will reveal the attitudes that our ancestors held and that we as a culture are therefore predisposed to hold" (para. 5)?

3. Define and describe the categories of language that Nilsen subtitles in her essay:

    Women Are Sexy; Men Are Successful

    Women Are Passive; Men Are Active

    Women Are Connected with Negative Connotations, Men with Positive Connotations

4. What other examples of sexist or biased language can you think of? Think about other examples of language that either support or refute Nilsen's findings.

5. In addition to sexism, what other values and attitudes from your culture are expressed in language? Try to think of examples that show positive traits about the culture and examples that demonstrate negative characteristics.

# TECHNIQUES FOR WRITING: LASTING IMPRESSIONS— WRITING THE CONCLUSION

What do you remember when you finish watching a movie or reading a good book? Chances are you remember the ending—how it made you feel, how satisfied you were with that ending. Essays are similar; the ending creates a lasting impression for your reader and helps your reader determine whether or not your essay lives up to what you said it would be in the introduction. Conclusions that are well-written leave us thinking about the essay, considering its thesis, contemplating its examples; they give us a reason to continue thinking about what the writer said. By contrast, the worst conclusions illustrate the writer's lack of thought or concern for the reader. Sometimes they simply restate the introduction in the same or almost the same words that the reader was presented with in the introduction. Sometimes a conclusion is missing altogether; the essay or paragraph just ends. Read the following conclusion examples:

> And that's all I have to say about that subject.
> In conclusion, I'd like to say that we really do need to stop crime in America.
> I'm not really sure how to bring this to a close, but I do want to say that I think that stopping crime is important.
> As I said before, "Let's stop crime."

What do all of these have in common? One feature that they share is their lack of audience. Notice they all use "I" as a way of personalizing the conclusion. In other words, the writer uses "I" to tell us that what he or she writes is his or her opinion. Is this necessary? If I tell you a point of view, do I really need to tell you it is what I believe, or will you already know that? Notice that the first three also tell the reader that this is the conclusion. One key to writing a good conclusion is providing the feeling of conclusion. If your reader does not know he or she is reading the conclusion, then just writing "in conclusion" will not make the conclusion work; instead, major revision is necessary. The poorest conclusion technique is the one shown in the first example, because it not only fails to recognize that someone will be reading this, but it seems like an afterthought—a haphazard ending that is designed for the writer's convenience. Most readers are likely to find this irritating and unsatisfying.

A well-written conclusion should acknowledge the reader by providing a sense of closure and satisfaction. It should bring some kind of resolution to the discussion provided in the essay. Most important, it should bring the essay to a close in a way that is anticipated by everything else in the essay. If the essay argues against crime, for example, the conclusion should provide a reasonable solution to this problem or a set of questions that the reader is left to consider. It should not try to oversimplify a problem that has already been discussed in the essay, and it certainly should never simply say, "I do not know the answer," because that takes all credibility away from the writer.

Below are many techniques for writing powerful, thoughtful conclusions. Many of them were discussed as techniques for introductions as well, but when they are used for conclusions, the requirements and the methods for using them can be very different. Try to apply some of these techniques in your writing when appropriate, but even if you do not use one of these specific techniques, remember that your conclusion will to some extent determine how much your reader trusts you and whether or not the reader is persuaded by your essay.

### Ending with Questions

Questions at the end of an essay, if they are thoughtful questions and if they are not simply a replacement for a real conclusion, can be a thought-provoking, stimulating way to end an essay. Ending an essay with questions can backfire, however, if the questions are not very significant, if they seem unrelated to the thesis, or if they seem like a quick fix offering no conclusion. When questions create concern, fear, or involvement on the part of the reader, they can be very effective. Questions can expand and augment the conclusion, leaving the reader to consider the significance of a problem, the effect of this problem on his or her life, and even what solutions he or she might offer.

### Ending with Short Narratives or Anecdotes

Another effective way to conclude an essay is to close with an amusing, heart-wrenching, or relevant story or joke. Choose a worthwhile and thought-provoking anecdote or narrative. The ending you choose must easily sum up the point and should evoke an emotional response from the reader. This can help the reader to remember what he or she has read and to understand the significance of the issue or topic discussed in the essay. Of course, these effects only work if the story's significance and relationship to the topic is clear, so choosing the anecdote carefully is very important.

### Ending with Statistics

Statistics used in the conclusion can sum up the magnitude of a problem and motivate the reader to take action. This technique can be very persuasive if it is used in conjunction with a persuasive essay conclusion that presents a resolution and if the essay's body has effectively set up the conclusion. Statistics by themselves are not very effective, though. The statistics need a context, so be sure to use them with questions, discussion, or some explanation.

### Ending with Quotations

Quotations can work well in essays, but when an essay ends with a quotation, as with an anecdote, great care must be taken to choose one that is significant and clearly related to the topic. Quotations can also be used in conjunction with other conclusion techniques, but should never be used simply to end the essay without having a clearly stated reason or significance. Quotations should either present a summation or significant commentary on the main idea or topic in the essay, or they should in some way make the reader think about the implications of this topic in his or her life or in the world.

### Using Endings with Shock Value

Ending an essay with a shocking story, question, or scenario takes skill and a great deal of forethought. Remember that you want your audience to remember your essay not because it was the most disgusting or horrific thing they ever read, but because it made them think or inspired them to change, or even just made them question their own firmly held beliefs. Of course, the major determining factor in whether or not to use something shocking is your audience. If your topic lends itself to this type of treatment, then once you choose your quote, story, scenario, questions, or whatever other shocking material you plan to use, you must evaluate how well your audience will receive this shock and how it will communicate your point.

### Referring Back to the Introduction

Another effective way to conclude an essay begins when you set up a goal in the introduction that you fulfill in the conclusion. This works particularly well in essays where a question serves as the thesis and the reader is led through the essay to a logical, thoughtful conclusion. This technique is particularly good for argumentation essays, especially essays with controversial topics. Never simply restate your introduction or thesis, though; that is not the same as referring back to a point for final comment.

### Giving Your Reader Options

Thoughtful solutions, options for solutions, or even an acknowledgment that there is no clear resolution can make for an effective conclusion, particularly in cause/effect and argumentative essays. Emphasizing the significance of the problem or topic you discuss will highlight your concern for this topic, and providing solutions or some sort of resolution shows that you have given the problem some thought. You might also tie in surveys, recent discussions, statistics, or regulations regarding the problem to show that others have ideas about solving this problem or situation. Avoid at all costs, though, the kind of conclusion that simply restates the problem. This will show the reader that you have not given the topic much thought.

When you think about your conclusion, you might think about what it feels like to watch a movie. When we watch movies we build expectations about how the conflict or topic in the movie will be resolved. At the end of the movie, sometimes we are surprised, sometimes amused, sometimes even angry. The worst reaction, however, is one of disappointment. Think about the last time you saw a movie that ended and left you thinking, "How could the director have ended this movie this way?" Typically, audiences can understand and be satisfied with the main character losing his life, the two lovers falling out of love, or some other less-than-happy scenario. What watchers typically object to is the type of ending that leaves major issues unresolved. Be careful in your conclusion to satisfy any expectations that you build for your reader throughout your essay. Providing the reader with a feeling of completion makes your essay more persuasive and you as a writer more credible and trustworthy.

## Building Your Skills

### Assignment 1

In her essay "Sexism in English: A 1990s Update," Alleen Pace Nilsen describes words that illustrate sexism in language and by extension in our culture. What other biases and prejudices exist in language and in culture; think about the other forms of discrimination based on age, race, religion, job qualifications, and so on. Make a list of words that illustrate the existence of this discrimination. For example, if you identified race as your topic, you could make a list of words that show bias for and against race. After you have chosen a topic and created a list of words that illustrate this bias or discrimination exists, write an essay defining what this type of discrimination is and in what situations it takes place. Use several of the words from your list as examples and evidence. When you finish your rough draft, look at the preceding section about conclusions for ideas for an effective conclusion that is somewhat different than the way you typically conclude your essays. Write your final draft by making the necessary changes and writing a very effective conclusion that leaves your reader thinking.

### Assignment 2

Using an essay you have written recently, write each sentence of your essay on a separate 3″ × 5″ card. Place the essay itself in a folder or other place out of sight. Shuffle the cards to mix them up well and then look at each individual sentence to find bland words, awkward or confusing words or phrases, or any words or sentences that can be rewritten and improved with restructuring, adding, deleting, or rewording. Once you have given each sentence individual attention, reconstruct the essay by putting the cards in a logical, effective order. If you have sentences that do not fit at all, leave them out. If, when you finish, you have sentences that do not go together, add connecting sentences to provide coherence. When you have completed all of the reordering and the cards go together in a logical, unified, and coherent manner, rewrite what is written on the cards to form a new essay. After you have reordered the essay, find an anecdote, story, quotation, or joke to replace the conclusion or add to the existing conclusion. Compare this essay with the original form. Which one is better?

### Assignment 3

Brainstorm or list the types of violence that exist in our society. After listing several forms, divide a piece of paper into two sections. On one half, identify the types of violence that are acceptable to society. On the other side, identify the types of violence that are not condoned or acceptable in our society. Compare the two sides and write an essay response to the following:

> Can or should all violence be eliminated? What types of violence are accepted in society as normal? What types are discouraged and viewed as inappropriate? What do these two types of violence tell us about the society in which we live?

At the end of your essay, try two of the conclusion techniques discussed in this chapter.

## READING A STUDENT ESSAY

### Peer Review Strategy: Revising for a Lasting Impression

When you finish reading an essay or even a book, what do you expect? What should the end of the essay do if the writer wants you to remember his or her point or message? In this chapter, many techniques for conclusions are presented. Revising a conclusion requires some creativity, as well as putting yourself in the reader's shoes.

Perhaps the best kind of conclusion is one that leaves the reader surprised, shocked, emotional, or in some way affected. This is tough to measure because each reader is a bit different, but the magnitude of the effect is probably less important than the fact that the conclusion does impact the reader.

Revising for impact in the conclusion requires that you go with your gut reaction to a piece of writing. If you read another student's essay, you will have no trouble knowing whether the essay leaves you with an emotional reaction or whether it leaves you with no reaction at all. The difficulty comes when you are revising your own essay. How do you judge the power of your own conclusion? One way is to get reactions from other readers, but a second way is to put the essay away for twenty-four hours and then come back to it with fresh eyes. If you do not have some reaction to your own conclusion, chances are your reader will not have a reaction either.

Read the following essay and notice the expectations the writer creates throughout the essay for an outcome or a solution. What techniques has she used for her conclusion? When you finish reading, think about whether your expectations as a reader are met. Also, notice any reactions or feelings the conclusion leaves you with.

## The Summit

### by Michelle Efseaff

It was a historical gathering of leaders and sol- [1]
diers who have been mortal enemies for generations.
Their coming together marked a milestone in an effort
to end a war that has torn apart their homeland for
decades. Blood has been spilled on both sides. The
mothers' anguished cries reverberate off the walls of
churches during Mass. White crosses mark the proud
and fallen warriors who have sacrificed their lives for
a cause they believed was worth dying for. Children,
without fathers, play in the streets with toy guns and
imitate a life they have known first hand.

Common culture, language, and traditions link [2]
these two sides. Both have descended from the great
warrior civilization and lay claim to the oldest occu-
pied European settlement in the continental United
States. Both are proud, but they have come to the real-
ization that resolution is necessary to end the years of
strife and bloodshed.

When these two sides meet, the designated meet- [3]
ing place must be held secret from the public. For a
successful outcome, the negotiator must be unbiased,
the site free from outside threat. Many people with
good intentions have tried to organize such negotia-
tions in the past, but the outcome has always been the
same: their own selfish reasons have been exposed.

When the meeting takes place, it is hard to [4]
breathe in the room. The air is heavy with feelings of
uncertainty, hatred, and fear. A big question looms
over all the participants, "Can this meeting really
solve the years of hostility? If so, then how?" Who will
be willing to take the first step, to put the past behind
them and move forward toward a peaceful existence?

The moment comes and two leaders face each other with their soldiers flanked and ready for any confrontation. The list of rules governing conduct during the meeting specifies that no weapons are allowed and that each person will be searched before entering. Respect is given to the oldest leader as the two sides meet and begin to address his grievances.

José is seventeen years old, second generation Mexican-American and leader of the Norteños. The Norteños are a California gang with roots deep in their Mexican-American culture. They make no claims of being politically correct and feel the title "Hispanic" groups them with people outside their ethnicity. Graffiti, often called tagging, marks the area's businesses with their logo, either X4 or X14. The fourteenth letter of the alphabet is "N," the letter beginning Norteños.

Sitting across the table from José is Aaron, his enemy and rival gang leader of the Sureños. Aaron is fifteen years old, and his immigration status is questionable. An outside observer might be fooled by his youth and quiet demeanor, but he has commanded drive-by shootings against Norteños for over two years and with no remorse for his victims. His group of young men are compiled primarily of sons of migrant farm workers in Southern California. Their signs are X3 and X13. They tag this sign over the Norteños X14 to show domination and territorial ownership of Norteños-marked claims. X13 comes from the thirteenth letter of the alphabet, "M." Sureños lay claim to ties with the notorious Mexican Mafia.

The dividing line that separates the Norteños and the Sureños is Bakersfield, California, but territory lines become less definite when one moves south or north out of their gang's territory. Sureños commonly claim territory all the way to Fresno, California, over one hundred miles into territory the Norteños claim. The friction

5

6

7

8

between the two groups is based on this boundary line and gaining ownership of territory for the gang.

The negotiator sits at the table with José and Aaron. He has tried to bring these two groups together for a meeting for so long that he has become weary of the many demands each side has made and their inability to concede anything. Finally, frustrated and angry, the negotiator decided to set the rules for the meeting himself and then simply did not back down once they were established. 9

After hours of bitter arguing and a few muttered threats, the gang leaders declared that the high school would be neutral territory, a learning environment. Agreeing to this means no gang colors, red for the Norteños and blue for the Sureños. They also must agree not to tag on school property or to make the usual gang signs or gestures in the hallways. Every new student would be informed of this gang policy by the school and the gang leader. 10

After this meeting, at the high school, a fragile peace looms over the hallways and schoolyard. Any small change could undo the efforts of José, Aaron, and the negotiator, bringing back the days of violence and bloodshed. All agree that more needs to be done to maintain this fragile peace so that the school will remain a learning environment and all gang activity will cease. 11

## Building Your Skills

1. Make a list of words that build your expectations as a reader. Why do you think Efseaff waits so long to tell us she's writing about high school students?

_____

_____

_____

_____

_____

_____

_____

_____

_____

2. What is Efseaff's main point? Where does she make this point?

_____

_____

_____

_____

_____

_____

_____

_____

3. What reaction did you have when you finished this essay? How well do you
   think Efseaff's conclusion fits with the rest of her essay?

_____

_____

_____

_____

_____

_____

_____

_____

_____

_____

4. As if you were discussing Michelle's paper with her, list three features of her essay that work very well or that really appeal to you as a reader. Then, recommend three changes she could make to improve her essay.

   Describe three features that are effective for you as a reader:

   a. _____

   b. _____

   c. _____

   Describe three improvements or changes Michelle could make to create a more effective, interesting, or informative essay:

   a. _____

   b. _____

   c. _____

## USING GRAMMAR: MAKING SURE REFERENCES AGREE

When we read, we understand ideas through recognizable patterns and connections between words. No grammatical concept makes this clearer than agreement between the grammatical parts of a sentence. In sentences, we expect the subjects and pronouns to agree; we also expect the verbs to agree with the subjects. You might ask, "What do you mean by *agree?*" but in reading, you probably recognize the concepts very well even though you may never have heard them described as agreement.

### Subject–Pronoun Agreement

Pronoun agreement is a good example of a concept you probably recognize in most cases even if you do not know this term. It is certainly a concept you use every day in speech and in writing. Does the following sentence make sense?

A person should never fail my tests.

Does the writer mean that someone else is taking his or her tests? We cannot tell. The pronoun *my* does not agree with the subject *person*. Pronouns are words that replace proper names, people, things—any noun—to keep from repeating the same word in the same sentence. In the following chart, you can see that each box in each column represents a different classification.

| Subject | Singular (only one) | Plural (more than one) |
|---|---|---|
| *First Person* | I | We |
| *Second Person* | You | You |
| *Third Person* | He<br>She<br>It | They |

First-person singular refers to the box that contains *I*. The box for second-person singular contains *you*, and the box for second-person plural also contains *you* because we can refer to more than one person using the word *you*. Pronouns that replace or refer back to nouns must stay in the same person or category. If we use the word *they* as the subject of a sentence, we cannot replace it or refer back to it with the pronoun *he*, because *they* is third-person plural while *he* is third-person singular.

If **they** are going, **he** should call us first.

Change *they* to *he* and the sentence makes sense; change *he* to *they* and again the sentence makes sense.

If **he** is going, **he** should call us first.
If **they** are going, **they** should call us first.

The pronoun must agree with the other nouns and pronouns when it refers to the same person or thing. We cannot replace a noun with any other pronoun except one that is consistent in person, or, referring back to the chart, one that belongs in the same box.

Look at the following examples to see if you can detect problems in subject–pronoun agreement.

> Suzy left the movie because she thought it was too violent.
> Every person should learn to protect themselves.
> First I tried to change the tire myself; then you called a tow truck.

The pronoun in the first example agrees with the subject, but the other examples are out of agreement.

Refer back to the chart in this chapter as you read the explanation of each sentence.

*EXAMPLE ONE:*

> **Suzy** left the movie because **she** thought it was too violent.

In this example, the pronoun *she* refers back to *Suzy* and because both are third-person singular, they agree.

*EXAMPLE TWO:*

> Every **person** should learn to protect **themselves**.

In this example, the pronoun *themselves* refers back to *person*, but *person* is third-person singular, while *themselves* is third-person plural. To make this reference agree with *person*, we must change it to third-person singular. It should read

> Every **person** should learn to protect **himself or herself**.

*EXAMPLE THREE:*

> First **I** tried to change the tire **myself**; then **you** called a tow truck.

This example reflects a trend in speech and writing to use *you* instead of being consistent with references. The writer in this sentence uses the word *you* to describe his own action. If *you* referred to a second person who made the call, this sentence would be fine, but in this case let's pretend for the sake of discussion that the writer means that *he* called the tow truck. What pronoun would we use to replace *you?* The sentence should read

First **I** tried to change the tire **myself**; then **I called** a tow truck.

The key to using the appropriate pronouns, then, is to use the pronoun that agrees in person with the subject or noun it replaces or refers back to. Keep a copy of the chart in this chapter for reference if this is a problem that you find often when you edit. Some hints can also help:

## ❏ Don't switch to *you*.

One problem many writers have because of a popular speech pattern is switching to *you* when they really mean *I*. Look at the following paragraph and pay special attention to where the writer switches to an inappropriate use of *you*.

> Whenever **I** go to the bank, **I** try to take out only as much money as **I** need. **You** never take more than **you** need because it is dangerous. When **people** do take a lot of money, for example, from an automated teller, **you** should always be extremely careful and lock **your** car doors and drive away before someone comes to rob **you**.

This paragraph begins by discussing the writer's viewpoint and experience; in grammatical terms, it begins in first-person singular. Then the writer is still discussing how he or she takes money out of the bank, but switches to *you*, which is second person. In the third person, the writer makes recommendations to *people*, which is third-person plural, but then switches back to second person again. This could be rewritten in the following way:

> Whenever **I** go to the bank, **I** try to take out only as much money as **I** need. **I** never take more than **I** need because it is dangerous. When **I** do take a lot of money, for example, from an automated teller, **I am** always extremely careful and lock **my** car doors and drive away before someone can rob **me**.

When you revise a rough draft of an essay, read it for the word *you*. This word is almost always inappropriate in a formal essay. Avoid using overly conversational phrases like *you know* or switching to *you* as if you were having a casual conversation. Notice that the rewrites above are consistent in their presentation, which makes them clear and easy to read.

## ❏ Use the appropriate reflexive pronoun when referring back to a person or to people.

In addition to the use of *you*, another common speech pattern is to use *themselves* to refer back to a person or to people. Look at the two following examples:

> A person can always better themselves.
> People can always better themselves.

Which sentence demonstrates pronoun agreement? *Themselves* is plural and third person, which means that it is appropriate only when the word it refers back to is also third-person plural. In other words, the second sentence uses *themselves* grammatically when it refers back to *people.* The first one is a good example of a common pronoun agreement problem. How would you change the first sentence to use the appropriate pronoun?

singular                               singular
A **person** can always better **himself or herself**.

The most important idea demonstrated by these two examples is consistency. You can learn to recognize singular and plural forms, especially in third person, and then you will know how to use them grammatically by always being consistent: use singular with singular, plural with plural.

## ❑ Use gender-neutral possessive pronouns.

Some older grammar handbooks will show a grammatical form for using third-person singular that is out of date. For example, an older grammar handbook might recommend that you use a male pronoun as the third-person singular pronoun in the following case:

A **person** should always follow **his** instincts.

This is consistent in that both *person* and the pronoun *his* are third person and singular. However, it does not recognize that the *person* referred to could also be female. What happens if we use the opposite approach?

A **person** should always follow **her** instincts.

Each of the sentence examples above is sexist, unless the activity described is uniquely male or female. Instead of choosing male or female, we reflect the gender-neutral nature of the word *person* by using the pronoun combination *his or her.*

A **person** should always follow **his or her** instincts.

Though this example demonstrates the appropriate use in most cases, can you think of any examples where gender-neutral pronouns would be ridiculous? Some cases do exist. Read the following group of sentences to determine where the gender-neutral pronouns belong and where the pronouns should be changed either to gender-specific or gender-neutral pronouns.

1. After giving birth, a person needs his or her rest.
2. As part of the National Football League, each player needs to do his or her part.
3. In the ocean, every fisherman must do his or her part.

The decision on when to use gender-neutral pronouns is not always crystal clear. The first two sentences in this set of examples are fairly easy. Men do not give birth and currently women do not play in the NFL, so each of these can be gender specific, using *her* in the first sentence and *his* in the second. The third sentence is more difficult. "Fisherman," even though it includes *man*, is often used to describe anyone who fishes. We do not often say "fisherwoman," "fisherboy," or "fishergirl." So using *his* or *her* with "fisherman," though it may look a bit odd, is actually appropriate.

Making gender-neutral references can impact the readability level of your writing as well as your own credibility, particularly with female members of your audience who may resent being ignored. Even though pronouns seem like a minor consideration, they are a major part of how we get meaning out of what we read. Using forms that exclude at least as many people as you include is certainly not a way to communicate effectively.

### Subject–Verb Agreement

Sometimes in speech and within our own community dialects, we use a variety of nonstandard patterns when combining subjects with verbs. Look at the following examples:

**They was** driving your car when I saw them.
**Each** of us **are** going.
Neither the **man** nor his **relatives were** happy.

Each of these uses a nonstandard verb form. In Standard English, subject–verb agreement refers to the subject agreeing in person and number with the verb. If the subject is plural, the verb must also be plural; if the subject is singular, then the verb must also be singular. Observe the subjects and verbs in the following sentences:

More often than not, every person work his hardest.
More often than not, every person works his hardest.

One letter makes these two sentences different: one is grammatical, one is ungrammatical. The *-s* on the verb *works* makes the second sentence grammatical. What is the big difference between using *-s* or not using *-s?* The verb *works* adds an -s ending in present tense when it describes the action of a third-person singular subject. Although this may seem like a minor difference, it affects how the reader understands the writer's message.

### Indefinite Pronouns

Indefinite pronouns are those words that replace a noun of an unknown quality or nature. These pronouns are often used with more information about the subject occurring directly following the indefinite pronoun. These are very common in speech and writing, but sometimes a problem arises when writers and speakers need to choose the appropriate verb form for showing the action or state of the indefinite pronoun. This is difficult because many people have difficulty determining whether to use a singular or plural form of a verb to accompany an indefinite subject. Test your own knowledge of this type of agreement.

> Everyone (is/are) invited to the party, but each of us (is/are) planning to
>
> attend. In fact, everyone (has/have) made plans to carpool.

Did you choose the verb that would be appropriate with singular nouns (*is* and *has*)? If not, this is probably an important skill for you to learn.

The following lists show whether several pronouns common in speech and writing are singular, plural, or can be used in both situations. The third group can be used followed by prepositional phrases (such as "of us") to indicate either a singular or plural subject, and as you may have guessed, these can be especially troublesome.

| Singular | Plural | Singular or Plural |
|---|---|---|
| anybody/anyone | few | all |
| everybody/everyone | many | none |
| nobody/no one | several | neither |
| somebody/someone | | either |
| anything/everything | | any |
| nothing/something | | some |
| each | | most |

Indefinite pronouns listed in the Singular column are used with verbs appropriate for third-person singular, for regular verbs this means the form that adds an -s ending.

Subject                                      Verb in third-person singular

**Anybody** who has expensive sports cars **needs** good insurance.
**Everyone likes** to be in love.
**Nothing keeps** a person from accomplishing his or her goals.
**Each** of the charter members **has** his or her own card.

Plural indefinite pronoun subjects are used with the form of the verb appropriate for third-person plural:

Subject   Verb in third-person plural

**Few** people **are** ever handed anything on a silver platter.
**Many** of my friends **have** enormous music collections.
**Several** students **think** the grades were unfair.

The trickiest use of indefinite pronoun subject–verb agreement occurs when an indefinite pronoun can be either singular or plural. Once you have determined how the indefinite pronoun is being used, apply the rules above using third-person singular verbs for indefinite pronouns that are singular and third-person plural verbs for indefinite pronouns that are plural. Look at the following examples, in which the clues to whether the indefinite pronoun is singular or plural have been underlined:

**All** except for one **was** there.
**All** of the students **were** there.
**Some** of what she said **was** true.
**Some** people **were** able to tell that she was lying.

When choosing the appropriate verb, look for exceptions (words like *except* and *but* occurring directly after the subject) as in the first sentence. These are likely to be singular. Also look at the prepositional phrases following the subject. In the second sentence above, "of the students" is a prepositional phrase. If you read the sentence without the prepositional phrase, "All were there," you can quickly choose the appropriate verb. In the third sentence, "Some of what she said" works as a whole subject, and notice that we could substitute the word *it* for "some of what she said" and simply write "It was true." This is your clue that this is a singular subject. If you get stuck, try substituting in this way to help determine the appropriate verb.

### Other Nouns Used with Subjects

Sometimes subjects in a sentence are linked with other nouns by the use of clauses directly following the subject. A few examples are listed below. The subjects and verbs are printed in bold, while the second noun is underlined.

The **ACLU**, as well as many community <u>leaders</u>, **was shocked.**
The **students**, along with their friend <u>Tom</u>, **think** the policy is unfair.

In each of these sentences, notice that the verb agrees with the subject of the sentence, not with the second noun. Sometimes this can be confusing, and some sentences, because of the second noun, can be written differently to make the subject and verb the most important focus in the sentence, as well as making the job of determining what verb to use easier.

### Subjects Linked by *and*

When subjects are linked by *and,* they can create confusion in choosing the appropriate verb. For example,

subject        subject
The magazine **editors** and **Tom want** to settle the lawsuit.
plural verb form

This sentence includes two subjects—otherwise known as a compound subject—and because the subjects together are plural, they require a plural verb form. When you have two subjects, however, you do not always need a plural verb form. If the subjects work as one idea or thing, you will need a singular form. Sometimes this happens through modifying words such as *each* and *every,* but they do not consistently affect the subjects, as you can see from these examples:

**Rock and roll is** here to stay.

<u>Each</u> **student** and **teacher is** at risk for violence.
modifies subject, producing singular form

The **student** and **teacher** <u>each</u> **are** at risk for violence.
does not modify subject

### Using *neither . . . nor* and *either . . . or*

Sentences structured with *neither/nor* or *either/or* statements may take practice in choosing the appropriate verb; however, simply put, the verb form must agree with the subject closest to it:

plural subject       singular subject
Neither the football **players** nor the **coach was** happy.
singular verb form

singular subject                plural subject
Either the test **format** or the individual **questions were** not clear.
plural verb form

This brief discussion cannot cover every possible subject–verb agreement question you may have, and for further help you can always consult a good handbook or a series of handbooks. Furthermore, you might want to watch for these problems in your papers. If you have consistent problems, practice in using that specific pronoun or subject–verb combination will help you overcome a phrase or use that gives you trouble.

## Building Your Skills

### Assignment 1

Each of these sentences contains a problem with subject–verb or subject–pronoun agreement. Read each and then make changes wherever necessary.

1. Each person should have their own books for a class. Sharing a book can be difficult for you.

   _____

   _____

2. My father and my brother both like to ski, but neither like to ski more than the other.

   _____

   _____

3. People can always take care of themself. You just need to save your money and be prepared.

   _____

   _____

4. He need a new car, but he did not buys one.

   _____

   _____

5. Each of us are going to the concert.

   _____

   _____

6. Dance lessons and piano lessons is expensive. This is two expensive types of entertainment.

_____

_____

7. Every student needed to keep their receipt for the books they bought.

_____

_____

8. A person should always follow his instincts.

_____

_____

Now that you have practiced, write two of your own sentences using a pronoun or subject–verb combination with which you have trouble.

9. _____

_____

_____

10. _____

_____

_____

## Assignment 2

Look back at the essays you have written and find several examples of subject–verb or subject–pronoun agreement problems. If you cannot find any examples in your own papers, look at another student's work. Write these examples in your grammar journal or on another piece of paper (write at least ten examples each of subject–verb disagreement and subject–pronoun disagreement). Identify any specific problems you have with either or both of these concepts. For example, you may have trouble using the appropriate verb form when you use the subject "each." Rewrite the twenty example sentences, changing them to the appropriate grammatical form, and then write a short paragraph about your strengths and weaknesses in using pronouns and subject–verb agreement.

*Assignment 3*

Using one of the essays in this book, either a student essay or one of the professional essays, choose a paragraph of at least fifteen lines and write this paragraph on a separate piece of paper. Underline the subjects and draw a line from subject to verb showing the verbs with which they agree. Identify the pronouns and draw a line back to the nouns with which they agree wherever possible. When you finish, change the subject in each case and then change the verb or pronoun so that it agrees with the new form. For example, if the subject is in third-person singular then change it to third-person plural and then write the appropriate form of the verb. If the subject is plural and agrees with a plural pronoun, change it to singular and make the necessary changes to accommodate the singular form.

## SEEING THE CONNECTIONS: APPLYING YOUR SKILLS

*Assignment 1*

Read Efseaff's "The Summit" in this chapter. Notice her technique for making the reader's expectations build as he or she reads. When you finish, think about momentous decisions, battles, or agreements that you have witnessed or been part of. Brainstorm if necessary to come up with a few events similar to the summit Efseaff describes.

Write a first draft that describes a significant decision, battle, or agreement. Tell what happened, who was there, all of the necessary details. Then reread your first draft and mark any place that can be rewritten in more emotionally stimulating words. For ideas, look at Efseaff's essay again and notice words and phrases such as "When the meeting takes place, it is hard to breathe in the room." Include details like this one so that your reader can experience the emotions you describe. Identify how long something seemed to take or how frustrated you felt. Help your reader to picture and feel what you are describing. Remember that sensory details, as we discussed in Chapter 2, will create a more effective essay for the reader.

Write a final draft of your essay and try to add a conclusion that will leave the reader with a strong overall feeling or reaction. Put your essay away for twenty-four hours, if you can, and reread it to see if the reaction you were hoping for occurs. Another option is to allow your friends or family to read and evaluate your essay.

## Assignment 2

Read Alleen Pace Nilsen's essay in this chapter. Evaluate how effectively she introduces and concludes her ideas. Evaluate the unity, coherence, and clarity of Nilsen's essay. Does she move from point to point smoothly? Are all of her points related and developing a single thesis? How clear are her points?

Write a letter to Nilsen responding to one or more points in her essay. Agree or disagree with her view and describe for her why her essay was convincing or unconvincing for you as a reader. Also identify any structural strengths or weaknesses that helped or hindered your reading of the essay.

Using your finished letter, go back and highlight or underline all of the pronouns and decide if each is used properly (see the guidelines in the grammar section of this chapter). Make changes if your pronouns do not agree with the nouns they are replacing. If you are using several different pronouns, such as *I, she,* and *you* within your letter, decide which should be replaced or changed so that your letter is more consistent. Rewrite your letter so that it provides a unified, coherent, clear statement of your views.

## Assignment 3

Read Nilsen's essay in this chapter. Identify the ways in which your language reflects your belief systems. To get started, freewrite for ten minutes about the following questions:

> What do your writing and speech patterns say about you?
>
> How comfortable do you feel with the image they project?

Choose one of your past essays and evaluate the style of your essay. You might use more than one essay and make a catalog of your style. List the major features of your writing style: your word use, punctuation use, whether you use many clauses, how you like to begin and end your essays, and so forth. Identify the features of your writing you would most like to change, including both the structural elements you would like to make stronger and the punctuation and more technical concerns you would like to improve or change.

Write an essay that discusses your writing strengths and weaknesses. Compare your writing ability with your speaking ability if you would like. The focus of your essay, though, should be on the qualities of your writing style that you like or feel good about compared with the qualities that you feel you need to improve.

When your first draft is finished, go back to your list of desired improvements. List each improvement on a piece of paper, leaving space for a response. Evaluate the essay you have just written and look for ways to make the improvements you have listed. If your list says you want to use better vocabulary, then your response might be that you can change five words in this essay. After you have created a list and responses or plans for how to accomplish these improvements, make the improvements you have listed. Compare your final draft with your first draft.

# Chapter 8

## Improving Your Writing Through Revision

In this chapter you will learn

★ to recognize and use global and local revision;
★ to develop a revising routine to produce your best writing;
★ to gauge the difficulty of reading materials and to adjust your reading speed accordingly;
★ to avoid informal writing styles in formal essays;
★ to avoid passive voice in formal essays;
★ to combine ideas and use modifiers to add variety to your sentences.

Take a moment to answer the following questions:

1. How do you revise your writing? Approximately how much time do you spend revising each essay you write?

_____

_____

_____

2. What are the biggest advantages and disadvantages to revising?

_____

_____

_____

3. What do you feel are your writing strengths? What are your weaknesses?

 

 

 

4. When you revise, what is your purpose? Do you ever skip revising? If so, when and why?

 

 

 

# REVISING AS A PROCESS

Often when students think about revision, they think of a one-step process that requires them to "correct" or "fix up" their essays. However, if we look at revision as a process that improves an essay, we can explore techniques that will improve the content, writing, and readability of an essay. We can then very easily see that revision means more than simply correcting spelling or fixing a comma.

Revision is an essential part of the writing process because it helps the writer to see whether or not he or she is communicating the intended message or purpose to a specific audience. It allows the writer to step outside of himself or herself to view a piece of writing as his or her audience might. Many times when we write, we lose our objectivity; we become too involved. Though this is good for the writing process, it can be counterproductive during the revision process because a writer may feel defensive or overly concerned about keeping an essay exactly as it is. Revision helps writers get beyond that initial need to protect what is already on paper and to look critically and carefully at how well the essay accomplishes the writer's goal of communication.

### Being Critical
When you hear the word "critical" what do you think? Is it good when someone is critical of your paper? Should you be critical of your own work? Typically, students believe that being critical means pointing out the faults or failures of a work, but during revision, this word should not carry that

connotation at all. When we revise, we should spend at least as much time looking at what works for our audience as looking for ways to improve an essay. If you are focusing on "correctness" and finding fault, you are missing the very point of the revision process.

In the context of revising, the word "critical" is not negative at all. Instead, it means that you look carefully at your own work to see where it meets, exceeds, or falls short of either your or your reader's expectations. Correctness is relative; when you revise, look for what is effective, what will best serve your own purpose and your audience. Probably the best way to do this is to develop a routine for revising that works well for you. Although every writer uses a different routine, all good revision routines will include some combination of reading for content and reading for form. Content is what your essay says—the point it makes. Form is the structure and grammar you use to make your point clear. Revision has been called by many writers the real work of writing. If you are leaving out this necessary process, your writing has not yet become what it can. When you struggle with revision, you are simply doing what all writers do. Professional writers, though they may love this part of writing, are often as frustrated and challenged by revising as anyone else.

## Global and Local Revision

We can discuss revision in two parts: global and local. *Global* revision looks at the paper as a whole:

> Title
>
> Thesis
>
> Overall structure
>
> Transitions between paragraphs and ideas

Anything that affects how easy or difficult an essay is to read and understand as a whole is the focus of a writer's efforts in the process of global revision. *Local* revision, on the other hand, concentrates on the smaller details in an essay and can generally be described as working with sentence-level features within the essay, such as the following:

> Sentence structure
>
> Sentence punctuation
>
> Spelling
>
> Word use
>
> Vocabulary

Though both global and local revision are necessary and important, think for a moment about the difference in effect for the reader. If a writer changes a feature of the essay that affects the whole essay, is that different from changing something that affects one or two sentences? Of course, the obvious answer is yes. But many students become so focused on spelling or small grammatical concerns that they forget about the big picture: global revision. Think for a moment about two essays. Essay A is easy to read, makes a clear point, and uses very persuasive examples, but has seven misspelled words and a problem with commas. Essay B seems to make no point at all, uses no clearly related examples, but is exceptionally grammatical and has no spelling errors. Though neither paper is an English teacher's dream, as a reader, which one would you rather read, the one that makes a point or the one that has no point? Does the grammatical correctness of an essay matter if it has no point? Though this example does not use real papers, it does use a very real challenge for writers. What should a writer pay attention to or focus on while revising? The answer is everything. However, this answer is misleading; of course, a writer cannot pay attention to everything at once. Instead, a writer should develop a routine that pays close attention to different concerns at different times. Before looking for grammatical problems and misspelled words, a writer first needs to see whether or not he or she has made his or her message clear for the reader. When that has been accomplished, then the writer should worry about sentence-level concerns.

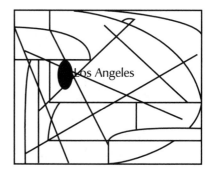

| Global | Local |
|---|---|
| Read whole essay aloud | Read essay sentence by sentence |
| Read for specific qualities |   Begin at the end |
|   Introduction, conclusion |   Read aloud |
|   Thesis and support | Read for recurring punctuation problems |
|   Development and unity | Read for word choice and vocabulary |
|   Expand the details | Read for sentence structure and variety |
| Read for a recurring structural | |
|    problem | |

Revising globally is the process of rereading your paper to observe and detect whether the essay makes a clearly defined and supported point, establishes and fulfills the thesis, develops the topic fully, and is unified, coherent, and readable. Revising locally includes looking at each sentence carefully to determine whether it uses the best word choices and vocabulary and whether it includes the appropriate punctuation and spelling. This is traditionally called editing, and it focuses on specific and limited areas for each change; in other words, these changes affect small areas of an essay rather than the essay as a whole. In addition to making a distinction between types of revision, we can discuss developing a routine for revising. The following is a discussion of one specific revision routine that you may want to try, adopt, or adjust to meet your personal style and needs.

### Reading in Stages

Reading your essay in a series of stages allows you to concentrate on specific features during each reading without being distracted by focusing on too many things at once. It is a good example of a revising routine that you could follow each time you revise an essay.

#### First Reading

Read the essay once carefully, looking only for the thesis and how well everything else in the essay relates back to the thesis. If your thesis is not carried throughout the whole essay, you can either take out the parts of the essay that do not fit with your thesis or you can rewrite your thesis to include the parts of your essay that were not included. If your essay does stick to your thesis, congratulate yourself and begin to read the essay again.

#### Second Reading

Read the essay focusing only on structure. Look for unity and development. Is each topic expanded to a reasonable point? Does every part of the essay contribute to the overall point in a meaningful way? How do the parts work together? Do any places need transitions? Overall, how easy is your essay to read? Pay special attention to audience at this point. Ask yourself whether your audience has enough information to get from one paragraph to the next or from the key point in paragraph two to the key point in paragraph three. Depending on your answers to these questions, you may want to take out or add paragraphs or sentences. Make any changes that are necessary before moving to the next reading.

#### Third Reading

On the third reading of your essay, move from global revision to local revision and read each sentence looking for clear structure, spelling, and punctuation. In addition, look for sentence variety, verbs that are bland

and lifeless, and for any sentence-level problems you have had difficulty with in the past. An unusual but very effective method for reading an essay closely is to read it backwards. Begin with the last sentence and read and evaluate it. Is it a complete sentence? Is it grammatical, well-structured, properly punctuated? Then move on to the second-to-last sentence and follow the same procedures. Then move to the third-to-last, and keep doing this until you have read the whole essay in reverse order. This technique forces you to focus your full attention on each sentence. In this stage, have a handbook, dictionary, and thesaurus nearby so that you can easily look up answers to any questions. If you are keeping a grammar journal, you should also have it nearby.

Though revision is a process of reading, it is also a process of rewriting. If you simply recopy words, sentences, and paragraphs from one piece of paper to another, you are transcribing or recopying; you are not revising or rewriting. No matter how well you read your essays to revise them, the only way this process can be helpful is if you actually act on what you see in your essays. If your introduction lacks character or a thesis, rewrite it. If you need a transition between two paragraphs, write a transition to insert between those paragraphs. If you are not sure whether a comma or a semicolon is appropriate punctuation in a sentence, find a handbook and look for the answer. Revising is part of the writing process, but clearly it is not the last part of this process, because between revising and actually turning in an essay, a lot of work takes place: rethinking, rewriting, rewording. All of these activities can transform a mediocre or even ineffective essay into a unified, thoughtful essay that is easy to read and clearly written. If communication is your goal, you can see here how important revising is to written communication. Develop your own revising process and pay attention to your particular needs in revising as a way of making this process particularly well suited to you and to your writing habits.

# READING AN ESSAY

## Strategy for Reading: Gauging Your Reading Speed

Readability of a written work is determined and measured by several factors: the number of words in a sentence, the length of the words, the difficulty of the words used, the complexity and organization of the sentences, and the experience of the reader. Each of these factors determines how quickly a reader will be able to read and comprehend a piece of writing.

Sometimes we mistake reading fast for reading well. In fact, commercials sometimes tell us that if we learn to speed read, we can read through any book or magazine in minutes. Like most things that sound too good to be true, this certainly is. People who read well know that sometimes they must slow down to read efficiently, while at other times they may need only to skim to understand what they are reading.

Learning to gauge your reading speed and get the most out of what you read comes with experience, but some features of written materials let you know that reading more slowly will be required and that comprehension will take more work. Comprehension occurs when the reader understands a writer's message and how this message is significant or important. Reading quickly does not always allow the time and concentration necessary to read more difficult works. For example, if you compare a newspaper article and a physics textbook, which one do you think would probably take the most time to read and comprehend? Obviously the textbook is filled with new terms and new concepts that require more concentration and thought from most readers. In addition, the newspaper article is designed for an audience that reads at a high school or junior high school level, so it assumes that a reader may need more information and detail to understand the point.

When you decide how quickly or slowly to read an article or essay, what should you look for? Remember that SQ3R, as discussed in Chapter 1, is a good technique for improving comprehension and memory, but while you perform the survey function of this technique, you might also gauge the difficulty of the work you are about to read to determine how carefully and how quickly to read the work. As you survey, you can begin to pay attention to the factors that require more concentration and that make it imperative to read more carefully:

 Read more slowly and more carefully if the topic is unfamiliar.

 Read at a slower pace when the sentences are long and complex. Complex sentences are longer and have more dependent and independent clauses; they present essential relationships and important connections.

 Read more carefully when an article or essay includes many words that are unfamiliar or when it includes vocabulary or terms you are trying to learn. Mark words you want to look up in a dictionary and remember.

 Read more slowly and annotate when you are reading textbooks and other learning materials, especially when you will be tested on the material.

 Read at a comfortable speed and try not to compare how fast you read with others. Comprehension is the focus of reading.

If you are worried about your reading speed, the way to improve your ability in reading is to practice. Set aside time each day for reading. If you have children or young relatives, you can even practice by reading to them.

The following essay is one of the most difficult in this book. As you prepare to read it, survey and answer the Before You Read questions. Gauge the difficulty by looking at length, sentence structure, and vocabulary. As you read, annotate by making notes about major ideas or points beside each paragraph. A place to write your start time and a place to figure total reading time is included. Read at your regular pace and when you finish, answer the questions to determine how well you comprehended Murray's point.

---

### BEFORE YOU READ

1. How important is revising for you when you write an essay? About how much time do you usually spend revising?
2. What steps do you use when you revise? How do these steps change with different writing assignments?
3. Write the time you started reading here _____.

---

## The Maker's Eye: Revising Your Manuscript*

### by Donald Murray

When the beginning writer completes his first draft,          1
he usually reads it through to correct typographical errors and considers the job of writing done. When the professional writer completes his first draft, he usually feels he is at the start of the writing process. Now that he has a draft, he can begin writing.

*Source: Murray, Donald M. "The Maker's Eye: Revising Your Own Manuscripts."
From *The Writer* by Donald M. Murray. Copyright © 1973 by Donald Murray.
Reprinted by permission of the author and Roberta Pryor, Inc.

The difference in attitude is the difference between amateur and professional, inexperience and experience, journeyman and craftsman. Peter F. Drucker, the prolific business writer, for example, calls his first draft "the zero draft"—after that he can start counting. Most productive writers share the feeling that the first draft—and most of those that follow—is an opportunity to discover what they have to say and how they can best say it.

2

To produce a progression of drafts, each of which says more and says it better, the writer has to develop a special reading skill. In school we are taught to read what is on the page. We try to comprehend what the author has said, what he meant, and what are the implications of his words.

3

The writer of such drafts must be his own best enemy. He must accept the criticism of others and be even more suspicious of it. He cannot depend on others. He must detach himself from his own page so that he can apply both his caring and his craft to his own work.

4

Detachment is not easy. Science fiction writer Ray Bradbury supposedly puts each manuscript away for a year and then rereads it as a stranger. Not many writers can afford the time to do this. We must read when our judgment may be at its worst, when we are close to the euphoric moment of creation. The writer "should be critical of everything that seems to him most delightful in his style," advises novelist Nancy Hale. "He should excise what he most admires, because he wouldn't thus admire it if he weren't . . . in a sense protecting it from criticism."

5

The writer must learn to protect himself from his own ego, when it takes the form of uncritical pride or uncritical self-destruction. As poet John Ciardi points out, "the last act of the writing must be to become one's own reader. It is, I suppose, a schizophrenic process, to begin passionately and to end critically, to begin hot and to end cold; and more important, to be passion-hot and critic-cold at the same time."

6

Just as dangerous as the protective writer is the despairing one, who thinks everything he does is awful, terrible, dreadful. If he is to publish, he must save what is

7

effective on his page while he cuts away what doesn't work. The writer must hear and respect his own voice.

Remember how each craftsman you have seen—the carpenter eyeing the level of a shelf, the mechanic listening to the motor—takes the instinctive step back. This is what the writer has to do when he reads his own work. "The writer must survey his work critically, coolly, as though he were a stranger to it," says children's book writer Eleanor Estes. "He must be willing to prune, expertly and hard-heartedly. At the end of each revision, a manuscript may look like a battered old hive, worked over, torn apart, pinned together, added to, deleted from, words changed and words changed back. Yet the book must maintain its original freshness and spontaneity."

8

It is far easier for most beginning writers to understand the need for rereading and rewriting than it is to understand how to go about it. The published writer doesn't necessarily break down the various stages of rewriting and editing, he just goes ahead and does it. One of our most prolific fiction writers, Anthony Burgess, says, "I might revise a page twenty times." Short story and children's writer Roald Dahl states, "By the time I'm nearing the end of a story, the first part will have been reread and altered and corrected at least 150 times. . . . Good writing is essentially rewriting. I am positive of this."

9

There is nothing virtuous in the rewriting process. It is simply an essential condition of life for most writers. There are writers who do very little rewriting, mostly because they have the capacity and experience to create and review a large number of invisible drafts in their minds before they get to the page. And many writers perform all of the tasks of revision simultaneously, page by page, rather than draft by draft. But it is still possible to break down the process of rereading one's own work into the sequence most published writers follow and which the beginning writer should follow as he studies his own page.

10

Many writers at first just scan their manuscript, reading as quickly as possible for problems of subject and form. In this way, they stand back from the more technical

11

details of language so they can spot any weaknesses in content or in organization. When the writer reads his manuscript, he is usually looking for seven elements.

The first is *subject.* Do you have anything to say? If you are lucky, you will find that indeed you do have something to say, perhaps a little more than you expected. If the subject is not clear, or if it is not yet limited or defined enough for you to handle, don't go on. What you have to say is always more important than how you say it.

12

The next point to check is *audience.* It is true that you should write primarily for yourself, in the sense that you should be true to yourself. But the aim of writing is communication, not just self-expression. You should, in reading your piece, ask yourself if there is an audience for what you have written, if anyone will need or enjoy what you have to say.

13

*Form* should then be considered after audience. Form, or genre, is the vehicle which will carry what you have to say to your audience, and it should grow out of your subject. If you have a character, your subject may grow into a short story, a magazine profile, a novel, a biography, or a play. It depends on what you have to say and to whom you wish to say it. When you reread your own manuscript, you must ask yourself if the form is suitable, if it works, and if it will carry your meaning to your reader.

14

Once you have the appropriate form, look at the *structure,* the order of what you have to say. Every good piece of writing is built on a solid framework of logic or argument or narrative or motivation; it is a line which runs through the entire piece of writing and holds it together. If you read your own manuscript and cannot spot this essential thread, stop writing until you have found something to hold your writing together.

15

The manuscript which has order must also have *development.* Each part of it must be built in a way that will prepare the reader for the next part. Description, documentation, action, dialogue, metaphor—these and many other devices flesh out the skeleton so that the reader will be able to understand what is written. How much develop-

16

ment? That's like asking how much lipstick or how much garlic. It depends on the girl or on the casserole. This is the question that the writer will be answering as he reads his piece of writing through from beginning to end, and answering it will lead him to the sixth element.

The writer must be sure of his *dimensions*. This means                17
that there should be something more than structure and development, that there should be a pleasing proportion between all of the parts. You cannot decide on a dimension without seeing all of the parts of writing together. You have to examine each section of the writing in its relationship to all of the other sections.

Finally, the writer has to listen for *tone*. Any piece of                18
writing is held together by that invisible force, the writer's voice. Tone is his style, tone is all that is on the page and off the page, tone is grace, wit, anger—the spirit which drives a piece of writing forward. Look back to those manuscripts you most admire, and you will discover that there is a coherent tone, an authoritative voice holding the whole thing together.

When the writer feels that he has a draft which has                19
subject, audience, form, structure, development, dimension, and tone, then he is ready to begin the careful process of line-by-line editing. Each line, each word has to be right. As Paul Gallico has said, ". . . every successful writer is primarily a good editor."

Now the writer reads his own copy with infinite care.                20
He often reads aloud, calling on his ear's experience with language. Does this sound right—or this? He reads and listens and revises, back and forth from eye to page to ear to page. I find I must do this careful editing at short runs, fifteen or twenty minutes, or I become too kind with myself.

Slowly the writer moves from word to word, looking                21
through the word to see the subject. Good writing is, in a sense, invisible. It should enable the reader to see the subject, not the writer. Every word should be true—true to what the writer has to say. And each word must be precise in its relation to the words which have gone before and the words which will follow.

This sounds tedious, but it isn't. Making something right is immensely satisfying, and the writer who once was lost in a swamp of potentialities now has the chance to work with the most technical skills of language. And even in the process of the most careful editing, there is the joy of language. Words have double meanings, even triple and quadruple meanings. Each word has its own tone, its opportunity for connotation and denotation and nuance. And when you connect words, there is always the chance of the sudden insight, the unexpected clarification.

22

The maker's eye moves back and forth from word to phrase to sentence to paragraph to sentence to phrase to word. He looks at his sentences for variety and balance in form and structure, and at the interior of the paragraph for coherence, unity, and emphasis. He plays with figurative language, decides to repeat or not, to create a parallelism for emphasis. He works over his copy until he achieves a manuscript which appears effortless to the reader.

23

I learned something about this process when I first wore bifocals. I thought that when I was editing I was working line by line. But I discovered that I had to buy reading (or, in my case, editing) glasses, even though the bottom sections of my bifocals have a greater expanse of glass than ordinary glasses. While I am editing, my eyes are unconsciously flicking back and forth across the whole page, or back to another page, or forward to another page. The limited bifocal view through the lower half of my glasses is not enough. Each line must be seen in its relationship to every other line.

24

When does this process end? Most writers agree with the great Russian novelist Tolstoy, who said, "I scarcely ever reread my published writings, but if by chance I come across a page, it always strikes me: all this must be rewritten; this is how I should have written it."

25

The maker's eye is never satisfied, for he knows that each word in his copy is tentative. Writing, to the writer, is alive, something that is full of potential and alternatives, something which can grow beyond its own dream. The

26

writer reads to discover what he has said—and then to say it better.

A piece of writing is never finished. It is delivered to a                27
deadline, torn out of the typewriter on demand, sent off
with a sense of frustration and incompleteness. Just as the
writer knows he must stop avoiding writing and write, he
also knows he must send his copy off to be published,
although it is not quite right yet—if only he had another
couple of days, just another run at it, perhaps . . . .

## Building Your Skills

### READING STRATEGY NOTE

Write your finish time          _____
Subtract your start time        _____
Total time                      _____

How readable is this essay? Did it take you a long time? A short
time? Why?

### *Focus on Words*

Look up the following words or parts of phrases in a dictionary. Consult the preceding essay and identify the meaning that best fits the way the
author uses the word in this essay. Each word or phrase is followed by the
number of the paragraph in which it appears.

| | |
|---|---|
| typographical errors (1) | virtuous (10) |
| prolific (2) | simultaneously (10) |
| progression (3) | metaphor (16) |
| detachment (5) | authoritative (18) |
| manuscript (5) | tedious (22) |
| euphoric (5) | connotation (22) |
| schizophrenic (6) | denotation (22) |
| instinctive (8) | nuance (22) |
| prune (8) | figurative language (23) |
| spontaneity (8) | parallelism (23) |
| altered (9) | |

**Focus on the Message**

1. What process does Murray recommend for revision?
2. Describe his primary audience and identify the clues that help you to determine his audience.
3. What is a zero draft? What advantages and disadvantages can you see to viewing a first draft as a "zero draft"?
4. In what ways is Murray's advice practical for students who are revising their writing?
5. In what ways is his advice unlikely to work for students who are revising their writing?

# TECHNIQUES FOR WRITING: DEVELOPING YOUR OWN STYLE

Many beginning writers do not realize that they have already developed a writing style. Unfortunately, this style sometimes sounds exactly as if they were speaking aloud. Think back to our discussion in Chapter 2 about the differences between speech and writing. Remember that speakers can use gestures, ask for feedback, elicit responses through questions, and even look at their listeners as a way of determining how listeners feel about what they are saying.

When we write we use techniques that work well in writing, and we develop techniques that meet our expectations about how writing should sound and how well we feel we are expressing what we want to say. Gaining your own style requires several important steps. First, as a writer, you must participate in the activities of language: you must read, write, think, and listen. Second, you must incorporate the techniques and ideas you acquire from reading and writing experiences to form a repertoire of techniques. For example, we have discussed using quotations and stories to end essays; if you do not at some time try this technique, you will not have actually gained anything in your own writing. You will, however, probably have learned to see these in what you read.

The third step you must take in developing your own style is being vulnerable. Because using new techniques and writing in new formats requires taking risks, you must be willing to experiment to increase your writing ability. Even when a technique does not work as well as you hoped, you will have the satisfaction of having tried a new approach. Also remember that a technique that did not work for one reader may work for another.

The fourth step in developing your own style is avoiding techniques that confuse or annoy readers. No one likes to read materials that are puzzling. When your meaning is not clear, your reader is unlikely to appreciate your style. Likewise, if your point is clear and creatively stated, your reader is likely to be very appreciative. To eliminate the qualities that often make writing seem confusing or your points meaningless, you need to be able to recognize and change a few important types of distractions for readers. Some of these are grammatical; some are more related to overall structure.

## ❏ Avoid Shifts in Person.

Read the following paragraph:

> Finally, winter had come and we were going skiing. We began by driving to our favorite ridge in the nearby mountains. The mountains looked like they had been covered by blankets of snow. Then you had to unpack all of the gear and get ready for the slopes. Because there was so much snow, you had to be careful not to sink in it too deep. We were so pleased to see that the lifts were fully in operation and that everyone had not followed us and made the mountain crowded.

Can you detect a problem in this paragraph? Does anything cause you to stop because you are unsure or confused? Notice that the writer begins telling the story using *we*, a word that signifies that the writer is a participant and that at least one other person is accompanying the writer. Then, in the fourth sentence, the writer switches to *you*, a word used to address others. This changes the person from third-person plural to second-person. The chart below demonstrates person by showing that *I* is used for first-person singular, *we* for first-person plural, and so on.

| Subject | Singular (only one) | Plural (more than one) |
|---|---|---|
| *First Person* | I | We |
| *Second Person* | You | You |
| *Third Person* | He<br>She<br>It | They |

Each person presents a different perspective; *I* tells us what one person who actually participated in the experience or thing being discussed believes or feels. When we use *he*, we are discussing a male person and what he did, thought, or felt. Switching from one person to another not only confuses the reader, but it makes the task of telling who did what very difficult, thus making an essay harder to read.

The most common shift in person is demonstrated by the example paragraph at the beginning of this section that switches from *we* to *you*. As we write, sometimes we switch to *you* out of nervousness or because we speak this way. When you revise your own essays, be sure that you are consistent in your presentation by checking for agreement in person. Read your essays for the word *you* and after you have highlighted this word in your essay, go back to see if it is appropriately addressing the reader, or if it needs to be changed to first or third person. For more information about pronoun agreement, refer to the discussion in Chapter 7. Even though in speech, people switch from one person to another, in writing this can be hard to follow, especially if the switches are erratic.

## ❏ Avoid Informal Styles.

Another stylistic concern in essay writing is developing a formal style. Even though formal style would be inappropriate in personal letters, diaries, and creative writing, in essays it is often required. Formal essay style includes stating your thesis clearly, providing adequate support and detail, and developing the essay logically. It does not include addressing the reader informally, as in phrases such as "this is what I mean when I say . . ." or "I'm sure you know what I mean." In fact, formal essays are most often written in third person, although first-person plural is also a reasonable option. The reason for the formality is that typically these essays are written to analyze a topic or to provide a serious discussion—a situation in which informal phrases, cute words, and directly addressing the reader would be inappropriate. This is a style all writers can use and most must use at some time, so this is one technique you will certainly want to be able to use when it is necessary.

## ❏ Avoid Passive Voice.

Another drain on effectiveness and style is the use of passive voice. Many writers have acknowledged the power of words to motivate and express action, but using verbs in passive voice takes the action out of the verb and makes the sentence lose its effectiveness. Passive voice occurs when a sentence is organized so that the person, people, or thing doing the action is not the subject of the sentence. In fact, the result of the action may actually serve as the subject in passive voice.

subject     verb
The **test** <u>was taken</u> by the students.

In the example above, notice that *test* is the subject of the sentence. Who took the test? The students took the test, but the word *students* is not the subject of this sentence. If we want to write this sentence in active voice, we must change the wording so that the word *students* is the subject of the sentence.

subject     verb
The **students** <u>took</u> the test.

Look at the other changes that occur. In addition to the change in the order of the words, the verb changes, too. Though these changes may seem minor, on closer inspection you will begin to see why these small changes make a big difference. Read the following paragraph very carefully. Do you notice anything unusual about it?

> The test was taken by the students. It was thought by all that the test was very difficult. The problem-solving questions were failed by most of the students, while the essay question was responded to by all with more success. Poor grades were received by many disappointed students.

How do you feel when you read this paragraph? Does it seem difficult or monotonous to read? If you did not like the way this was written, can you identify why? The writer uses passive voice in each of the sentences in this paragraph. This technique makes the writer seem tentative and unsure of his or her ideas. It also creates a paragraph that is harder to read and less interesting. The action that should be emphasized is described so that it seems as if no action took place at all. If we reword the paragraph, changing the verbs to active voice, we can see that it is more direct and clear.

> The students took a test. Everyone thought it was very difficult. In fact, most students failed the questions requiring problem solving, while they did much better on the essay question. The disappointed students received poor grades.

Recognizing active and passive voice is an important skill in developing style. Writers may occasionally use a sentence written in passive voice, and this can actually add variety to their style; it becomes a problem when it is pervasive throughout an essay or paragraph. Not only will passive voice frustrate your reader, it is likely to keep you from communicating your message with any real impact. An interesting feature of passive voice is that it is often used by writers who are uncomfortable with writing—for example, students who are writing for new instructors. Active voice clearly communicates the actions and relationships between subjects and the results of their actions, whereas passive voice leaves ideas vague and may keep the reader at arm's length, guessing about meaning and relationships.

To recognize this type of writing, look at the following example of passive voice and note how it is changed to active voice. Then try changing the sentences that follow from passive to active.

*EXAMPLE:*

| The car <u>was wrecked</u> by the <u>student</u>. | The <u>student</u> <u>wrecked</u> the car. |
|---|---|
| past participle    person doing | person    verb is |
| form    action is | acting is   simple past |
| of verb    not subject | subject   tense form |

1. The mountains were enjoyed by the campers.

_____

Sometimes you must add a subject when you change a sentence to active voice because the actor is not included in the sentence. Try the following example:

2. The door was left open.

_____

Although passive voice is not always a problem for writers, if responses to your essay assignments mention passive voice as a problem, or if, while you are revising, you notice that many of your sentences are passive, then you need to strengthen your style by avoiding this stylistic pitfall.

## ❏ Choose Words Carefully.

Another aspect of editing is word choice, often called *diction*. As you use a thesaurus, you will be exposed to many new words, and hopefully by using them in papers and in your speech you will expand your vocabulary. You will also encounter new words in reading. Expanding your vocabulary allows you to make exact and meaningful word choices to more effectively and creatively communicate your meaning.

As you search for appropriate and concise words or phrases to express your meaning, take the following guidelines into account:

> **Avoid clichés and colorless words.** *Clichés* are words or phrases that have been used so often that they have lost most of their original

meaning. Arguably, "Have a nice day" has become a cliché; it is not viewed as a deeply sincere comment, but a way of responding to someone politely. *Colorless words,* such as "special" and "nice," do not communicate a concise meaning. They give a general feeling or meaning, but they neither emphasize nor drive home a point. As you develop your vocabulary and learn new words, try to revise your work so that it includes the best wording possible for your purpose and audience. Look for words that accent your point.

**Avoid being wordy or using elevated or fake styles.** Always use the language best-suited to your audience. Using elevated language or what some people refer to as "big words" does not mean that your essay will be effective. Though you should try to expand your vocabulary to improve your writing style, taking a pompous or arrogant approach will probably not help you communicate your ideas. Pretending to be an authority or know-it-all will also prove to be equally ineffective as a technique.

*Above all other techniques to avoid,* **never try to impress your readers by sounding esoteric or "smarter" than they are.** If you are trying to intimidate your readers, not only will they realize what you are doing, but they will resent you for it. Along the same lines, acting less intelligent or doubting yourself in an essay is not a trust-building technique either. In fact, when a writer uses phrases like "I don't really know but . . ." or "I think that is what happened," he or she loses the trust and respect of the reader.

The key to presenting ideas well and using concise and well-chosen words and phrases is expressing your ideas, point of view, and knowledge, while at the same time showing the reader respect. Some of the greatest writers, past and present, are known for their ability to choose the perfect word to express an idea. This is a very important skill in developing your own effectiveness and style.

## ❏ Develop Style Through Reading.

In addition to developing style through writing essays, many writers develop style through what they read. They may do this on purpose, or they may do it simply by reading for pleasure. Sometimes writers begin to use new phrases, sentence structures, or other techniques simply as a result of exposure to them through what they read. Obviously, reading is an important way to learn about language and the effect it has on readers, just as riding a Harley Davidson is important to knowing what it feels like to ride a Harley Davidson. Reading, then, develops basic style patterns and helps writers to understand how to reach potential readers. In addition to acquiring stylistic techniques while we read, we learn information, ideas, and creative approaches that make us more learned people and more creative, insightful writers.

These recommendations for building style will help you become a more effective writer, as well as helping you to bring out your own personal viewpoints effectively. However, to build and develop your style, you must write, and you must be willing to try new techniques and approaches such as using new or untried rhetorical modes, trying different essay structures, enhancing your vocabulary through reading for pleasure and for assignments, even trying new types of writing to get a new perspective. As you take chances, you will have successes and failures, but most important, you will always be improving your ability to say what you want to say and to have others listen to you and appreciate the way you express yourself.

## Building Your Skills

### Assignment 1

Gather several essays you have written recently. Divide a piece of paper into two columns. Read each essay, and in one column make a list of good stylistic qualities in your essays, such as consistent person references, sentence variety, active voice, clear word choice, and grammatical punctuation. Use actual examples from your essays. In the second column, make a list of needed improvements. For example, if you seem to use the same punctuation marks repeatedly without ever including semicolons, you might suggest that you use more semicolons. If your essays have very simple sentences that never go beyond a few words, then you might suggest that you develop your sentence structure. As you read, evaluate your style. When you are finished and have a list of at least ten items per side, create a portfolio of your writing by ranking your essays from best to worst. Then choose one to rewrite and follow your own suggestions to create a better essay.

### Assignment 2

Brainstorm about the effects reading has on your life. Create a list of benefits people receive from reading well. Write an essay, based on the information in your brainstorming and listing, that persuades other students that they will benefit from learning to read well. If you want to be creative, you might write this as an advertisement for the National Endowment for the Humanities and illustrate your campaign with pictures, drawings, excerpts from things you enjoy reading, and so on. When you finish the first draft, first revise globally by reading the whole essay and looking for needed additions, cuts, or changes; then, revise locally by reading the essay again to make changes to sentences, words, and punctuation. Using the rules in the previous section, make sure that you have avoided all the stylistic problems described.

### Assignment 3

Brainstorm or freewrite about someone or something you really miss. Think about what makes you miss this person or thing so much. Write an essay that describes this person or thing in detail, discusses why you miss him or her or it so much, and then presents some insight on why people feel loss or react to loss as they do.

Because this essay topic has several components, you will probably want to decide in what order you would like to present these ideas, what examples would help your reader best understand your loss, and the details that will create an accurate picture or impression. Include all three parts in your essay, but the order of presentation will depend on your focus and what you want to accomplish.

When you finish the first draft, annotate your essay, as described in Chapter 2, by writing the main topic of each paragraph in the margin. Underline and label the examples and details. Also underline any words that are well-chosen and will appeal to your reader. Rewrite this essay by looking for gaps. Where are you missing examples or details? What part of your essay uses the best word choice? Which parts might benefit from more careful word choice? Rewrite your essay so that your reader can better identify with and feel your loss or other feelings about this person or situation.

## READING A STUDENT ESSAY

### Peer Review Strategy: Revising for Style

Revising for style requires careful reading and thinking, as well as a clear understanding of the techniques that work for readers and those that do not. When you read another student's essay or your own with the intent of revising to make the essay more readable and well-written, you will want to remember the elements of style discussed in this chapter. In fact, reading for style can mean simply looking at the way someone writes, but revising for style means that you look for inconsistencies or problems that detract from the effectiveness of the essay. This type of revising should only be done after you recognize that an essay already includes unity, coherence, clarity, and good essay structure. Revising for style is something like polishing a car. You can see the paint without waxing, but after waxing the true color and shine come through. In the same way, revising for style polishes your message and reveals your best ability.

The following is a list of the main points from the writing section above about style. Each element on the list will improve your style and your reader's ability to read your essay with ease.

❏ **Avoid Shifts in Person.**

❏ **Avoid Informal Styles.**

❏ **Avoid Passive Voice.**

❏ **Choose Words Carefully.**

For a review of these elements, read the preceding writing section in this chapter. Then read the following student essay and evaluate this student's style. Mark any places in the essay that exhibit particularly good features of Connie's style and any examples of stylistic choices that make her essay more difficult for you to read. You might practice reading this in stages, as described early in this chapter, focusing each time on a different point of observation.

### Affirmative Action

#### by Connie Perez

In today's society, it is commonplace for people to 1
want to be preferred rather than unpreferred. We are
raised with the idea that we should belong to a special
group or that we should be preferred socially. African-
Americans have often lived with being unpreferred or
segregated in America. They have been fighting to be
treated as equals, and in some people's opinion their
fight has not been totally successful. They have

achieved a number of accomplishments through their persistence in the fight to be seen and treated as equals. Affirmative action has been one of their biggest accomplishments, even though opponents believe it has set their fight for equality back a step.

Racial preferences have always existed and will                 2
continue to exist, not only in our society, but every-where in the world. African-Americans, unfortunately, have not been the preferred race historically. Some people have even viewed African-Americans as inferior, when clearly they are not. Americans have been trying to come up with a way to do away with preferential treatment of particular races, but racial preference is not an issue that can easily be done away with. If we look back in history, African-Americans had to deal with being racially unpreferred simply because of their skin color. White men treated them as subhuman and even made slaves of them. It would be a great accom-plishment, not only for African-Americans, but for the whole human race, if we could find a way to end racial preferences.

Shelby Steele in an essay titled "Affirmative                 3
Action: The Price of Preference" writes "Affirmative action tells us that racial preferences can do for us what we cannot do for ourselves." In some cases, his argument may be true, but there are some cases in which people succeed without the help of preferential treatment. Sometimes when African-Americans or other ethnic or supposedly preferred groups are hired or accepted into a school, people assume they received the job or acceptance into a school based on their race. However, many African-Americans have outstanding qualifications that allow them to be hired or accepted into the school of their choice. As a recent speaker in our English class said, "Affirmative action may get you

into college, but only you can get you out." Affirmative action was designed to give African-Americans equal opportunity in the hiring and enrollment process. Once affirmative action places a person where he or she rightfully belongs, it is up to that person to succeed. If this person is unable to fulfill his or her part of the process, then he or she will be fired or kicked out of school.

Contrary to what some people believe, Whites are not superior to Blacks or any other race. There may be people who are superior in their ability to do something better than someone else, but this does not make anyone racially superior. Shelby Steele in the aforementioned essay also states that "racial preferences implicitly mark Whites with an exaggerated superiority just as they mark Blacks with an exaggerated inferiority." Some people may argue that affirmative action marks Whites as superior to Blacks because affirmative action does not often apply to Whites and was designed by Whites. To some extent this argument may be true. If affirmative action did not exist, perhaps many African-Americans with high-paying jobs and those attending good schools would not be there. For Whites, this would not matter because they would have access to the best simply because of their race. Racial preference marks Blacks with inferiority and superiority because it allows them to obtain the jobs and school opportunities that otherwise may have been given to Whites, but it uses their race as a determining factor for this preference.

Respect from others, motivation, and self-respect are often lost due to the negative effects of racial preference. Competence and not preference should be the main consideration when hiring people into a new job or admitting them into a school.

4

5

## Building Your Skills

1. What are the strengths of Perez's style in this essay? Do any stylistic qualities detract from the effectiveness of her essay?

_____

_____

_____

_____

_____

_____

_____

_____

2. What is Perez's main point? How does she argue this point? What rhetorical modes does she use? Is she primarily writing to people who agree or disagree with her point of view? How can you tell?

_____

_____

_____

_____

_____

_____

_____

_____

3. How does Perez create unity in this essay? Does she present a coherent point of view? How do transitions play a role in this?

_____

_____

_____

_____

_____

_____

_____

_____

_____

_____

4. As if you were discussing Connie's paper with her, list three features of her essay that work very well or that really appeal to you as a reader. Then, recommend three changes she could make to improve her essay.

Describe three features that are effective for you as a reader:

a. _____

b. _____

c. _____

Describe three improvements or changes Connie could make to create a more effective, interesting, or informative essay:

a. _____

b. _____

c. _____

# USING GRAMMAR: ADDING VARIETY TO SENTENCES

Sentence variety will make your writing more interesting and expressive for your readers. Variety, though, can be derived from many types of patterns for presenting information. Each of the patterns discussed here is best suited for a particular format and a particular type of message. The techniques discussed here will benefit your writing, but use them according to your own needs and style, and learn how to use them in the appropriate places and with the appropriate punctuation by paying special attention to those features in the varieties of sentences below. Remember the discussion of the four sentence types in Chapter 4 (pages 104–107)? Referring back to this section may be helpful as you look at these ways to add variety to your sentences.

### Combining Information Through Parallel Structure

Sometimes without actually meaning to, writers use the same type of sentence structure over and over again. This not only bores the reader, but it fails to show the relationships between ideas. In addition, sometimes information is repeated from sentence to sentence because the sentences use the same information but add different details or ideas to accompany that information in each successive sentence. Read the example below.

> Students enjoy having Monday holidays. Students can enjoy these holidays by getting extra sleep. Students can enjoy these holidays by doing fun activities with friends. Students can enjoy these holidays by studying or getting extra work finished. Overall, most students enjoy these holidays a lot.

The phrase "students enjoy" is repeated several times in this paragraph. While most writers use this kind of repeated structure at some point in their writing, sometimes combining the information into one sentence or a series of more effective sentences can make a paragraph more meaningful and more enjoyable to read. Adding variety to your sentences will probably give you more options and ideas for expressing yourself.

The information in the preceding example paragraph could easily be combined into one or two sentences by leaving out the repeated elements and rewording. Look at all of the repeated words and phrases.

> Students enjoy Monday holidays. Students can enjoy these holidays by getting extra sleep. Students can enjoy these holidays by doing fun activities with friends. Students can enjoy these holidays by studying or getting extra work finished. Overall, most students enjoy these holidays a lot.

If we break down the sentences and look at the components, we can see that it is a list of details about what students enjoy.

Students enjoy Monday holidays

by getting extra sleep.
by doing fun activities with friends.
by studying or getting extra work finished.
a lot.

How can we combine these ideas? The following are some possibilities, but the most important reason to combine ideas in a sentence is to express them more effectively and retain your reader's interest. One effective way to combine ideas is to write them so that they use parallel structure. A sentence that uses parallel phrases, words, or concepts creates almost a list of details to develop the subject or topic of the sentence. Making ideas parallel requires that the sentence list ideas of the same type or part of speech so that each parallel item begins with the same kind of word. The example below demonstrates this by using the core sentence "Students enjoy Monday holidays" and then filling in the details by adding the parallel phrases in the box.

Students enjoy Monday holidays by _____.
                                    **insert parallel parts**

| | |
|---|---|
| parallel sentence parts ending in *-ing* ‖ | **getting** extra sleep |
| | **doing** fun activities with friends |
| | **studying** or **finishing** extra work |
| This part is not parallel. | a lot |

By listing the parallel elements, we can produce the following sentence:

> Students enjoy **getting** extra sleep, **doing** fun activities with friends, **studying**, or **finishing** extra work on Monday holidays.

Compare this sentence with the initial paragraph. Is it more effective? Is it easier to read? Probably most readers will read this sentence without noticing the parallel structure, but readers would definitely be affected by the monotony and repetition of the paragraph.

As we combine sentences, note that the goal of combining is never just to make sentences shorter. An occasional short sentence can be very effective, but having one short sentence after another adds to the monotony and difficulty of reading. Rewriting and combining sentences helps to avoid these problems.

### Combining Information to Demonstrate Equal Importance

Sometimes we use coordinating phrases to combine sentences and information within sentences to show that two or more points in the sentence have equal value or importance. This is a technique similar to parallelism, which usually combines equally important elements, but coordination rarely uses lists of items as we saw with parallel structure.

Coordination can be defined simply as combining equally important ideas or concepts in one sentence in a way that demonstrates their relationship of equality. Combining coordinating sentence parts can be done with words, punctuation, or a combination of the two. Let's use two sentences for an example.

> I have a very important math test.
> I have an essay due in English.

The sentences above have equal importance. Notice that one did not cause the other, and neither depends on the other. We might choose to combine these into one sentence to avoid repeating "I have" or even to convey a feeling of being overwhelmed by the two assignments. To combine these into one sentence, we have several options:

❏ **Combine two equal elements by making them parallel and using a coordinating conjunction.** (See the list in the Appendix.) Notice that no comma is necessary here because we dropped "I" from the second sentence.

I have a very important math test **and** an essay due in English.

❏ **Combine two equal elements using a semicolon.** (Refer to Using Grammar in Chapter 5 for more information.)

I have a very important math test; I have an essay due in English.

❏ **Combine equal elements using a coordinating conjunction and a comma.** Notice the comma here is necessary because the coordinating conjunction *and* is followed by an independent clause. (Refer to Using Grammar in Chapter 5 for more information.)

I have a very important math test, **and** I have an essay due in English.

Look at these three options carefully, and you will easily see that they maintain the idea of the separateness of each assignment, while emphasizing that each must be done. Notice that the first example combines the two sentences into one independent clause, but the other two examples use two independent clauses combined into a compound sentence that uses an appropriate form of punctuation (semicolon or comma and coordinating conjunction).

### Combining Ideas Through Subordination
To demonstrate cause/effect, dependent, or other relationships, you will want to use subordination. Subordinating ideas does not necessarily mean that you make one idea less important, but it does mean that you add a particular emphasis to one of your ideas. Instead of showing an equal relationship, subordination uses words, phrases, and punctuation to show the clear relationship of one idea to another. Observe the following example. Insert the words below it in the blank space and read the sentence that is created.

clause subordinated or made dependent

_____ I have a very important math test,

independent clause

I have an essay due in English.

after

before

whenever

How is each sentence different? What relationship between the math test and the English essay does it emphasize? When we change the word from *after* to *before*, we change the order of events. If we use *whenever*, we indicate an ongoing relationship between math tests and English papers.

To combine ideas using subordination, we can add a subordinating conjunction to an independent clause and make it dependent. What this will emphasize or highlight depends on the sentence and the dependent word that is used. These sentences can occur with either the subordinating conjunction or the independent clause first, as in the following examples:

**Because** I left my purse in the restaurant, I had to go back.
dependent clause first requires a comma before independent clause

I had to go back **because** I left my purse in the restaurant.
dependent clause after independent clause requires **no comma** before dependent clause

Subordination, like coordination, adds to the variety of your sentences, but it also allows you to make the relationships between ideas clear and to emphasize your point by making your most important idea the focal point of your sentence. As with the other sentence variety ideas here, you will want to try using this technique—but making all of your sentences parallel, coordinating, or subordinating will leave you with a monotonous, repetitious paragraph. Learn to use each of these sentence-combining techniques to increase your competence and your confidence in writing.

### Combining Ideas Through Modifiers

Modifiers are single words, phrases, or clauses that give additional information about another word, phrase, or clause. When we focus on sentence variety, we are primarily focusing on adding information to a single sentence instead of using a different sentence for every detail; thus in sentence-combining, modifiers are phrases made from kernels of meaning taken out of a full sentence and then embedded within another sentence. Modifiers, like subordinating clauses, show relationships between ideas and sentence parts. For example, the following three sentences can be changed by using the core idea in one sentence to modify the other sentences.

Amy Woo is a bright young woman. She has a future as a scientist. She is one of the best students in my physics class.

Each sentence states a point about Amy Woo. Because her name is included in the first sentence, let's use that as the base for combining the other sentences.

Amy Woo is a bright young woman.

What other information is important to combine into a single sentence expressing the same idea?

> future as a scientist
> one of the best students in my physics class

*EXAMPLE WITH MODIFIERS:*

> modifier created from the third sentence
> Amy Woo, **one of the best students in my physics class**, is
>
> modifier created from the second sentence
> a bright young woman with a **future as a scientist**.

Notice that the two ideas taken from the sentences after the main sentence develop the idea. In this case, the single sentence describes Amy better because it highlights Amy's positive qualities. The sentence could easily be rewritten to produce a different relationship.

> Amy Woo, a bright young woman in my physics class, is
> a future scientist.

In this version, the emphasis is changed. The fact that the writer has Amy in a class is less important than her possible career as a scientist. The point of this demonstration is that simply changing the modifier or way that the information is combined in a single sentence changes the message and emphasis of the sentence.

Modifiers are typically formed by creating a clause or a phrase that embeds or inserts a meaning from another sentence into a related sentence, sometimes with commas, sometimes without. The form and order of modifiers can be extremely important to achieving the meaning you want in a sentence; these two considerations can also determine whether or not your sentence makes sense. Look at the following examples and try to determine the meaning; the modifiers have been underlined.

> While making a sandwich, Jack's hand was cut.
> Her books are difficult reading for school.
> Running out of time, the paper needed considerable revision.
> Without enough money, the car had to be returned.

Each of these sentences demonstrates a problem that can occur with modifiers. Though you may be tempted to say, "Why should I bother using modifiers if they can cause so many problems?," recognize first that you already use them every day in your speech. Second, realize that they can be very effective in communicating meaning when they are used properly. And third, using common sense and close observation in revision will help you to catch any problematic modifiers, as the following discussion will show.

### Dangling Modifiers

*Original Example:*

> While making a sandwich, Jack's hand was cut.

*Revised Example:*

> While making a sandwich, Jack cut his hand.

Technically, Jack's hand probably is making the sandwich, but it makes more sense to say that Jack, the owner of the hand, is making the sandwich. The modifier "while making a sandwich" is described as dangling because the subject following it is not what it modifies. In fact, if you look at the original sentence, the hand is the subject of the sentence, not Jack. When we make Jack the subject, we understand that *he* cut *his* hand while making the sandwich. Revise for dangling modifiers by making sure that a modifier describes the subject it precedes.

*Original Example:*

> Running out of time, the paper needed considerable revision.

Does an essay run out of time to revise itself? The problem here is obvious—we need to add the writer. Rewrite the sentence in the space provided.

_____

_____

### Misplaced Modifiers

*Original Example:*

> Her books are difficult reading for school.

*Revised Example:*

> Her books for school are difficult reading.

*REVISED EXAMPLE:*

> She has difficulty reading her books for school.

The original sentence makes is unclear because we are not sure what "for school" modifies. The two revised sentences have different meanings and clarify what the original does not. The modifier must be placed next to what it modifies; when it is not, it is called a misplaced modifier. Always place a modifier as close to the item it modifies as possible. Try the following example yourself. What is the problem in this sentence? How would you rewrite it so that it makes sense?

*ORIGINAL EXAMPLE:*

> The car had to be repossessed without paying the bills.

_____

_____

Three keys to using modifiers are

❏ **Always make sure you are adding meaning or description to the right word or concept in the sentence;**

❏ **Do not allow your sentences to become burdened with modifiers—using too many is as bad as never using any at all;**

❏ **Always place the modifier next to what it modifies.**

### Other Techniques for Combining Sentences for Variety

In addition to using coordination, subordination, parallel structures, and modifiers, you can change sentences with several other techniques. You can, for example, invert the word order in a sentence. Of course, when you use this technique you want to make sure that you retain your meaning and that the sentence is still easy to understand. You can invert sentences by using the subordinating clause first as described previously, by moving a prepositional phrase to the beginning of the sentence, or by moving conjunctive adverbs or other phrases to the beginning of the sentence to vary the style. Look at the examples below of a prepositional phrase and subordinating conjunction in inverted order.

*ORIGINAL EXAMPLE:*

> She keeps a stash of money in the back room.

*Revised Example:*

In the back room, she keeps a stash of money.

*Original Example:*

Butterflies will land on a variety of plants although they prefer purple flowers.

*Revised Example:*

Although butterflies prefer purple flowers, they will land on a variety of plants.

Though the meaning does not greatly change, the inversion of these sentences is an important technique to use to make your essays more readable and to develop an educated, skillful writing style. Combining sentences, working with sentence structure to reflect meaning and capture interest, and learning to use the appropriate forms of punctuation and modifiers to accompany these changes is important to your style as a writer, as well as to your own sense of being able to communicate effectively. Keeping a grammar journal that reflects the successes and possible pitfalls you have experienced with these concepts may help you to employ them in your writing and to learn to use them as a natural, even unplanned part of your style and revision process.

## Building Your Skills

### Assignment 1

Combine the following sentences in the way specified. For additional practice, on a separate sheet of paper, combine each of the sets of sentences using three other techniques.

1. Combine the following sentences into a sentence using parallel sentence structure.
   The teacher graded the papers.
   She was very tired.
   She spilled coffee on the papers.
   She decided to get some sleep.

   _____

   _____

2. Combine the following sentences into a sentence using coordination.

Each of the firefighters was exhausted.

They had been working through the night.

They were trying to put out an industrial building that caught fire.

_____

_____

3. Combine the following sentences into a sentence using subordination.

The students prepared for the test until 4:00 a.m.

They were really tired.

They hoped they would do well.

_____

_____

4. Combine the following sentences into a sentence using modifiers.

Ryan Lee and his sister Dicsie were both hard-working students.

Ryan was almost finished with mortician school.

Dicsie was pursuing a degree in music.

_____

_____

## Assignment 2

In this chapter, we examined parallel structure, coordination, subordination, and modifiers. Using a recent essay you have written, change fifteen sentences using all four of these structures. Evaluate whether the essay still communicates the same message. If it doesn't, how has the message changed?

## Assignment 3

Create a style journal or guide that you can use as you write. (If you did Assignment 1 in this chapter's writing section, then you can make this a continuation of that assignment.) Review the grammar discussion in Chapter 7 and in this chapter, and create a list of the ways you can change or improve your use of grammar and variety in sentence structure and punctuation. When you have a clear list with at least eight to ten suggestions, write at least five sentences for each of the techniques you feel you could improve.

## SEEING THE CONNECTIONS: APPLYING YOUR SKILLS

### Assignment 1

Read Connie Perez's essay in this chapter and respond in a fifteen-minute freewriting exercise where you discuss your view of what she says, your view of affirmative action, or your view based on some other point in her essay. After writing for fifteen minutes, reread your freewriting and choose a specific view or idea for a thesis statement. Using this thesis statement, write a one-page response to Perez's essay that either agrees or disagrees with one of her main points. When you finish, follow the directions in this chapter for reading your rough draft in stages (page 229); in the third reading, read your essay backwards as directed and mark any weak sentences. Use sentence-combining techniques from this chapter to improve these sentences. Make at least ten changes.

### Assignment 2

Read a local or major newspaper and pick out three issues covered in the paper that affect you personally. Write a thesis statement presenting a view about each issue. Choose one of the thesis statements, and identify or list the ways this issue affects you or the ways you agree or disagree with this issue. After preparing this information, go back to the newspaper and find the letters to the editor. Read one or two of them. Is a letter to the editor different from a typical essay? Make a list of the necessary elements for a letter to the editor based on the examples you read. Then in the same style, write a letter to the editor of that newspaper that presents the issue you thought about and wrote a thesis statement for. Explain your view of this issue and use an example to support your view. As you are writing your letter, remember to incorporate the elements of style you noted in the letters to the editor, but avoid any ungrammatical usage or organizational problems you see in the sample letters you read.

### Assignment 3

Read Donald Murray's essay in this chapter. Make a list of his guidelines. Respond to Murray's description of how to revise a manuscript by writing an essay that tells students the process for revising a student essay. You can write this as a serious essay that describes the process for writing an effective essay, or you may want to write this as a humorous look at how to write a rotten essay.

Revise your essay using the style guide or list of changes you wrote either in Assignment 1 following Techniques for Writing (page 245) or in Assignment 3 following Using Grammar (page 261), or both. If you did not do either assignment, follow the guidelines for one of these assignments, and then use the style guide to make at least ten changes in your essay.

# Chapter 9

# Integrating and Testing Your Skills

In this chapter you will learn

☆ to recognize the influence reading has on writing, grammar, and thinking;
☆ to identify three levels of thought in reading;
☆ to write and revise a summary;
☆ to take tests well;
☆ to develop and use a routine in essay test situations;
☆ to recognize grammatical relationships and their meaning.

Take a moment to answer the following questions:

1. How often do you read? What do you enjoy reading? Approximately how many books have you read?

_____

_____

_____

2. When you read, do you feel you understand what you are reading? How well do you think you read?

_____

_____

_____

3. Have you ever written a summary? What purpose do you think summaries serve?

_____

_____

_____

4. How is grammar related to the ideas and the meaning of the things you read? How can grammar change or influence meaning?

_____

_____

_____

# USING YOUR WRITING AND READING SKILLS TOGETHER

The relationship between reading and writing can seem at once obvious and obscure. Most writers know on a conscious level that they are writing to someone (i.e., a reader) and most readers know that someone has written what they are reading (i.e., a writer), but many readers and writers overlook the significant connection between reading and writing. For example, many writers do not recognize how much their writing is influenced by what and how often they read. Many skills link reading and writing. Both focus on communication. As writers, we try to present ideas so that other people can understand them, and as readers, we try to understand ideas being presented to us. Many of the skills we use for one affect how well we do the other.

### The Effects of Reading on Writing

When we read, we use a myriad of intricate skills. If you learned to read easily in the first or second grade, you may not recognize how complex and sophisticated this combination of skills and abilities is. If you struggled when you learned to read, or you still struggle with reading well, chances are you already have realized how much skill is required to read effectively.

People who read well understand the differences between reading materials, use the appropriate speed for different types of reading, have good vocabulary skills that allow them to understand and use the words they read, and recognize structural elements that help them to comprehend what they read. Although this may sound like a formidable list of skills to learn, each of these skills plays an important part in the writing process and is acquired readily during reading.

Just as readers recognize different types of reading, writers must understand the different types of writing they are asked to do. For example, a personal letter, a formal essay, a summary, or a research paper all require different writing techniques and processes. Writers also use the skill of recognizing the level of difficulty in a piece of writing. In their own writing, they must use appropriate language and formats to present ideas in a way that is appropriate to their audience. For example, a writer would not want to write a term paper in the form of a personal letter to his or her instructor. In addition to recognizing the difficulty and format of the material he or she must write, every writer realizes the effect of having a broad vocabulary because words are the primary devices of writing. The greater the variety of words the writer knows, the greater the ability he or she has to express an idea exactly and completely. As readers we become aware of the effect that clear writing, well-chosen words, and easy-to-read prose have on us; as writers, we practice these skills for ourselves and learn to employ them in ways that are relevant and that fit with our own style of communication.

One of the most profound influences that reading has on writing is in the use of grammar. Most people originally learned grammar from the language they heard as children while listening to the adults speaking around them. In fact, some people use this same grammar in their writing. However, people who read, especially those who are visual learners and learn best by what they see, have learned much of the grammar they use in writing from what they see in the writing they read. If you do not read very often or if you read materials that are not well written, this can have a significant influence on the way you write and, in particular, on your sentence structure and use of grammar. Most students who write very well when they enter college could not tell you the definitions for many grammatical terms and probably could not even tell you why they use a particular punctuation mark or type of sentence structure, but they will all tell you that they do a lot of reading and that they read many high-quality reading materials.

Writing, as a hobby or for school assignments, also affects reading. When we write, we learn how to present ideas to an audience, but of course, we use what we know from being an audience member when we read. The relationship between reading and writing is cyclical; as we write, we are constantly employing the words, formats, and types of presentation we have seen as readers. This also makes us more sensitive as readers. As readers, we get an opportunity to see how well a writer's expression of an idea helps us to understand his or her idea. Then we can employ this technique at a later time when it is useful in our own writing.

Using your skills in writing and reading simultaneously can greatly improve your abilities in both of these related areas, as well as increasing your ability to evaluate, discuss, and interpret pertinent information. One of the best ways to use the skills you learn in reading and writing is to use both of these abilities to produce an assignment that makes you use your reading skills, writing skills, and for that matter, your thinking skills too. Several kinds of assignments do this: summaries, analytical papers written about an essay or story, and research papers. Each of these assignments uses a variety of reading and writing skills, forcing the student to perform more careful reading, thinking, and writing. Of course, this is why instructors give these assignments and why many students groan and complain when they do. Each of these reading-and-writing combination assignments involves some important skills. They also require that students analyze the works they read before they write about them and that they learn presentation techniques appropriate for presenting summary, analysis, and other ideas obtained through reading.

As a writer, you use the skill of analysis to think out your presentation to a reader. In assignments that require both reading and writing, the difficulty lies within the analysis process. While it takes much time and effort to write an essay, it often takes more time to prepare to write an analytical essay than it does to physically write it. Most combined reading and writing assignments require some kind of summarizing or paraphrasing, as well as knowing the difference between simply summarizing and analyzing information. Quoting and paraphrasing will be discussed more specifically in Chapter 10, but essentially a quote is the use of the exact words of another writer or speaker. Quotes must be enclosed in quotation marks (" ") to indicate that the words have been quoted. A paraphrase, on the other hand, is the presentation of another person's ideas through your own words. This requires interpretation of those ideas, as well as giving credit to the person who originally presented the ideas by indicating that these ideas came from a particular source—an essay, speaker, and so on. Summaries and analytical writing employ both paraphrasing and quoting. A well-written summary requires thought, careful reading, and clearly presented discussion. It differs from analyzing, but is often the foundation of a clear analysis because it forces the reader to clearly identify what information is contained within a written work and then evaluate and discuss that information. Analytical writing and research paper writing are processes that require a clear understanding of the differences between summarizing and analyzing. Let's examine these two forms in more detail.

## Writing a Summary

A summary presents the ideas contained within a written work in a shorter, more concise form. A summary has three essential parts: an introduction that includes the writer's name, the writer's title if applicable, and the title of the written work being summarized; a concise presentation of the writer's major ideas; and an evaluation of the ideas or information presented in the original work.

Begin writing a summary by organizing your ideas—just as with any other essay. In a summary, though, instead of using your own ideas, remember that you are presenting and evaluating someone else's ideas. Every summary should begin by identifying the work being summarized and its author. For example, an introduction might begin

> In Bruce Catton's essay "Grant and Lee: A Study in Contrasts," Catton compares the influence of these two historical figures on American politics. He believes that the demeanor of these men at such a crucial time in American history made all the difference.

Notice that the first sentence tells the reader of the summary that the essay was written by Bruce Catton and identifies the essay title. A summary that is reader-based will identify these important points, as well as using phrases like the one we see in the second sentence: He believes. This writer does not try to take credit for Catton's ideas, but clarifies instead that this is Catton's belief and point. In addition, this introduction includes another important feature. The thesis or main idea of Catton's essay is discussed in the first sentence and further detailed in the second. The summary writer even indicates the dominant rhetorical mode for this essay when he uses the word "compares." These features allow the reader to understand the original essay while giving the writer an overall thesis for his summary. How would he finish his summary? He would go on to give examples of Catton's ideas about the characteristics of these men and then he would evaluate Catton's ideas.

A few other techniques will help to produce a readable, well-written summary. Use the writer's name and identify the person who wrote what you are summarizing. For example, use phrases like "Catton asserts," "he presents the idea that," and other phrases that include the author's name or a pronoun like he. Also, use quotations from the original essay to illustrate a viewpoint, a writing style, or a particularly good example. Remember to use quotation marks if you are using the author's exact words. When you are not quoting, use paraphrases of a few significant supporting details as you summarize. Make sure that you do not simply list the supporting details; instead, use phrases like "he offers several examples to prove his thesis" and then go on to give a few examples. In addition to discussing what the essay covers, and how well the author covers the topic, be sure to offer the reader your own ideas and evaluation as well. A good summary should give your reader a clear idea of the material contained within a written work, the viewpoint taken, and your view about the effectiveness or validity of the reading.

To write an effective summary, you need to carefully read the writing to be summarized, take notes, find the main idea, and then prioritize the supporting ideas to see what is most important. Your summary should focus at all times on the writer's work and should discuss how effectively the author makes his or her point. The following is an essay by Bruce Catton titled "Grant and Lee: A Study in Contrasts." Read the essay and make notes about the main idea and the supporting ideas that would be important to include in a summary.

## Grant and Lee: A Study in Contrasts*

### by Bruce Catton

1    When Ulysses S. Grant and Robert E. Lee met in the parlor of a modest house at Appomattox Court House, Virginia, on April 9, 1865, to work out the terms for the surrender of Lee's Army of Northern Virginia, a great chapter in American life came to a close, and a great new chapter began.

2    These men were bringing the Civil War to its virtual finish. To be sure, other armies had yet to surrender, and for a few days the fugitive Confederate government would struggle desperately and vainly, trying to find some way to go on living now that its chief support was gone. But in effect it was all over when Grant and Lee signed the papers. And the little room where they wrote out the terms was the scene of one of the poignant, dramatic contrasts in American history.

3    They were two strong men, these oddly different generals, and they represented the strengths of two conflicting currents that, through them, had come into final collision.

*Source:* Catton, Bruce. "Grant and Lee: A Study in Contrasts." From *The American Story.* Reprinted by permission of the U.S. Capitol Historical Society.

Back of Robert E. Lee was the notion that the old                    4
aristocratic concept might somehow survive and be dominant in American life.

Lee was tidewater Virginia, and in his background                    5
were family, culture, and tradition . . . the age of chivalry
transplanted to a New World which was making its own leg-
ends and its own myths. He embodied a way of life that
had come down through the age of knighthood and the
English country squire. America was a land that was beginning all over again, dedicated to nothing much more complicated than the rather hazy belief that all men had equal
rights and should have an equal chance in the world. In
such a land Lee stood for the feeling that it was somehow
of advantage to human society to have a pronounced
inequality in the social structure. There should be a leisure
class, backed by ownership of land; in turn, society itself
should be keyed to the land as the chief source of wealth
and influence. It would bring forth (according to this
ideal) a class of men with a strong sense of obligation to
the community; men who lived not to gain advantage for
themselves, but to meet the solemn obligations which had
been laid on them by the very fact that they were privi-
leged. From them the country would get its leadership; to
them it could look for the higher values—of thought, of
conduct, of personal deportment—to give it strength and
virtue.

Lee embodied the noblest elements of this aristocratic          6
ideal. Through him, the landed nobility justified itself. For
four years, the Southern states had fought a desperate war
to uphold the ideals for which Lee stood. In the end, it
almost seemed as if the Confederacy fought for Lee; as if
he himself was the Confederacy . . . the best thing that
the way of life for which the Confederacy stood could ever
have to offer. He had passed into legend before Appomattox. Thousands of tired, underfed, poorly clothed Confederate soldiers, long since past the simple enthusiasm of the
early days of the struggle, somehow considered Lee the
symbol of everything for which they had been willing to
die. But they could not quite put this feeling into words. If

the Lost Cause, sanctified by so much heroism and so many deaths, had a living justification, its justification was General Lee.

Grant, the son of a tanner on the Western frontier, was everything Lee was not. He had come up the hard way and embodied nothing in particular except the eternal toughness and sinewy fiber of the men who grew up beyond the mountains. He was one of a body of men who owed reverence and obeisance to no one, who were self-reliant to a fault, who cared hardly anything for the past but who had a sharp eye for the future.

7

These frontier men were the precise opposites of the tidewater aristocrats. Back of them, in the great surge that had taken people over the Alleghenies and into the opening Western country, there was a deep, implicit dissatisfaction with a past that had settled into grooves. They stood for democracy, not from any reasoned conclusion about the proper ordering of human society, but simply because they had grown up in the middle of democracy and knew how it worked. Their society might have privileges, but they would be privileges each man had won for himself. Forms and patterns meant nothing. No man was born to anything, except perhaps to a chance to show how far he could rise. Life was competition.

8

Yet along with this feeling had come a deep sense of belonging to a national community. The Westerner who developed a farm, opened a shop, or set up in business as a trader could hope to prosper only as his own community prospered—and his community ran from the Atlantic to the Pacific and from Canada down to Mexico. If the land was settled, with towns and highways and accessible markets, he could better himself. He saw his fate in terms of the nation's own destiny. As its horizons expanded, so did his. He had, in other words, an acute dollars-and-cents stake in the continued growth and development of his country.

9

And that, perhaps, is where the contrast between Grant and Lee becomes most striking. The Virginia aristocrat, inevitably, saw himself in relation to his own region. He lived in a static society which could endure almost any-

10

thing except change. Instinctively, his first loyalty would go to the locality in which that society existed. He would fight to the limit of endurance to defend it, because in defending it he was defending everything that gave his own life its deepest meaning.

The Westerner, on the other hand, would fight with     11
an equal tenacity for the broader concept of society. He fought so because everything he lived by was tied to growth, expansion, and a constantly widening horizon. What he lived by would survive or fall with the nation itself. He could not possibly stand by unmoved in the face of an attempt to destroy the Union. He would combat it with everything he had, because he could only see it as an effort to cut the ground out from under his feet.

So Grant and Lee were in complete contrast, repre-     12
senting two diametrically opposed elements in American life. Grant was the modern man emerging; beyond him, ready to come on the stage, was the great age of steel and machinery, of crowded cities and a restless burgeoning vitality. Lee might have ridden down from the old age of chivalry, lance in hand, silken banner fluttering over his head. Each man was the perfect champion of his cause, drawing both his strengths and his weaknesses from the people he led.

Yet it was not all contrast, after all. Different as they     13
were—in background, in personality, in underlying aspiration—these two great soldiers had much in common. Under everything else, they were marvelous fighters. Furthermore, their fighting qualities were really very much alike.

Each man had, to begin with, the great virtue of utter     14
tenacity and fidelity. Grant fought his way down the Mississippi Valley in spite of acute personal discouragement and profound military handicaps. Lee hung on in the trenches at Petersburg after hope itself had died. In each man there was an indomitable quality . . . the born fighter's refusal to give up as long as he can still remain on his feet and lift his two fists.

Daring and resourcefulness they had, too; the ability     15
to think faster and move faster than the enemy. These

were the qualities which gave Lee the dazzling campaigns of Second Manassas and Chancellorsville and won Vicksburg for Grant.

Lastly, and perhaps greatest of all, there was the ability, at the end, to turn quickly from war to peace once the fighting was over. Out of the way these two men behaved at Appomattox came the possibility of a peace of reconciliation. It was a possibility not wholly realized, in the years to come, but which did, in the end, help the two sections to become one nation again . . . after a war whose bitterness might have seemed to make such a reunion wholly impossible. No part of either man's life became him more than the part he played in this brief meeting in the McLean house at Appomattox. Their behavior there put all succeeding generations of Americans in their debt. Two great Americans, Grant and Lee—very different, yet under everything very much alike. Their encounter at Appomattox was one of the great moments of American history.

16

What is the main idea of this essay? Catton identifies the elements of Grant's and Lee's characters that are important to an understanding of each man and of his effect on American history. How, then, would you write a summary about this essay? You would need to introduce Catton and his essay title, the main idea of his essay, and some of his major points. What else would you need to provide in addition to this information? You would need to offer an evaluation or discussion of the benefits or drawbacks to reading this essay. You would also agree or disagree with the ideas presented. For an example, look at the summary included in Reading a Student Essay in this chapter.

# READING AN ESSAY

## Strategy for Reading: Analyzing What You Read

Many students read the surface level of an essay and never look for the thesis or controlling idea. In other words, they read the words, but they do not get the point. In Chapter 5, we discussed figurative language and connotation, both of which require analysis and interpretation. Analyzing an essay is a skill requiring thought and careful observation. Analysis helps readers to make connections between what they read and what they already know. Three levels of understanding divide a reader who gets the point and thinks about information from other, less careful readers. First, a reader may look only for literal information and gain a literal understanding, which means that the reader understands what an essay or story actually says in words, but does not see how this point is significant or meaningful. This level of understanding requires the least amount of thought and does not go beyond the obvious content in a written work. A second level of understanding occurs when a reader interprets what the author is saying by paying attention to how the writer makes a statement, to the writer's attitude, and to the specific language he or she uses and the different meanings it provides. This is usually described as interpretive thought because the reader looks beyond the surface meaning to find a deeper, more meaningful point. On the third level, serious readers seek out a true understanding of what they read by analyzing. Readers who analyze discover the meaning presented, evaluate that meaning, and decide how significant that meaning is to their lives and the lives of others. Obviously, this takes real work—thinking, pondering, considering—and consequently many readers simply read the surface of a written work. However, analyzing what you read has many advantages.

The first advantage of analysis is that the more you analyze what you read, the more sensitive you become to language and how language communicates. As you analyze, you notice attitudes and relationships that the author communicates through his or her use of words and sentence structure. A second advantage to analyzing is that it helps you avoid the feeling that you have missed something. If when you read you feel that you really do not understand what you have read and you do not see its significance, analyzing what you read can make reading easier, more enjoyable, and more meaningful to you, especially after practice. A third advantage to analyzing what you read is that it aids memory and retention. If you think about what you read, you are much more likely to actually remember specific and important ideas, as well as their relationships to one another. As a student, you will find this invaluable because it saves you from having to reread materials for classes and tests. The fourth advantage to analyzing is that it gives you freedom of thought. When you do not analyze, often you allow someone else to interpret what is written for you; when you analyze, on the other hand, you can read and understand for yourself and evaluate what you read given your own value system and personal opinions. Obviously, analysis requires thought and careful reading, but even more, it produces better thinking and more careful reading in anyone who practices it.

In the following essay, Richard Rodriguez presents his experience and views of reading. As you read, identify the literal content (what happens), interpret the irony (words or ideas that seem to mean one thing but really mean another) or other meanings that go beyond the surface, and finally, analyze his overall point, the significance of it, and what it means to your life and the lives of others. What is he really saying about reading?

---

### BEFORE YOU READ

1. How did you feel about reading in third and fourth grade? Did your parents or guardians do a lot of reading?
2. Has reading played an important role in your life? In what ways did reading seem frustrating or even unimportant in your experience?
3. As a college student, what reading skills have an impact on your success in school? What reading skills influence your success outside of school ( jobs, home life, family, business, and so on)?

---

## Reading for Success★

### by Richard Rodriguez

From an early age I knew that my mother and father could read and write both Spanish and English. I had observed my father making his way through what, I now suppose, must have been income tax forms. On other occasions I waited apprehensively while my mother read onion-paper letters air-mailed from Mexico with news of a relative's illness or death. For both my parents, however, reading was something

1

★*Source:* Rodriguez, Richard. "Reading for Success." From *Hunger of Memory* by Richard Rodriguez. Reprinted by permission of David R. Godine, Publisher, Inc. Copyright © 1982 by Richard Rodriguez.

done out of necessity and as quickly as possible. Never did I see either of them read an entire book. Nor did I see them read for pleasure. Their reading consisted of work manuals, prayer books, newspapers, recipes. . . .

In our house each school year would begin with my mother's careful instruction: "Don't write in your books so we can sell them at the end of the year." The remark was echoed in public by my teachers, but only in part: "Boys and girls, don't write in your books. You must learn to treat them with great care and respect."                                                                           2

OPEN THE DOORS OF YOUR MIND WITH BOOKS, read the red and white poster over the nun's desk in early September. It soon was apparent to me that reading was the classroom's central activity. Each course had its own book. And the information gathered from a book was unquestioned. READ TO LEARN, the sign on the wall advised in December. I privately wondered: What was the connection between reading and learning? Did one learn something only by reading it? Was an idea only an idea if it could be written down? In June, CONSIDER BOOKS YOUR BEST FRIENDS. Friends? Reading was, at best, only a chore. I needed to look up whole paragraphs of words in a dictionary. Lines of type were dizzying, the eye having to move slowly across the page, then down, and across. . . . The sentences of the first books I read were coolly impersonal. Toned hard. What most bothered me, however, was the isolation reading required. To console myself for the loneliness I'd feel when I read, I tried reading in a very soft voice. Until: "Who is doing all that talking to his neighbor?" Shortly after, remedial reading classes were arranged for me with a very old nun.                                                                        3

At the end of each school day, for nearly six months, I would meet with her in the tiny room that served as the school's library but was actually only a storeroom for used textbooks and a vast collection of                                                                         4

*National Geographics.* Everything about our sessions pleased me: the smallness of the room; the noise of the janitor's broom hitting the edge of the long hallway outside the door; the green of the sun, lighting the wall; and the old woman's face blurred white with a beard. Most of the time we took turns. I began with my elementary text. Sentences of astonishing simplicity seemed to me lifeless and drab: "The boys ran from the rain. . . . She wanted to sing. . . . The kite rose in the blue." Then the old nun would read from her favorite books, usually biographies of early American presidents. Playfully she ran through complex sentences, calling the words alive with her voice, making it seem that the author somehow was speaking directly to me. I smiled just to listen to her. I sat there and sensed for the very first time some possibility of fellowship between a reader and a writer, a communication, never *intimate* like that I heard spoken words at home convey, but one nonetheless *personal.*

One day the nun concluded a session by asking me why I was so reluctant to read by myself. I tried to explain; said something about the way written words made me feel all alone—almost, I wanted to add but didn't, as when I spoke to myself in a room just emptied of furniture. She studied my face as I spoke; she seemed to be watching more than listening. In an uneventful voice she replied that I had nothing to fear. Didn't I realize that reading would open up whole new worlds? A book could open doors for me. It could introduce me to people and show me places I never imagined existed. She gestured toward the bookshelves. (Bare-breasted African women danced, and the shiny hubcaps of automobiles on the back covers of the *Geographic* gleamed in my mind.) I listened with respect. But her words were not very influential. I was thinking then of another consequence of literacy, one I was too shy to admit but nonetheless trusted. Books were going to make me "educated." *That* confidence enabled me,

5

several months later, to overcome my fear of the silence.

In fourth grade I embarked upon a grandiose reading program. "Give me the names of important books," I would say to startled teachers. They soon found out that I had in mind "adult books." I ignored their suggestion of anything I suspected was written for children. (Not until I was in college, as a result, did I read *Huckleberry Finn* or *Alice's Adventures in Wonderland.*) Instead, I read The *Scarlet Letter* and Franklin's *Autobiography.* And whatever I read I read for extra credit. Each time I finished a book, I reported the achievement to a teacher and basked in the praise my effort earned. Despite my best efforts, however, there seemed to be more and more books I needed to read. At the library I would literally tremble as I came upon whole shelves of books I hadn't read. So I read and I read and I read: *Great Expectations*; all the short stories of Kipling; *The Babe Ruth Story*; the entire first volume of the *Encyclopedia Britannica* (A–ANSTEY); the *Iliad*; *Moby Dick*; *Gone with the Wind*; *The Good Earth*; *Ramona*; *Forever Amber*; *The Lives of the Saints*; *Crime and Punishment*; *The Pearl.* . . . Librarians who initially frowned when I checked out the maximum ten books at a time started saving books they thought I might like. Teachers would say to the rest of the class, "I only wish the rest of you took reading as seriously as Richard obviously does."

6

But at home I would hear my mother wondering, "What do you see in your books?" (Was reading a hobby like her knitting? Was so much reading even healthy for a boy? Was it the sign of "brains"? Or was it just a convenient excuse for not helping around the house on Saturday mornings?) Always, "What do you see . . . ?"

7

What <u>did</u> I see in my books? I had the idea that they were crucial for my academic success, though I couldn't have said exactly how or why. In the sixth grade I simply concluded that what gave a book its

8

value was some major idea or theme it contained. If that core essence could be mined and memorized, I would become learned like my teachers. I decided to record in a notebook the themes of the books that I read. After reading *Robinson Crusoe*, I wrote that its theme was "the value of learning to live by oneself." When I completed *Wuthering Heights*, I noted the danger of "letting emotions get out of control." Rereading these brief moralistic appraisals usually left me disheartened. I couldn't believe that they were really the source of reading's value. But for many years, they constituted the only means I had of describing to myself the educational value of books.

In spite of my earnestness, I found reading a pleasurable activity. I came to enjoy the lonely good company of books. Early on weekday mornings, I'd read in my bed. I'd feel a mysterious comfort then, reading in the dawn quiet—the blue-gray silence interrupted by the occasional churning of the refrigerator motor a few rooms away or the more distant sounds of a city bus beginning its run. On weekends I'd go to the public library to read, surrounded by old men and women. Or, if the weather was fine, I would take my books to the park and read in the shade of a tree. Neighbors would leave for vacation and I would water their lawns. I would sit through the twilight on the front porches or in backyards, reading to the cool, whirling sounds of the sprinklers.

9

I also had favorite writers. But often those writers I enjoyed most I was least able to value. When I read William Saroyan's *The Human Comedy*, I was immediately pleased by the narrator's warmth and the charm of his story. But as quickly I became suspicious. A book so enjoyable to read couldn't be very "important." Another summer I determined to read all the novels of Dickens. Reading his fat novels, I loved the feeling I got—after the first hundred pages—of being at home in a fictional world where I knew the names of the characters and

10

cared about what was going to happen to them. And it bothered me that I was forced away at the conclusion, when the fiction closed tight, like a fortune-teller's fist— the futures of all the major characters neatly resolved. I never knew how to take such feelings seriously, however. Nor did I suspect that these experiences could be part of a novel's meaning. Still, there were pleasures to sustain me after I'd finish my books. Carrying a volume back to the library, I would be pleased by its weight. I'd run my fingers along the edge of the pages and marvel at the breadth of my achievement. Around my room, growing stacks of paperback books reinforced my assurance.

11    I entered high school having read hundreds of books. My habit of reading made me a confident speaker and writer of English. Reading also enabled me to sense something of the shape, the major concerns, of Western thought. (I was able to say something about Dante and Descartes and Engels and James Baldwin in my high school term papers.) In these various ways, books brought me academic success as I hoped that they would. But I was not a good reader. Merely bookish, I lacked a point of view when I read. Rather, I read in order to acquire a point of view. I vacuumed books for epigrams, scraps of information, ideas, themes—anything to fill the hollow within me and make me feel educated. When one of my teachers suggested to his drowsy tenth-grade English class that a person could not have a "complicated idea" until he had read at least two thousand books, I heard the remark without detecting either its irony or its very complicated truth. I merely determined to compile a list of all the books I had ever read. Harsh with myself, I included only once a title I might have read several times. (How, after all, could one read a book more than once?) And I included only those books over a hundred pages in length. (Could anything shorter be a book?)

12    There was yet another high school list I compiled. One day I came across a newspaper article about the

retirement of an English professor at a nearby state college. The article was accompanied by a list of the "hundred most important books of Western Civilization." "More than anything else in my life," the professor told the reporter with finality, "these books have made me all that I am." That was the kind of remark I couldn't ignore. I clipped out the list and kept it for the several months it took me to read all of the titles. Most books, of course, I barely understood. While reading Plato's *Republic*, for instance, I needed to keep looking at the book jacket comments to remind myself what the text was about. Nevertheless, with the special patience and superstition of a scholarship boy. I looked at every word of the text. And by the time I reached the last word, relieved, I convinced myself that I had read *The Republic*. In a ceremony of great pride, I solemnly crossed Plato off my list.

## Building Your Skills

### Focus on Words

Look up the following words or parts of phrases in a dictionary. Consult the preceding essay and identify the meaning that best fits the way the author uses the word in this essay. Each word or phrase is followed by the number of the paragraph in which it appears.

| | |
|---|---|
| apprehensively (1) | grandiose (6) |
| "toned hard" (3) | "moralistic appraisals" (8) |
| remedial (3) | bookish (11) |
| intimate (4) | epigrams (11) |
| literacy (5) | solemnly (12) |

### Focus on the Message

1. Why does Rodriguez explain that he observed his parents reading "work manuals, prayer books" (para. 1) and other necessary readings, while at the same time pointing out that he never saw them reading for pleasure? Does Rodriguez want readers to be critical of his parents?

2. As an elementary school student, Rodriguez questioned the purpose of reading and considered reading "only a chore" (para. 3). How does his perspective
   change? Why does he show us this earlier view?

3. How is reading aloud different from reading silently? What changed reading
   from an activity of "isolation" (para. 3) to an activity "intimate" and "personal"
   (para. 4) for Rodriguez? Why does he describe this for us?

4. What is Rodriguez's major point about reading in this essay? What differences
   do you notice between Rodriguez's attitude about the value of reading as a
   child and the theme or message about reading in his essay?

5. In what ways was Rodriguez "not a good reader" (para. 11)? What does
   Rodriguez mean in paragraph 12 when he writes, "I looked at every word of
   the text" of Plato's *The Republic* and then "crossed Plato off my list"?

# TECHNIQUES FOR WRITING:
# IN-CLASS ESSAYS AND TIMED WRITING

One of the most difficult types of writing for most students is writing that
is timed or writing that the writer has not had a chance to prepare for by
thinking at length about the subject matter. Sometimes students feel very
frustrated when presented with a writing assignment in class; they may even
feel "blocked" or unable to write. Coping with this situation is a skill, not
an automatic ability that some writers have and others do not. When you
are asked to write an essay or a written response in class, how do you feel?
What do you think about or worry about? What fears or feelings do you
experience during this type of assignment? Do you feel as comfortable writing in class as you do at home? Believe it or not, some people feel more
comfortable in class than they do at home. While you do not necessarily
need to become as comfortable writing in class as you are at home or in the
computer lab, you can develop coping skills that will make writing in class
less frustrating, easier, and more satisfying. Most instructors in classes such
as composition, history, psychology, anatomy, and many other subjects
require some kind of in-class essay responses, either on tests or as
impromptu or pop quizzes. Therefore, learning to write effectively in class
can greatly increase your ability to do well in college courses and can build
your skills for the job market too. Many interview processes require appli-
cants to write impromptu responses prior to an interview.

Taking timed tests or writing timed essays reveals how well you
understand the information being tested, but it also demonstrates how

effectively you manage time and how well you think when you are given a time limit. This lack of control often makes students uncomfortable. The trick is becoming comfortable in test situations by gaining as much control as possible and using this to your advantage. In a timed situation, focusing too much of your attention on the time element or pressuring yourself to perform may keep you from demonstrating skills you have learned and may affect your performance on an exam or essay in very pronounced ways. Almost everyone has had the experience of "freezing" on a test or in an essay situation. The following are some suggestions for performing well and becoming comfortable with timed tests and essays. One advantage to timed tests, by the way, is that when the time is up, the test is over. You cannot work with a timed essay for hours or days—you must turn it in, usually within an hour or two. Thus, on a positive note, timed essays can be liberating for college students who already have many demands on their time.

## ❏ Psych yourself up for the test!

Before a test or timed essay, build your confidence and ability by giving yourself positive feedback. Instead of thinking "I'm not very good at tests or in-class essays," think "I will do well in this test if I remain calm and keep my cool." Positive feedback is an important part of success, because if you tell yourself that you are likely to fail, you are setting yourself up for failure rather than preparing for success. Get ready for a test by giving yourself the edge of confidence. Being nervous is not necessarily bad, but being too nervous or jittery can certainly prevent you from doing your best. Try giving yourself positive and calming messages to prepare for your peak performance.

## ❏ Be prepared.

Preparation can be impossible in some situations, but when you know a test or essay is coming, prepare for it. In the case of a test, study for tests using your textbook, notes from your class, and consultations with the instructor or a tutor. Try to guess what questions will be asked by reviewing the subject matter the instructor emphasized the most. Try brainstorming about possible subjects that might be covered on the test, and make up your own questions with a study partner to project what the instructor may ask. Try also to study over a period of time rather than all in one night.

When you have an essay topic or you know an essay will be required in class, prepare either by brainstorming (if you know the topic) or by preparing mentally through writing a practice essay (if you do not know the topic). Preparation should be part of your routine when the essay begins, too. If you are given an impromptu essay topic, do not simply start writing hoping that something good will come out. Deal with this writing situation as you would any other. Allow yourself three to five minutes to brainstorm and get ideas on paper. Brainstorming allows you to get to work immediately: your brain starts working; your hand starts writing; you begin a routine that, after you have done it once or twice, will make you more comfortable with in-class writing. This technique helps to prevent you from freezing up because you begin writing from the very beginning, and you move from brainstorming to writing, which is a skill you have already used when writing out of class. The key to effectively preparing for in-class essays is to use the skills you already have in new ways.

## ❏ Don't let frustration overwhelm you.

If you find yourself blocked or unable to think clearly during an in-class essay or test, stop everything you are doing. Close your eyes; take a few deep breaths; tell yourself to relax, or repeat the word "relax" to yourself several times. Do not allow yourself to give in, but redirect your energy to the task at hand. If necessary, brainstorm some more, move on to the next question, or begin an essay in the middle—but do not become frantic. A single test or essay is just that. It does not determine your whole life, so try to keep it in perspective rather than making it more important or crucial than it is. As you take a test or write an essay, the most effective strategy is to focus on simply doing the best you can. This is the only real control you have, and remember that a test or essay shows how well you can perform on that particular day doing the specific task the test or essay asks for. Do not allow one test to completely threaten your self-confidence by making it an ultimatum, such as "If I don't do well on this essay, I might as well drop out of school." Positive messages help, whereas negative messages make test-taking and essay writing a frustrating and overwhelming activity. Try to remain positive and prepared to do your best.

## ❏ Read the test carefully!

One of the most important test-taking and in-class essay writing skills is reading the test or essay prompt or question carefully. How well you under-stand what needs to be done will affect your performance on tests and essays alike. In an essay situation, your response should directly address the topic specified in the prompt or essay question. It should not, however, begin with statements like the following:

> My essay is about. . . .
>
> I plan to write about. . . .
>
> I've thought about this topic a lot and what I want to say is. . . .

Each of the approaches above addresses the writing assignment rather than the person reading the essay. When you respond with sentences such as "I plan to write about . . ." you are not presenting ideas to a reader, but planning out your approach on paper. While planning is a good technique, your actual plan should be part of your preparation, not part of the final essay. Present your ideas to a reader and remember to use formal essay structure and language, unless you have been asked to do otherwise. If the introduction does not immediately come to you, then write what does, but be sure to come back to the introduction to see that it introduces what your essay discusses and that it grabs the reader's attention. When you write your essay, you may want to skip every other line so that you can insert parts of sentences and make changes without making your paper illegible.

When you read an essay prompt, look for the rhetorical mode it asks you to use (for a review of rhetorical modes consult Chapter 6, pages 139–146). For example, look at the essay question below and find the important words that tell you what techniques to use in your answer.

> Write an essay that defines the major reasons for U.S. involvement in World War II and discuss the different ways Americans perceived U.S. involvement.

What words give you important clues about what the instructor assigning this essay wants from the student writing the essay? Look at it again and identify what each of the words in bold type asks the student to do.

> Write an **essay** that **defines** the **major reasons** for U.S. involvement in World War II and **discuss** the **different ways** Americans perceived U.S. involvement.

The student who writes this essay needs to use essay structure to define major reasons and discuss different perceptions. This prompt specifically asks the student to "define" and to contrast "different ways" of perceiving World War II. When you define, you need to provide clear distinctions and qualities for something—in this case, reasons for involvement in a war. How do you define reasons? You must explain each reason clearly enough so that it is defined or very clear to your reader. When you show differences—in this case, in perceptions—you need to contrast or show the differences between one person's perception and the perceptions of others. Writing an introduction for an essay on this topic, then, involves both of these features and should provide a foundation for the discussion. A sample introduction might be the following:

> During World War II, Americans differed in their perceptions about U.S. involvement in the war, but American involvement was necessary for three important reasons.

Notice the way the student writer in this introduction uses words from the essay prompt to begin the essay and also narrows quickly to a specific focus by using the phrase "three important reasons." Of course, the introduction technique will be different depending on the type of essay, but careful observation of what the prompt actually asks for, and how much of the topic the essay should address, are important considerations.

Once you understand the question, you might want to brainstorm before you actually begin to write. To write about the question above, you might list reasons for U.S. involvement and then list perceptions about American involvement. Once you have created these lists, you could organize the information according to what information is necessary to effectively answer the question on the test. Identify, before you answer, what the question asks, how much information is important enough to include, and in what order these elements should be addressed within the essay. Identifying these features ahead of time and taking quick notes about the order in which to present your ideas will allow you to take control of the situation and produce clearer writing.

## ❏ Survey before starting, and answer what's comfortable first.

When you are taking a non-essay test, you should always survey or look over the entire test before you begin. Surveying will help you understand the contents of the test, and then you can begin at whatever point is most comfortable for you. If you see many questions that you know you are unprepared for, then begin with what you do know. Many times this will help you remember other answers. If you forget items that occur in a series of ideas that are interrelated, try writing what you can remember and coming back to this list after answering easier questions. Whatever you do, do not allow yourself to stare at a blank test or piece of paper. The sooner you begin to write, the sooner you will become comfortable. Surveying, like carefully reading an essay question, is an important test-taking skill. Work to develop this as part of your normal test-taking routine.

## ❏ Use time effectively without clock watching!

One of the biggest mistakes students make while taking tests is rushing through the test to finish early or to finish at the same time as other students. In essays especially, taking the time allotted to you can make a big difference in how clearly written your essay is. If you finish writing your essay early, use the extra time to reread your essay, and revise anything that is not as clearly written or as detailed as it might be. If you usually do not finish writing within the time given, try to organize your time to include time for brainstorming and organizing, time for the introduction, body, and conclusion, and at least five minutes to reread and revise your essay.

Time presents us with an interesting balancing act in class. If you watch the clock too much, it will most likely make you nervous and jittery. If you do not watch the clock at all, you may not finish the essay or test in the allotted time. Two ways to practice balancing time with quality writing or test-taking are to practice at home and to figure out how to spend your time before you get to class. For example, if you know in advance that you will be asked to write an in-class essay, you might give yourself an essay assignment or ask your instructor for a topic and then use a timer at home to practice completing an essay in the time you will be given in class. Another way to do this is to figure out approximately how much time is necessary for you to write each part of the essay; look at the following example schedule:

| | |
|---:|---|
| 5 | minutes for brainstorming or note-taking on separate paper |
| 15 | minutes for the introduction |
| 25 | minutes for the body of the essay |
| 10 | minutes for the conclusion |
| +_5_ | minutes for rereading and rewriting |
| 60 | minutes total |

Experiment with the amount of time you allow yourself for each part, and during a real essay test allow for some flexibility. By deciding how long it will take you to do each part of the essay and practicing this at home, you can dispel your fears about writing a timed essay, as well as discover a timing arrangement that gives you a greater sense of control over your writing process.

## ❏ Establish a routine.

After you have written a few essays in class, you can begin to establish a routine both in and out of class. This is important for test-taking as well. On the day of a test or an in-class essay, try not to change your life drastically.

If you typically wake up at 6:00 A.M., then wake up at 6:00 A.M. as usual. Whatever is usual behavior for you is the best way to get your test day started without creating anxiety. If something does go wrong, try to avoid linking it with the test or essay with statements like, "Well, this day is sure not going well; I'm probably going to fail that test!" Sentiments such as this create more opportunity for failure than success. Try to be positive and keep your day as normal as possible.

Try also to begin an in-class routine for test-taking. Before a test, decide whether last-minute studying or review is helpful or if it creates anxiety or confusion that makes the test more difficult. During a test or in-class essay, use brainstorming, note-taking as ideas occur to you, careful reading of test questions and rereading of answers, and good time management that includes occasional checks on the time, not constant clock-watching. After tests or in-class essays, evaluate your own performance, and if you feel that your actual knowledge or performance is not reflected well on the test or essay, discuss this with your instructor for study and writing advice.

Writing in class provides you with an opportunity to develop your ability to express yourself within time limits and in particular formats. Learning to write well under these constraints can help you perform well in interviews, where you may have only a few minutes to answer an involved question, and can make speaking and writing one of your personal strengths.

## Building Your Skills

### Assignment 1

Carefully read the five essay questions/prompts below. Underline the rhetorical modes and other hints about technique requested by each prompt, and write an opening thesis sentence that addresses the prompt and would begin a good essay answer. The first one is done for you.

*EXAMPLE:*

identifies rhetorical mode

Describe the most effective <u>process</u> students can use <u>for</u>

<u>tells what type of process to discuss</u>          <u>tells how to discuss topic</u>

<u>writing an effective essay</u>. Provide a <u>step-by-step</u>

identifies audience

<u>explanation</u> that addresses <u>fellow students taking their first</u>
<u>college-level writing course.</u>

EXAMPLE THESIS:

> A student taking writing in college for the first time may be afraid of what awaits him or her in that first writing course, but several helpful hints can make writing effective essays much easier and even enjoyable.

1. Describe your most embarrassing moment. How important was this event at the time it happened? Has it changed your life in any significant ways?

   _____

   _____

2. Identify and explain three major causes of alcoholism and three major effects. What role do you think society should play in helping alcoholics?

   _____

   _____

3. Compare the advantages and disadvantages of being either single or married. Use one or two carefully chosen examples to illustrate your point.

   _____

   _____

4. In a three-page essay, describe the process an average student could use to become a better writer. Identify why a student would benefit from this process in your essay.

   _____

   _____

5. Write an essay that argues for or against the use of violent force by police officers. Take a specific point of view and support it using clearly related evidence.

   _____

   _____

Once you have written a thesis statement that addresses each prompt, choose one and time yourself for fifty minutes. During the fifty-minute time limit, begin by brainstorming for possible approaches. Next, begin with your opening line as you wrote it above. Continue writing the introduction, body, and conclusion, and save five minutes at the end of this timed exercise to reread your work and make any necessary changes. Once you have completed this exercise, evaluate how much time each of the essay parts took you and where your essay is its strongest and weakest.

### Assignment 2

Look in a newspaper and find two or three newspaper articles that are at least 200 words each. Read each of these articles carefully, and then write an opening sentence for a summary about each article. Allowing yourself twenty minutes per paragraph, write a one-paragraph summary of each of the newspaper articles including the main point, the most important details, and your own evaluation and analysis. When you finish, evaluate how well each summary employs the summary writing techniques discussed in this chapter.

### Assignment 3

To explore the three levels of understanding described earlier in this chapter (pages 273–275), find a magazine article or use one of the essays in this book. Write a separate paragraph that discusses each of the following:

> Identify the literal content, or what the essay actually says. In your paragraph, summarize the exact content of what you read.
>
> Identify several parts of the article or essay that are not literal or that require thinking to understand. In your paragraph choose one or two points that another reader might miss and explain them carefully for your reader.
>
> Identify the ways this essay or article may influence another person or the effect it has on you.

When you have written all three paragraphs, decide which was the most difficult to write and why. Then write a summary of essay length that discusses this article or essay and includes parts of each of these paragraphs. Use ideas from the following section about revising a student essay to revise your summary.

## READING A STUDENT ESSAY

### Peer Review Strategy: Revising a Summary

Summaries condense information and evaluate the validity or insightfulness of a writer's comments in an essay or longer work. A summary usually includes the main idea, the most important supporting details or examples, and an evaluation of the writer's work by the summary writer. When you revise a summary, these are important features to identify and evaluate. However, you should also include several other features in your revision process:

- ✔ Are the essay title and author introduced in the first paragraph? Does the thesis make clear to your reader that you are summarizing?
- ✔ When you quote do you use quotation marks (" ")? When you are not quoting, are you writing completely in your own words?
- ✔ Do you discuss the author's ideas using third-person references such as "the author believes," "he asserts," "she contradicts the popular view," and "in the author's view"?
- ✔ Are you evaluating the author's point rather than simply repeating it?
- ✔ Does your summary include some important supporting details or examples so that you provide your reader with enough detail?
- ✔ Does your essay have conventional essay structure including an introduction, body, conclusion, and transitions?

A well-written summary is easy to read and allows the reader to understand the main points in an essay without ever reading it. Like other essays, it should flow from point to point smoothly and logically. Read the student essay that follows and make notes as you read about which of the above points Dale Standfill uses in his essay. For example, you might underline when he refers to the author, when he uses quotation marks, and so on. If you have not yet read Catton's original essay (pages 269–273), you might want to read it before or after reading this summary. When you are finished, evaluate how well Standfill represents Catton's main points and evaluates them.

---

### A Summary of Catton's "Grant and Lee"

#### by Dale Standfill

Bruce Catton writes his essay "Grant and Lee: A Study in Contrasts" discussing mostly the contrasts between two Civil War generals, Ulysses S. Grant and Robert E. Lee. The issue that Catton addresses first is the contrasts between the places where the two men were raised. Lee was southern born and came from a [1] near royal society of "family, culture, and tradition." The south had an aristocratic air, complete with shades of old-world chivalry. Lee embodied these elements to such an extent that Catton believed Lee was the very heart of the Confederacy. Unfortunately, Lee also represented the aristocratic south and its inability to change. Catton points out that the south had no interest in the progress and competition that the north valued. Its only goal was to maintain the status quo under which a system of rights for some and few or no rights for others had thrived and provided marked benefits for those in power.

Grant, on the other hand, was "everything that Lee was not." Catton describes him as coming from a stock of men who believed in themselves and owed their fortunes not to their families, but to themselves. This was the ideal of the industrial north and the frontier west. Catton, in his comparison, points out that Grant, much like Lee, embodied the ideals of the land from which he came. He was fiercely nationalistic and believed the only way to prosperity was unification of the nation, to grow and accomplish everyone's success. Grant was a believer in a harsh system of competitive democracy.                                    1
                                                                 2

Catton does acknowledge the fact that Grant and Lee also shared qualities. As a general should, both of these men showed great abilities as leaders and an unwavering commitment to never giving up. This, of course, would allow both men to inspire their men in the face of sure defeat.                                         3

Catton's study is accurate and well thought out. He is able to describe two completely different men and yet still find their similarities. However, in the war between the north and the south, more than just two men were the embodiment of their respective lands. Catton goes too far when he says that Lee "was the       4

Confederation," when in reality the south held a diversity of cultures with the dominant one fighting against its extinction by the north. Although this essay is interesting to read, Catton invests too much in these generals. Grant and Lee were the focal point of two societies that contrasted greatly. So, in fact, the true importance is the society that produced these ideals, not the men who lived by them.

## Building Your Skills

1. What points from Catton's essay does Standfill choose to include? What does he omit? Are there any omitted ideas you think should have been included?

_____

_____

_____

_____

_____

_____

_____

_____

_____

2. How does Standfill evaluate this essay? Do you agree or disagree with his evaluation? Why?

_____

_____

_____

_____

_____

_____

_____

_____

_____

3. How well does Standfill's summary follow the summary structure and check-
   points discussed in this chapter?

_____

_____

_____

_____

_____

_____

_____

_____

_____

4. As if you were discussing Dale's paper with him, list three features of his essay
   that work very well or that really appeal to you as a reader. Then, recommend
   three changes he could make to improve his essay.

Describe three features that are effective for you as a reader:

a. _____

b. _____

c. _____

Describe three improvements or changes Dale could make to create a more effective, interesting, or informative essay:

a. _____

b. _____

c. _____

# USING GRAMMAR: RECOGNIZING GRAMMATICAL CLUES TO MEANING

One of the most important connections you can make, as a reader and writer, is the connection between what a writer puts on the page and what the reader perceives. Because this connection often involves grammatical concepts like the placement of words, the use of phrases, and the use of punctuation marks, grammar in reading determines to some extent our understanding and ease in reading a written work.

### Equal and Subordinate Relationships

Grammar helps to set up our expectations in what we read. It tells us when to expect equal relationships and when to expect subordinate relationships. It tells us when to expect a list or clarification of a point. Because grammar is so embedded in our reading and writing and is intuitive or subconscious, often we fail to recognize how important it is to both our writing and our reading. Grammatical use of semicolons, commas, conjunctions, conjunctive adverbs, and other forms by an author helps us to understand ideas, even if we do not know what a conjunctive adverb is. You might wonder, "How is that possible?" But after years of reading, most people have already become accustomed to using and easily recognizing words and punctuation marks that express relationships between ideas. Let's look at a few examples so that you can test your own knowledge.

*EXAMPLE:*

> We came home. We left again.
> We came home; however, we left again.
> We came home, but finally, we left again.
> We came home, and then we left again.
> We came home; we left again.

Do each of the combinations above haves the same meaning? What differences in meaning does each have? When we add words or phrases—"however," "finally," "and then"—we change the meaning even if just a little. We can make the same types of changes through punctuation marks, although the results tend to be less noticeable. Learning to pay attention to these seemingly minor details and reading for subtleties in meaning can help you to become a more efficient and better reader; at the same time, noticing these qualities as a reader also helps you begin to use phrases and punctuation more carefully and more meaningfully in your own writing.

Communicating ideas often requires us to establish priorities—to show the importance of one event or idea over another or to show that two events or ideas are equally important. We can show that one idea is subordinate to another by using subordinating conjunctions such as *because, after, even though, although* (see the Appendix for a more comprehensive list). For example, in the sentence "Because I was late, I missed the first question of the test" we know as readers why the person missed the first question on the test, but the sentence also tells us that the question was important—more important than the reason. If we change this sentence to "I was late; I missed the first question on the test," we no longer have the subordinating word *because* and each part of the sentence gets equal attention. Another way that information can play a subordinate role in a sentence is when it is embedded within the sentence. Instead of having two equally important statements, sometimes we compress one of the statements and place it within the other sentence.

If we use two sentences, we can emphasize two points equally:

> Mary is a doctor. She is the first woman in her family to finish college.

If we embed or move the information from one sentence into the other, we can make some information the focus while other information becomes secondary or less important:

Mary, a doctor, is the first woman in her family to finish college.
Mary, the first woman in her family to finish college, is a doctor.

Notice that the emphasis in these two sentences is different. In one sentence, we focus on Mary finishing college; in the other, we focus on Mary being a doctor. Although these may seem like minor differences, you understand this type of information and make judgments based on these kinds of impressions all the time. Has anyone ever said something to you that sounded very pleasant on the surface but seemed to carry another meaning under the surface? The judgment that the person was less than sincere was probably based on *how* that person made the statement, not on what he or she actually said.

Just as subordinate relationships can be expressed through subordinating conjunctions, relationships of equal importance can be communicated through coordinating conjunctions, conjunctive adverbs, and punctuation marks like the semicolon. When we use coordinating conjunctions (*and, but, or,* and so on), we coordinate or bring together two ideas of equal significance. This makes the reader focus on each idea rather than drawing his or her attention to one idea and then showing related but less important ideas. Conjunctive adverbs work in a similar way, but depending on the word you choose, different messages may be communicated. Let's look at a few examples.

We went to the movies; we had a great time.

If we use a semicolon to bring two independent clauses together, we really do not change the meaning a lot, but we do bring the two ideas together as equal units. Notice that the changes in meaning occur when we use other words such as coordinating conjunctions.

We went to the movies, **and** we had a great time.
We went to the movies, **but** we had a great time.

The two examples above both use coordinating conjunctions. Even though the meaning is different in each, the two independent clauses are equal with respect to their importance. The fact that the two went to the movies seems to be as important as the two having a great time. In the next two examples, look at the way the conjunctive adverbs can change the meaning of the whole sentence.

We went to the movies; **therefore**, we had a great time.
We went to the movies; **furthermore**, we had a great time.

In the first example, it seems as though the two are having a great time because of the movies, and in the last example, the couple has gone to the movies and, in addition, is having a great time. Although these examples are made up and presented here to make a point, as you can see, the connecting words used in each case influence the meaning the reader gets from the sentence, the impression the reader gets about the subjects of the sentence, and the overall ability of the reader to understand the message.

### Logic Through Grammar

Grammar also influences the presentation of logical ideas through wording, the way we establish connections between ideas, and the way we connect sentences. When we use words that show cause or effect, time relationships, sequence, priority, dependence, or other important relationships between ideas, we must use them grammatically and logically. Read the following example:

> When buying a car requires money and patience; the salesperson was really nice to me, but wanted money all at once.

How well do you understand the connections between the ideas in this sentence? What words keep you from clearly understanding the sentence? Try to rewrite it in a way that makes sense.

_____

_____

The main problem in this sentence comes from the lack of clear wording to establish a logical connection between each of the ideas. Some possible ways to reword this sentence are as follows:

> Buying a car requires money and patience; salespeople want money, no matter how nicely they may behave.
> To buy a car, I needed money and patience; the salesperson was really nice to me, but mostly he wanted my money.
> What no one tells the person who is going out to buy a car is how much money and patience this purchase requires; salespeople seem nice, but they are actually just trying to make a sale.

Each of these sentences is very different from the original because a clear focus has been established and is now logically presented. When you tried to revise the sentence, did you notice that you had to establish a point or focus before you could rewrite the sentence effectively?

Another way logic is established in writing is through phrases that have two parts—for example, *neither/nor, either/or, if/then,* and so on. These two-part phrases may occur within one sentence or may present relationships established through several sentences. When we use these in writing, we set up expectations for our reader, and if we do not follow through or demonstrate clearly the relationship between these logical parts, we may frustrate our readers or lose them altogether. In the following examples, look at the way each connects ideas using these phrases.

> **Neither** the boy **nor** his mother was happy about the broken window.
> **Either** he must fix the window, **or** he must pay to have it fixed.
> **If** you break a window, **then** it is your responsibility to fix it.

In each sentence the phrase clearly relates pieces of information to form a logical unit. Look at the next few examples, and try to detect which ones are logical or illogical.

> Neither the teacher nor the test was easy to take.
> Either taking the bus or becoming serious about the environment is important to preserving our ecological balance.
> If a student wants to learn about grammar, then he or she must.

In each of the sentences above, the logic or sense of the sentence seems to be unclear or stated poorly. As a reader, do you feel perfectly satisfied with these statements? Do they clearly communicate an idea in the same way that the three examples before them did?

As readers we expect writers to connect ideas in a logical way. When they do not, we respect writers less and judge what they write more harshly. As a writer, strive to make logical connections for your reader, and as a reader, look for phrases that lead to logical connections. When you study textbooks for a variety of classes, you will notice that writers often begin major points with *if/then* phrases or other clues like "the most important reason is. . . ." By paying attention to these grammatical clues, you can read more efficiently and make better sense of what you read.

You also receive the added benefit of learning to write better through seeing the many effective techniques other writers use and by learning to avoid techniques you observe that are less than effective. As you annotate the margins, mark the connective phrases so that when you scan a book or essay again, you can easily pick out the important points and relationships.

As a reader, you must judge a writer's credibility, or whether that person is believable or not, based on what and how he or she writes. Likewise, your readers judge what you write using the same criteria. If you find many grammatical or logical problems in something you read, this is a clue that what is written may not be credible, unless the writing represents a dialect of English or is purposely exaggerating a point using faulty logic or grammar. As a reader, notice these qualities, and as a writer, know that others who are reading what you have written build expectations and draw conclusions based not only on what you say but on how you say it.

## Building Your Skills

### Assignment 1

In the sentences below, circle the grammatical elements that help to provide the meaning for each sentence. Then, as the example below demonstrates, change the meaning by omitting the word or punctuation you have circled and rewriting the sentence using a new method for connecting the ideas. The first one has been done for you.

*EXAMPLE:*

(First) students must give up any hope of free time; (second,) they must be prepared to pay for tuition; (third,) they must learn to enjoy meeting constant demands teachers make.

*CHANGED SENTENCE EXAMPLE:*

(When) beginning school, students (must give) up any hope of free time, (be prepared) to pay for tuition, and (learn) to enjoy meeting the constant demands teachers make.

1. The most challenging part of beginning a new job is learning the new people, the new routines, and the new rules; after a few months on the job, new employees become seasoned professionals.

_____

_____

2. Even though we prepared for our summer vacation, the whole vacation seemed to be a disaster; anything that could go wrong, did.

_____

_____

3. Besides buying a car, we sold our house and built a new one after winning the lottery.

_____

_____

4. In addition to watching television, we spend our evenings meeting the demands of family life: cooking, cleaning, preparing for the next day, and paying attention to our children.

_____

_____

5. Finally, despite years of going back and forth, they broke off the relationship and decided to see other people.

_____

_____

## Assignment 2

In one of your recent papers, highlight or circle all of the dependent words, conjunctive adverbs, coordinating conjunctions, and phrases like *neither/nor* and *either/or* (find at least fifteen). Using the lists in the Appendix, change each of the connecting words or phrases you use to something else, and make adjustments throughout the paragraphs to accommodate the new relationships and connections these changes create. Make sure that the changes you make are grammatical and that they make sense within the paragraph. Then, working with a partner, look at both the original paragraph and the rewritten version. Identify the changes in meaning in your paragraphs. Evaluate how much changing just a few words changed the overall meaning of your paragraph.

### Assignment 3

Using one of your own textbooks or copies of a textbook chapter from your library or from a friend, practice reading while annotating or making notes in the margin. Develop a system for identifying the major points, highlighting any connected ideas, and then use this as you read the chapter. When you have finished, look at the grammatical clues to meaning in at least five of the places you have marked as important. As a final step, write a paragraph that presents the most important ideas in this chapter. Evaluate how well this process has helped you to understand the chapter. Does it improve your ability to read the chapter actively rather than simply reading the words? Does it help you discover the major ideas more easily? What role does grammar play in your ability to use these skills?

## SEEING THE CONNECTIONS: APPLYING YOUR SKILLS

### Assignment 1

Read Paul Roberts's essay "Speech Communities" (pages 36–37) and Alleen Pace Nilsen's "Sexism in English: A 1990s Update" (pages 185–200). As you read, make notes about the main points, supporting details, and reactions you have as you read. Divide a piece of paper into two columns; on one side, list the points Roberts makes about the way we use language; on the other, list some of Nilsen's points. How are they similar or different in their views about the ways in which people use language?

Write a summary that compares Roberts's and Nilsen's views about language. Remember to summarize their most important points about this topic, and then include one or two important supporting details. Also remember to evaluate their views.

When you finish a first draft, consult the checklist on page 291 and evaluate how well your summary does each of the suggested tasks. Rewrite your summary so that it follows the guidelines given in this chapter.

### Assignment 2

Choose any essay in this book and read it carefully. First look for points that require analysis and think about their meaning. Second, mark words used figuratively or connotatively. Third, write three questions that would help someone else understand the meaning of this essay if they answered them.

When you have finished, reread the essay, but this time look for the most effective and the most ineffective parts of the essay. As you read, look for structure, grammar, creativity—whatever works or does not work for you as a reader.

Write an essay that describes what makes this essay either a great essay or a boring or poor essay. Argue your view so that someone reading your essay will see why you feel this way. In addition, point out specific qualities and use quoted material from the essay to support your view about the essay.

When you finish a first draft, revise your essay by adding five coordinating conjunctions, five subordinating conjunctions, and five conjunctive adverbs in combination with five new semicolons, five new commas, and at least one *neither/nor, either/or,* or *if/then* phrase.

### Assignment 3

Choose a chapter in a textbook and read it carefully, annotating it throughout. Design a test for this chapter that uses multiple choice questions, a set of fill-in questions, and a short essay question. When you finish, write an essay that describes for another student the process of reading a textbook chapter effectively and then preparing to take a test on it. Use the test you designed as an example throughout your essay. When you finish, put the test and essay away for two days. After two days, take your own test without looking back at the chapter, and then revise your essay adding any details you think you may have left out and making your meaning clearer wherever possible.

## Chapter 10

# Writing for College
# and Beyond

In this chapter you will learn

☆  to use sources to support your ideas and to read essays that use sources;
☆  to use different types of sources and to identify those that are credible;
☆  to paraphrase, quote, and avoid plagiarism;
☆  to write college admission essays, resumés, and cover letters;
☆  to revise a research-based essay;
☆  to avoid common grammatical errors.

Take a moment to answer the following questions:

1. How well do you know your school library?

_____

_____

_____

2. What kinds of research have you done in the past?

_____

_____

_____

3. What experiences have you had writing resumés, cover letters, or college admission essays? How important do you think these skills are for you?

_____

_____

_____

4. What do you think is the purpose of learning to find and use research materials? How might these skills be useful for you?

_____

_____

_____

# WRITING FOR COLLEGE: SUPPORTING YOUR IDEAS WITH RESEARCH

One of the most significant changes in a student's writing takes place through the requirement of research. Although most students are reluctant to begin researching, either because of their inexperience or because they are overwhelmed by the sight of so many books, magazines, and computer screens, once students have used research materials several times, they wonder how they ever lived without them. Many librarians would tell you that the most important place to know on a college campus is not the student center but the library. Within the library lies help for any assignment, information on an amazing number of topics, and peace of mind. When you begin to argue your ideas or to try to persuade others, you soon find out that your words or your friends' or parents' words are not enough to convince someone listening that your view is valid. What often will make the difference is evidence. Where do you find evidence? The library is a major source, although it is not the only resource. If you attend a college that has a very limited library, you may have to become very creative in your search for resources—but resources are available anywhere if you are willing to work to find them. Let's look at some of the varieties of resources available for student use at most schools. If you do not have access to one or two of these, though, do not despair. Creative thinking and consulting with your instructor and with library staff will help you find the resources available to you.

As you progress in developing your writing, you will find that simply clarifying your opinion is not enough; you must also support it. Many types of evidence are available to help you do this. Research is a great way to find persuasive and enlightening evidence and examples. But before you research, you need to remember a few rules that should govern your research process:

> Not everything that is published is accurate, worthy of your respect, or credible. Look for sources that are believable, scholarly, and preferably written by an unbiased or at least fairly objective author. If your source is very one-sided, find other sources to check its credibility.
>
> Find out who published the source and how respected the author, company, magazine, or newspaper you are using is.
>
> Try to get a diversity of sources. Do not use only books or only interviews; whenever possible, use different types of sources to provide a more convincing variety of evidence.
>
> Browsing can be a good way to find a topic, but it can be overwhelming and frustrating. When possible, begin research with a fairly clear topic in mind. If you can, begin research with a thesis statement in mind. You may want to change your topic or thesis later, but begin with some idea of what you would like to find.

### Types of Sources

Let's discuss some of the resources that may be available at the college or school you are attending. Find out from a reference librarian, your instructor, friends, or through your own investigation, which of these resources are available in your library or on your campus. You might also consult public libraries or other local school libraries that allow off-campus students to use their facilities.

#### Books

Although books can be a wonderful resource, for most short student papers they are overwhelming because of the amount of information they contain. You may be able to find some specific information in books, but see what is available in other sources as well.

#### Encyclopedias and Dictionaries

These resources are great for getting started or beginning your research, but many college-level instructors do not accept encyclopedia sources because they are usually very condensed and less than scholarly. If you use an encyclopedia, your audience may wonder why you did not seek out a more learned source, like a professional in the appropriate field of study. For example, if you are writing about affirmative action, the encyclopedia and dictionary will give you a definition of the term, but you need to seek out a more scholarly, in-depth discussion of the issue than the summary contained in an encyclopedia.

### Periodicals (Magazines or Journals)

Magazines, periodicals, and journals are names for essentially the same type of resource. Each is published on a set schedule (weekly, monthly, quarterly) and is usually focused on a subject or area of interest. Journals tend to be more scholarly and often contain articles about particular academic areas of study written by authorities in that field. Magazines and periodicals can be very helpful for researching current topics because they are published on a much shorter time schedule than a book would be and usually cover popular topics. To look for a subject published in magazines you can use the *Readers' Guide to Periodical Literature* or a magazine database (described below). These usually index topics and then list magazine articles that deal with that particular topic.

### Research Databases

Databases usually have thousands of sources on one computer. Often databases use CD-ROM disks that look just like CDs you might play in your stereo. These small disks hold an incredible amount of information. Most research databases have a specific area of focus, but some include a great variety of topics and specify only that the source is a magazine article or a newspaper article. When you use a database, type in a topic and the computer screen will show you all of the entries about that topic indexed in the database. For a topic like AIDS research or the death penalty, the computer might list 250 sources. Not all of them will work for a specific essay that you are writing, though. When you have many sources available, you must be selective and look for a good source, not just any source. In addition to telling you what magazines or newspapers to look in to find articles on a particular topic, some databases now print copies of articles with the push of a button. This is obviously a very convenient and modern way to research.

### On-Line Sources

Perhaps the newest research tool available to many people in their own homes is the Internet. By using a search resource such as yahoo.com or other available search engines, Internet users can find screens full of information. The biggest current question about this resource is how valuable much of this information is. As a new student of research, do not assume that the information on the Internet is either accurate or worthwhile. Much of what is available is compiled and presented by students or private individuals who do not have any special credentials or authority in the field of information they are presenting. Although many interesting ideas are presented in sites throughout the Internet, use this resource with great caution, and check your sources for bias or inaccuracy.

### Interviews

Interviews with individuals who are authorities in a particular field, or who have special knowledge about an event or have a particular perspective, can provide the researcher with valuable information and give the writer a compelling view to present to persuade readers. Consider the recent case of a student who was writing a paper about a water proposal that a private company had presented to an Indian reservation's tribal council. This student had to use interviews because the only people who actually knew about this issue were the residents of the reservation and the company making the proposal. Interviews can produce information that is unavailable in any other form, so be careful not to overlook this resource.

### Videos

Video collections in libraries are growing, and offerings at video stores now include a variety of educational videos. Though this is not the perfect resource for many essays, sometimes educational videos can provide long-term studies that contain very useful evidence. Looking for educational videos to increase your own knowledge about a historical or scientific concept can be a good way to start the research process.

### Pamphlets

Pamphlets come in three varieties: (1) pamphlets published by private companies or individuals; (2) pamphlets published by government agencies; and (3) pamphlet booklets published by educational companies on particular topics. Though each of these types of pamphlets can be valuable, the first type, published by private companies or individuals, must be examined carefully for accuracy or bias. If a company publishes a pamphlet presenting a product it makes money on or a product it wants outlawed, sometimes its presentation of the "evidence" can be very biased or one-sided. It may ignore evidence contrary to its view. Government publications, on the other hand, tend to include a variety of statistics and usually are reliable, unless they are produced by campaign staff members during an election year. The third variety, published by educational companies, can be very helpful in the research process. Two good examples of these pamphlets, sometimes published in paperback and sometimes in hardback, are *Taking*

*Sides* and *Opposing Viewpoints*. Each of these resources takes many different views on a variety of controversial issues. Simply by the way they are organized, they can assist a student who is trying to narrow a topic. Furthermore, they provide a variety of opinions, discussions, and evidence. They are an especially good source for learning argument techniques and different views of controversial issues.

### Surveys

Another source that can be useful when there are not many sources available on a topic is a student-conducted survey. This is a good resource, though, only if it is carefully conducted and if it produces evidence that is worthwhile to the writer and the reader. If you were writing an essay about a change that you felt should be made on campus or in your community, a survey of your fellow students or residents could produce persuasive evidence. If you simply ask people's opinions, though, this information may not be very valuable. Asking how others will be affected by a change, how they are impacted by a particular situation, how they would like to see a conflict resolved, and other such survey questions will produce more specific and thus more useful results. Write your questions for a survey very carefully and without your own bias. As you distribute a written survey or ask survey questions, be sure not to influence the results or try to force people into the response you want to hear.

### Using Sources in Your Writing

Just finding sources will not actually improve your writing; how carefully you read sources, evaluate them, and present them to your reader is the key to improving your essays with research. In presenting research, you need to be aware of the methods for quoting and paraphrasing other writers' and speakers' work appropriately. Although as you continue your education you will be taught different methods for giving credit to other writers and speakers, knowing how to quote and paraphrase is a good skill to acquire now.

Most writers work hard to produce the essays and informative articles we read, and are paid for what they write. When you use other people's writing, research, or ideas, you must always give them credit, even if you are using ideas in an original way. When we use other writers' ideas, we must use one of two techniques. The first way to use an idea from something you read is to quote it exactly as the writer wrote it. When we **quote** directly from someone else's writing, we use the exact words that that person used, and we give the person credit by placing necessary information in parentheses after the quote or by using a footnote, depending on the style of paper and the assignment. We never simply use someone else's words without quotation marks or without noting who wrote the quote originally. Using another writer's words or ideas without giving him or her credit is a type of cheating called **plagiarism.** For that matter, using most of another writer's words, but keeping the same structure and simply changing a few words or phrases, is also a form of plagiarism. When you want to use an idea that another writer has researched or thought of, you can do this without quoting if you paraphrase the writer's ideas. To **paraphrase** you must change the idea completely into your own words and you must still give the original writer credit. Though instructors deal with this serious problem differently, many schools take it so seriously that a student can be asked to leave the school or can receive an F in a class simply for one plagiarized sentence. You may think, "Then why should I use sources at all?" However, the way to avoid this is to use the appropriate style assigned by your instructor to cite or provide information to show where you found the information you discuss in your summary or essay. The following examples show an exact quote, a paraphrased sentence, and some examples of plagiarism.

*EXACT QUOTE EXAMPLE:*

> "So Grant and Lee were in complete contrast, representing two diametrically opposed elements in American life" (Catton 350).

*PARAPHRASED EXAMPLE:*

> According to the noted historian and writer Bruce Catton, Grant and Lee symbolized the two sides of America that led to the Civil War. Each man stood for a philosophy that was exactly the opposite of the other's (Catton 350).

*PLAGIARISM EXAMPLES:*

**Problem #1—Lack of quotation marks**
> So Grant and Lee were in complete contrast, representing two diametrically opposed elements in American life (Catton 350).

**Problem #2—Words moved, but idea and sentence structure is essentially the same**
> Grant and Lee, by their contrast, represented the opposed elements in American life (Catton 350).

**Problem #3—Nothing to indicate source for this quote**
> "So Grant and Lee were in complete contrast, representing two diametrically opposed elements in American life."

**Problem #4—Nothing to indicate source for paraphrased material**

According to the noted historian and writer Bruce Catton, Grant and Lee symbolized the two sides of American that led to the Civil War. Each man stood for a philosophy that was exactly the opposite of the other's.

Information taken from other sources must either be quoted exactly or the words must be completely changed and the original writer must be given credit in parentheses. This style, called MLA Style (for Modern Language Association) includes the author's last name and the page number in parentheses and then provides a Works Cited page at the very end of the essay to give more information about where to find the sources used in the essay. (For an example of MLA style, look at the student essay in this chapter.) In the examples of plagiarism above, notice that in each case information either is not quoted exactly, is quoted without quotation marks or without citation of an author, or is paraphrased and has no reference back to the original source. Respecting other authors is an important skill, but it is also important for building your integrity as a writer. Be sure to quote exactly or paraphrase completely, as well as giving information about your source, as you practice the types of assignments that are discussed below.

# READING AN ESSAY

## Strategy for Reading: Reading Essays with References

Writers use research to support their ideas, to add interest, to show experience or authority, and sometimes because they want to respond to a statement or idea that someone else has written or said. Essays that use references to other writers' works are really not that different from other essays, but they may look very different. Take a look at the Rachel Jones essay that follows (page 313) and then look at the student essay on page 325. Notice that Jones refers to another writer in her first paragraph, but that her essay looks very much like any other essay. Notice further that the student essay by Melanie Broaddus includes references that show where she obtained her information, as well as a final page that gives detailed information about where to find these sources. Although her essay may look a bit different on the surface, it has an introduction, a body, and a conclusion; it is like any other essay except that it includes references so that her reader can find the original information she used to write it. As you read essays with research, be sure that you are reading for audience and purpose as you would any other essay. Use the research for information and to evaluate credibility, but do not get lost in the references in parentheses or become overwhelmed by the information. As we discussed in Chapter 8, gauging your reading speed is important. When you read essays with references, recognize that these kinds of essays take time and concentration that others may not require. The following is a list of reading suggestions:

| **Do** | **Don't** |
|---|---|
| read as you would any other essay. | forget to look for the main point and supporting details. |
| evaluate the credibility of sources. | let the references overwhelm you. |
| look for transitions and expect the writer to explain the connection between research and the point. | forget that you may need to concentrate more and take notes. |

As you read the essay by Rachel Jones that follows, focus on the way she argues her point. Try also to identify her major point and the ways she supports it. Then evaluate what her use of the reference in the first paragraph adds to or takes away from her essay. In what situations would you want to refer to something you have read in an essay?

---

## BEFORE YOU READ

1. What is Black English? Do you speak it? Have you heard it before?
2. Do people ever judge others based on the way they speak? Have you ever laughed at, harassed, or made false judgments about someone else based on how they spoke? Think of examples to support your answer.

---

# What's Wrong with Black English?[*]

## by Rachel Jones

William Labov, a noted linguist, once said about the
use of black English, "It is the goal of most black Americans to acquire full control of the standard language without giving up their own culture." He also suggested that
there are certain advantages to having two ways to express
one's feelings. I wonder if the good doctor might also consider the goals of those black Americans who have full control of standard English but who are every now and then
troubled by that colorful, grammar-to-the-winds patois that
is black English. Case in point—me.

I'm a 21-year old black born to a family that would
probably be considered lower middle class—which in my
mind is a polite way of describing a condition only slightly
better than poverty. Let's just say we rarely if ever did the
winter-vacation thing in the Caribbean. I've often had to
defend my humble beginnings to a most unlikely group of
people for an even less likely reason. Because of the way I
talk, some of my black peers look at me sideways and ask,
"Why do you talk like you're white?"

The first time it happened to me, I was nine years
old. Cornered in the school bathroom by the class bully
and her sidekick, I was offered the opportunity to swallow
a few of my teeth unless I satisfactorily explained why I
always got good grades, why I talked "proper" or "white."
I had no ready answer for her, save the fact that my
mother had from the time I was old enough to talk
stressed the importance of reading and learning, or that
L. Frank Baum and Ray Bradbury were my closest com-
panions. I read all my older brothers' and sisters' literature textbooks more faithfully than they did, and even

[*]*Source:* Jones, Rachel L. "What's Wrong with Black English?" Originally published in *Newsweek* 12/27/82. Copyright © 1982 by Rachel L. Jones. Reprinted by
permission of the author.

lightweights like the Bobbsey Twins and Trixie Belden were allowed into my bookish inner circle. I don't remember exactly what I told those girls, but I somehow talked my way out of a beating.

*"White pipes."* I was reminded once again of my "white pipes" problem while apartment hunting in Evanston, Illinois, last winter. I doggedly made out lists of available places and called all around. I would immediately be invited over—and immediately turned down. The thinly concealed looks of shock when the front door opened clued me in, along with the flustered instances of "just got off the phone with the girl who was ahead of you and she wants the rooms." When I finally found a place to live, my roommate stirred up old memories when she remarked a few months later, "You know, I was surprised when I first saw you. You sounded white over the phone." Tell me another one, sister.    4

I should've asked her a question I've wanted an answer to for years: How does one "talk white"? The silly side of me pictures a rabid white foam spewing forth when I speak. I don't use Valley Girl jargon, so that's not what's meant in my case. Actually, I've pretty much deduced what people mean when they say that to me, and the implications are really frightening.    5

It means that I'm articulate and well versed. It means that I can talk as freely about John Steinbeck as I can about Rick James. It means that "ain't" and "he be" are not staples of my vocabulary and are only used around family and friends. (It is almost Jekyll and Hyde-ish the way I can slip out of academic abstractions into a long, lean, double-negative-filled dialogue, but I've come to terms with that aspect of my personality.) As a child, I found it hard to believe that's what people meant by "talking proper"; that would've meant that good grades and standard English were equated with white skin, and that went against everything I'd ever been taught. Running into the same type of mentality as an adult has confirmed the depressing reality that for many blacks, standard English is not only unfamiliar, it is socially unacceptable.    6

James Baldwin once defended black English by saying it had added "vitality to the language," and even went so far as to label it a language in its own right, saying, "Language [i.e., black English] is a political instrument" and a "vivid and crucial key to identity." But did Malcolm X urge blacks to take power in this country "any way y'all can"? Did Martin Luther King, Jr., say to blacks, "I has been to the mountaintop, and I done seed the Promised Land"? Toni Morrison, Alice Walker, and James Baldwin did not achieve their eloquence, grace, and stature by using only black English in their writing. Andrew Young, Tom Bradley, and Barbara Jordan did not acquire political power by saying, "Y'all crazy if you ain't gon vote for me." They all have full command of standard English, and I don't think that knowledge takes away from their blackness or commitment to black people. 7

*Soulful.* I know from experience that it's important for black people, stripped of culture and heritage, to have something they can point to and say, "This is ours, *we* can comprehend it, *we* alone can speak it with a soulful flourish." I'd be lying if I said that the rhythms of my people caught up in "some serious rap" don't sound natural and right to me sometimes. But how heartwarming is it for those same brothers when they hit the pavement searching for employment? Studies have proven that the use of ethnic dialects decreases power in the marketplace. "I be" is acceptable on the corner but not with the boss. 8

Am I letting capitalistic, European-oriented thinking fog the issue? Am I selling out blacks to an ideal of assimilating, being as much like white as possible? I have not formed a personal political ideology, but I do know this: It hurts me to hear black children use black English, knowing that they will be at yet another disadvantage in an educational system already full of stumbling blocks. It hurts me to sit in lecture halls and hear fellow black students complain that the professor "be tripping dem out using big words dey can't understand." And what hurts most is to be stripped of my own blackness simply because I know my way around the English language. 9

## Building Your Skills

### Focus on Words

Look up the following words or parts of phrases in a dictionary. Consult the preceding essay and identify the meaning that best fits the way the author uses the word in this essay. Each word or phrase is followed by the number of the paragraph in which it appears.

| | |
|---|---|
| linguist (1) | articulate (6) |
| patois (1) | well versed (6) |
| peers (2) | double negative (6) |
| bookish (3) | eloquence (7) |
| doggedly (4) | flourish (8) |
| concealed (4) | capitalistic (9) |
| flustered (4) | assimilating (9) |
| jargon (5) | political ideology (9) |
| deduced (5) | |

### Focus on the Message

1. Which dialects of English can Jones use effectively? What problems has speaking and writing different dialects caused her?
2. How does Jones's mentioning William Labov, whom she describes as "a noted linguist" (para. 1), affect you as a reader? How is this technique effective or ineffective?
3. Why do you think Jones mentions Martin Luther King, Malcolm X, and other African-American writers and public figures? If you read the Malcolm X essay in Chapter 6 (pages 149–151), identify and explain what reactions you think he might have to Jones's reference to him and his use of language.
4. When people say that Jones "talks white," what are they implying about her? What are they saying about Black English? Do you think this is a fair assessment of either her or the dialect?
5. Compare Jones's view of Black English and Standard English with Paul Roberts's view as he presents it in his essay "Speech Communities" in Chapter 2 (pages 36–37). Are their views of Standard English and dialects the same? In what ways do they agree or disagree?

# TECHNIQUES FOR WRITING: PRACTICAL WRITING— COLLEGE ADMISSION ESSAYS, RESUMÉS, AND COVER LETTERS

Writing instruction prepares students for college, but it also prepares them for many job-related and goal-oriented writing tasks. Two such tasks are the resumé and the college admission essay. Whether you plan to transfer to a four-year school or you want to enter or advance in the job market, the skills you learn in your writing classes will be the same skills that help you gain admission to the school of your choice or an interview for a job for which you have applied. The guidelines in this section are designed to give you some helpful hints for writing these incredibly personal and important types of writing, but do not use them without thinking about your audience or your purpose. Like any other type of writing, these are still the two determining factors in how to write well.

### College Admission Essays

Most college application forms that require essays ask for something similar to one of these three sample essay prompts.

> Describe in 500 words or less the most significant achievement in your life to date.
>
> Describe in 500 words or less an important challenge that you have faced.
>
> In an essay of no more than 1,000 words, describe your most important goals and accomplishments to date.

In each of these writing assignments, notice that the topic is very focused, that the word limit is clearly given to you, and that the audience for the essay is not named. How difficult is it for you to write to someone you have never met and with whom you may have little or nothing in common? How then can you assess your audience? Who do you think will be reading all of the essays of all the students who applied to the school where you are applying? Most of the time, a committee of teachers and administrative evaluators reads the essays that come to a campus, and they score them based on some criteria the committee has decided on beforehand. But knowing this still does not help your approach very much. Put yourself in the place of the reader. How many essays do you think you might have to read? Perhaps two hundred, five hundred, maybe even five thousand! If you had to read this many essays, what would you look for? Would you want the essay to get to the point? Maybe you would welcome an essay that took an unusual approach or an essay that made you laugh or cry. Although you cannot know exactly who will read your essay, you can write your essay using two guidelines. First, make the essay stand apart from the rest by being original in your approach. Second, rewrite your essay several times and let other people read it so that it makes sense, is easy to read, and is free from grammatical errors. If you had to read a thousand essays, you might really resent an essay you had to work hard to read, so keep in mind that easy reading is important. Also, be sure to use formal Standard English, avoid slang uses, avoid shifting to or using second person ("you"), and avoid using a conversational style with colloquial or unfamiliar phrases. Think about making your essay more creative by beginning with or including a brief quote, some poetry, or an unusual anecdote. If you follow these guidelines, you will create an essay that will express who you are, while at the same time using the appropriate form and fulfilling your readers' expectations.

### Resumés and Cover Letters

Resumés, unlike essays, have a definite set of writing requirements and a specific audience with experience and qualifications in a particular field. The most challenging part of writing a resumé is gathering information that will convey your experience and background with a clear sense of pride and accomplishment. To prepare to write a resumé, organize information about your educational and occupational past so that as you work, all of the information you need will be handy. Think about your audience. If you are applying for a job as a mechanic, think about what the manager of a repair shop might be expecting or wanting to see in your resumé. The aim of your resumé should be to meet these expectations. Even though writing an individual resumé for each job you want to apply for is time-consuming, it can make the difference in how favorably a potential employer views your resumé. Nothing is more obvious than a generic resumé that gives an overview but does not really address the skills required for the specific job. After reading twenty or thirty resumés, a potential employer will no doubt be able to tell the difference between those that have been written specifically for the job and those that the job seeker sends to every company or potential employer. One key is to make your resumé specific and to really sell your attributes for the specific job. A resumé is no place for modesty and humility. You do not want to seem pompous, but too much modesty will cost you the job. Another key to resumé writing is to make everything on the resumé easy to read and understand. Most employers glance over resumés looking for potential candidates to interview. If your resumé is sloppy or difficult to read, it will probably end up at the bottom or in the circular file—that is, the wastebasket.

The following is a guide for writing a resumé. Observe the categories and types of information contained in each section.

**Your Name**
**1236 Your Street**
**Your City, State, 12345**
**(209) 111-2222**

### Job Objective

In this section describe the job you are applying for,
your employment goals and personal strengths, as well
as reasons why you feel qualified for the position. This
should be a short, concise statement.

### Work History

Describe your last two or three jobs (or volunteer
positions) including the following:

Dates of employment          Position held
                             Company name
                             Address and phone
                             Name of supervisor or contact person
                             Description of duties

### Education

Describe your educational background or any special
training courses or workshops you have attended.

Dates of schooling           Educational institution
                             Type of education or training
                             Degree or certificate obtained

### Job-Related or Special Skills

Describe any job-related skills that you have that might
make you more desirable as an employee.

### Special Awards

Describe any personal accomplishments that may
make you more desirable as an employee.
Community or volunteer work or other types of
involvement could be listed here as well.

Along with your resumé, you should send a cover letter that addresses the person or committee making the final decision on who will be hired. If the person to whom you should write this letter is not named on the application materials, then address the letter "To Whom It May Concern." Otherwise address the letter directly to the person or company representative listed on the job application materials. The cover letter should discuss the job for which you are applying and the reasons you feel you are qualified, and should express your appreciation for the consideration you are being given.

The following is an example of a cover letter and resumé. The resumé is somewhat different from the guideline example just given. Either form would be appropriate for a variety of positions.

Ron Jones
9417 Anywhere Road
Some town, CA 91234
(916) 123-4567


March 14, 1997


First United Church
344 East Main
Somewhere, CA 91234


Dear Hiring Committee:


I am very interested in working for your church as a full-time
custodian. I have been employed as a maintenance worker with
Rental Maintenance since 1992 doing rental and home maintenance.
I am currently looking for a position that will not require as much
out-of-town travel as my current job. I would bring over ten years of
building and maintenance experience to your church. I have a strong
work ethic and am honest and hard-working. Enclosed please find a
resumé and references. I hope you will give me serious consideration
for this position; if you hire me, you will be pleased with my skillful,
quality work. If you have further questions about my qualifications,
please contact me at the above telephone number.
Thank you for your time.


Sincerely,


Ron Jones

**Ron Jones**
**9417 Anywhere Road**
**Some town, CA 91234**
**(916) 123-4567**

---

## EDUCATION

1988–graduate of Washington High School, Somewhere, WA
1989–certified for CPR at Community Center, Somewhere, WA

## EXPERIENCE

Employer: Rental Maintenance
Duties: perform all types of repair services for regular and one-time customers
Dates: January 1992–present
Supervisor: Bob Smith

---

Employer: Howard Reason Construction, San Diego, CA
Duties: Framing and general construction
Dates: 1990–1992
Supervisor/Owner: Howard Reason

---

Employer: Valley Care Center, Somewhere, WA
Job Title: Maintenance Person
Duties: Janitorial and maintenance
Dates: October 1989–January 1990

---

## JOB SKILLS

I have several years experience in the following:
• all facets of home building and repair
• landscaping and yard maintenance
• rental maintenance and management
• painting, plumbing, electrical
• pouring cement and foundations
• cleanup of construction sites and rentals

## REFERENCES

| Howard Reason | Fran Perez | Ida Boyles |
|---|---|---|
| San Diego, CA | Washington High School | San Diego, CA |
| (909)123-1234 | (909)223-2234 | (909)455-4467 |

# Building Your Skills

### Assignment 1

Write an admission essay to a college near you or to your dream school. Use one of the following sample essay questions:

> Describe in 500 words or less the most significant achievement in your life to date.
>
> Describe in 500 words or less an important challenge that you have faced.
>
> In an essay of no more than 1,000 words, describe your most important goals and accomplishments to date.

Follow the guidelines in the section above that describes the process of writing an essay of this type. Remember that even though this essay is for college admission, it is still an essay and it follows the same conventions as other essays. When you finish your first draft, evaluate what features a college entrance committee would use to determine whether or not to admit you based on this essay.

### Assignment 2

Look in the classified ads section of a local newspaper and find a job advertisement (preferably for a job you would like to apply for now or in the future). Write a cover letter demonstrating your interest in the position and describing either your current qualifications or the qualifications you hope to have five years from now. Follow the format discussed in this chapter. When you finish, prepare information for a resumé by listing your skills and job qualifications and gathering information about past employment or volunteer work. When you have as much information as you can produce, write a resumé that reflects your qualifications for this job. (If you do not have many of the qualifications for your dream job, make some up for this assignment.) Use the resumé format provided in this chapter and remember to edit for spelling and clear wording.

### Assignment 3

Visit or phone several employers and interview them about what they expect in a cover letter and resumé. Ask them about the kinds of responses they usually get from an advertised position. Do they usually receive cover letters and resumés? Ask them about the process they use to choose people for interviews and how much influence the letter and resumé have on this process. When you have completed three interviews, do one of the options below.

**Option 1:**   Using the information you received from these interviews, write a cover letter and resumé as directed in assignment 2 above and then revise it based on what you have learned from these interviews.

**Option 2:**   Write an essay that tells another student the methods for getting a good job. Include a discussion of training, application procedures, and interview techniques. You can use either your own experience or interviews as a basis for the information you provide.

# READING A STUDENT ESSAY

## Peer Review Strategy: Revising Research-Based Essays

Revising a research-based essay is very much like revising any other essay, except that essays that include references to research require an additional look at transitions and at how well the research material presented ties in with the argument and the rest of the essay. In other words, research in an essay should not stand apart from the essay, but instead should be an integral part of the essay and its point. Research may be used for support, to add interest, to enlighten the reader about a problem, or to provide examples—but no matter what it is used for, it must relate well with the point, and the writer must blend the research content into the essay so that the reader can read smoothly from point to point.

When you revise a research-based essay, begin by reading the essay carefully and identifying the purpose and audience for the essay. Then look at each piece of evidence presented and ask yourself, "How does this relate to the main point?" If the answer is not clear, then the writer needs to rewrite the essay to connect the evidence with the point. This may require a sentence or a whole paragraph, or it may require radical surgery in the form of cutting the material altogether. As you revise, keep in mind that researched material is only as valuable as the context in which the writer places it. If the evidence does not fit the context, omit it. If the evidence expands on or supports the point, use it and identify clearly how it is connected.

In an essay about drug abuse, would statistics about drug use in New York City fit the context? If the statistics showed a rise in drug abuse and you were making the point in your essay that drug abuse had increased in recent years, these figures might be very helpful. If your essay was about recovering from drug abuse, these statistics might seem out of place and unrelated, despite the fact that the figures and essay have to do with drug abuse. Be choosy about your evidence and be sure that you make the connections for the reader. One way to edit is to use this question: Do I explain the point and connection for the reader? If the answer is yes, your essay is probably making good use of evidence, but if you are not sure or your answer is no, then you should focus at least part of your revision time on making connections for your reader. The harder your reader has to work to get your point, the more he or she will resent your essay and be tempted to "tune out."

A second consideration in revising essays that employ research is to check the quotes, paraphrased material, and citations of sources to make sure that the evidence or examples used are presented with accuracy and clarity, and that credit is given in the proper format. Because plagiarism is such a serious concern, double-check quoted material to be sure that it is quoted completely and properly. Make sure that paraphrased material is indeed paraphrased and not plagiarized (see pages 309–311).

As you read the following student essay, pay attention to the way Broaddus uses references and the way she ties these references to her main point. Ask yourself; Does she explain her point and connect her evidence for me? How hard do I have to work to understand her point? Also, observe the way she gives the sources where she got her information.

## Normal, Isn't

by Melanie Broaddus

*"What do you read, my lord?"*
*"Words, words, words."*

Flipping through a magazine, I happened across an article entitled "Are You Normal?" The opening paragraph promised "an absolutely factual picture of how your habits, tastes, talents, and quirks stack up against the rest of the world's." Mildly curious, I scanned through the piece to discover a collection of factoids about how average Americans carry out everyday tasks, like getting up in the morning and dressing for work. Say, did you know that nearly four percent of women don't wear underwear (Kanner 97)?

1

I really didn't want to know that. But many of us   2
are a little curious to know just where we fit in. We all
want to be recognized for what we consider to be the
right reasons, and most of us don't want to be thought
of as total weirdos. We want to be normal. The problem is, no one seems to know what "normal" really
means.

The Oxford English Dictionary, possibly the most   3
complete collection of words and their meanings in
existence, marks the earliest use of the word "normal"
in a written work dated 1530. Back then all it meant
was "a regular verb"; just a simple, straightforward
term used to teach grammar (207). That innocuous little word would soon veer from its path, taking detours
into mathematics, physics, chemistry, medicine, sociology, and ultimately the realms of psychology and psy-
chiatry, stringing trails of misconceptions in its confused wake.

Where is the logic in a word that can mean "aver-   4
age," "a perpendicular," or "designating a price for a
commodity" depending upon its context (Webster
1001)? Imagine a tourist trying to make his way
through an American magazine for the first time. He
leans over to the guy sitting beside him on the plane
to ask "what is this word, 'normal'?" Having unknow-
ingly encountered a chemistry professor, he listens to
a brief litany about chemical equivalents and atomic
weight and wonders how this applies to his Cosmopolitan
questionnaire about kinky sex.

Fortunately, the more esoteric definitions of "nor-   5
mal" rarely pop up in daily conversation, yet, somehow, the common vernacular tends to make this term
more ambiguous than it was to begin with. Most people have a pretty good idea of what they think normal
isn't, but few can articulate what they think normal is.

In my quest for understanding I asked members   6
of my family and received a number of replies ranging

from the offhand to the sarcastic. They included "boring," "definitely not <u>you</u>," and "normal is, you know, normal." My favorite response came from my mother, who insisted that "there is no normal" then proceeded to ignore my protestations in favor of watching a talk show about transvestites.

A reverse dictionary provided me with a list of the usual synonyms, such as "mediocre," "regular," "conventional," and the like, which only left me wondering why people get so worked up about what's normal (<u>Reader's</u> 365). If all it amounts to is being average and dull, then what's the big deal? I would think no one would want to be normal, wouldn't you?

Yet, nobody wants to be considered <u>ab</u>normal. No one wants to hear the voice of Satan coming from their French poodle or to feel the burning need to build a bell tower. (At least, not on a Monday.) I turned to an introductory-level psychology text for a better idea of what being abnormal or deviant means and found this: "a behavior is considered abnormal if it deviates greatly from accepted social norms" (Plotnik 490). So, basically, if the mysterious entity called "society" doesn't consider the way you act to be normal, you must be abnormal.

Gee. That's enlightening.

An article in <u>Current</u> magazine further explores society's dilemma with deciding what's normal and what's not:

> . . . we have had an explosion of deviancy in family life, criminal behavior, and public displays of psychosis. And we have dealt with it in the only way possible: by redefining deviancy down so as to explain away and make "normal" what a more civilized, ordered and healthy society long ago would have labeled—and long ago did label—deviant. (Krauthammer 34)

The same article goes on to say "there is a complementary social phenomenon that goes with defining

7

8

9

10

deviancy down. . . . it is not enough for the deviant to be normalized. The normal must be found to be deviant" (34).

Feeling desperate, I turned to sociology for a better answer. I was only reminded that "some norms in a society apply equally to all members of the society, while others apply only to certain persons" (Stokes 73). In other words, not only are the meanings of normal and abnormal interchangeable, they were subjective to begin with. To top it all off, my psychology book also noted that "there is no absolute definition of abnormal behavior" (Plotkin 491).                                   11

So defining normal by defining its opposite is out, too. Yet the statistics would indicate that somebody, somewhere, believes that abnormality is rampant among us. About twenty percent of us suffer from at least one mental disorder (493), "almost no family in the nation is entirely free of mental disorders" (Friedrich 24), and about "half a million Americans go crazy every year" (22).                                   12

Well, is it any wonder? I'm going crazy just trying to get a straight answer to a simple question: <u>what is normal?</u> I say forget the experts. Forget the question "are you normal?" No human being is utterly average. No individual will ever totally fit in with the rest of society. And no one should. If it weren't for the unusual, the world would be an intolerably dull place.                                   13

"Normal" is a just a word with more than a dozen definitions and no meaning.                                   14

## Works Cited

Friedrich, Otto. <u>Going Crazy: An Inquiry into Madness in Our Time</u>. New York: Simon, 1975.

Kanner, Bernice. "Are You Normal, Strange, Really Weird?" <u>Mademoiselle</u> October 1995: 97+.

Krauthammer, Charles. "Defining Deviancy Up: Deviancy and Normality in America." Current March-April 1994: 34–39.

"Normal." Oxford English Dictionary. 1933 ed.

"Normal." Reader's Digest Illustrated Reverse Dictionary. Ed. John Ellison Kahn. Pleasantville, NY: Reader's Digest Association, 1990.

"Normal." Webster's New World Dictionary, 1957 ed.

Plotnik, Rod, and Sandra Mollenauer. Introduction to Psychology. New York: Random, 1986.

Stokes, Randall. Introduction to Sociology. Dubuque, IA: Wm. C. Brown, 1984.

## Building Your Skills

1. How do the references to dictionaries and other works affect your reading of Broaddus's essay? What value do these references have within the essay?

_____

_____

_____

_____

_____

_____

_____

_____

_____

2. What is Broaddus's main point? How clearly does she relate her main point to her evidence? How easy or difficult was this essay for you to read?

 

_____

_____

_____

_____

_____

_____

_____

_____

3. Without the research that Broaddus provides, how would this essay be different? Do you think you would like it better or not as much? Why?

 

_____

_____

_____

_____

_____

_____

_____

_____

4. As if you were discussing Melanie's paper with her, list three features of her essay that work very well or that really appeal to you as a reader. Then, recommend three changes she could make to improve her essay.

Describe three features that are effective for you as a reader:

a. _____

b. _____

c. _____

Describe three improvements or changes Melanie could make to create a more effective, interesting, or informative essay:

a. _____

b. _____

c. _____

# USING GRAMMAR: A PUNCTUATION REVIEW FOR PROFICIENCY

Basic punctuation is not something any writer learns from an easy, ready-made list, but you can use this brief review for quick reference. The following excerpts are from William Safire's "Never-Say-Neverisms" printed in his "The Fumblerules of Grammar," originally published in *The New York Times Magazine*. Safire uses examples in a humorous way to demonstrate ungrammatical phrases and usage. The sentences are listed using his numbers, and since some have been omitted they do not always follow numerical order. In each of these sentences, try to identify the problem. If you can detect the problem, you obviously understand the rule. If you cannot detect the problem, look in the grammar sections of this book or in a grammar handbook for help and for the definitions of unknown words or concepts.

1. Remember to never split an infinitive.
2. The passive voice should never be used.
3. Avoid run-on sentences they are hard to read.
4. Don't use no double negatives.

5. Use the semicolon properly, always use it where it is appropriate; and never where it isn't.

8. Verbs has to agree with their subjects.

9. No sentence fragments.

10. Proofread carefully to see if you any words out.

11. Avoid commas, that are not necessary.

12. If you reread your work, you will find on rereading that a great deal of repetition can be avoided by rereading and editing.

13. A writer must not shift your point of view.

15. And don't start a sentence with a conjunction.

16. Don't overuse exclamation marks!!!

20. Don't use contractions in formal writing.

28. Everyone should be careful to use a singular pronoun with singular nouns in their writing.

33. If a dependent clause precedes an independent clause put a comma after the dependent clause.

38. "Avoid overuse of 'quotation "marks."'"

Try to correct each of these phrases using the hint contained within each. For example, in number 1, "Remember to never split an infinitive," "infinitive" is the clue. An infinitive is the base form of a verb preceded by the word *to (to eat, to sleep, to think)*. What's wrong with number 1? The phrase "to never split" splits the infinitive "to split." If we rewrote the sentence using Safire's advice, we would change it to "Remember never to split an infinitive." Try figuring out the rest of these grammar mindbenders.

## Building Your Skills

### Assignment 1

Write each of Safire's "neverisms" giving the actual grammar rule. Then write a completely new sentence that demonstrates this rule.

### Assignment 2

Using an essay you have previously written, look for any of the problems Safire points out in his "neverisms." If you did Assignment 1 in this section, use your list of rules; if not, figure out the problems in the sentences in the above grammar section and find any evidence of these problems in your own essay. For example, look for split infinitives in your essay such as "to never split" (see number 1 in Safire's list). Rewrite the essay, making changes to any sentences in your essay that violate Safire's rules.

## Assignment 3

To test your ability to correct ungrammatical sentences, identify the grammatical problems in the following sentences and make as many changes as necessary to make them grammatical.

1. Last night, I had to rush my friend Ryan Lee to the emergency room to receive stitches, she cried.

2. The day is sunless opaque obscure but we still continue with our jobs careers and activities.

3. When I went to the beach and played in the sand I used a rake I used a shovel I used a bucket and I used my imagination to build a sandcastle.

4. I didn't understand what my English teacher told me as she explained the problem with my papers, I wish I understood.

5. This morning I woke up at 7:00 a.m., and take my little brothers and sisters to school, we arrived late.

6. I tried to do my best I wrote an 18-word sentence before the teacher asked for my paper.

7. While writing an essay I must always have everything organized and I especially like to have a fresh cup of coffee.

8. Even though I never seem to finish all the work I have to do I do seem to get everything done on time as well as saving just a little time to relax.

# SEEING THE CONNECTIONS: APPLYING YOUR SKILLS

*Assignment 1*

Brainstorm about the many controversial issues you hear about every day. Make a list of three issues about which people disagree and about which you have an opinion or viewpoint. Write a thesis statement that takes a view about each of them. Choose one and freewrite for fifteen minutes expressing your thoughts and feelings about this issue.

Go to your school or public library and find two or three resources about this topic. Read them to increase your knowledge and understanding about the topic. Then write an essay that clearly outlines or presents your view. Use at least one quote and one sentence that paraphrases to present evidence or examples from your resources. Be sure to use the exact words when you quote, and change the words completely into your own words and sentence structure when you paraphrase. Also, identify the sources you have used by listing the author, title, and any publishing information necessary in parentheses following the quote or paraphrase. Ask your instructor for guidelines if you are not sure how to do this.

When you finish your first draft, read the draft in two stages by answering the first set of questions below and performing any necessary revision, then going on to the next set:

Stage One:
1. Does your essay have a main point? Does everything else in the essay relate to the main point?
2. Does the essay move smoothly from point to point?
3. Do you make your meaning clear to the reader?

If you answer no to any of these questions, revise your essay to make it more readable and unified.

Stage Two:
1. Are the quotations and paraphrased sentences you provide important to your point? Do they make sense and seem to belong in the essay?
2. Is your evidence thoughtful and convincing? Did you use reliable sources?
3. Will your reader be interested in your evidence? Will your reader learn from your essay?

If you answer no to any of these questions, revise the evidence you use in your essay, either by presenting the evidence in a new way or by using new evidence that is better suited to your audience or topic. When you finish, write a final draft with all of the changes you have made.

## Assignment 2

Read Rachel Jones's essay in this chapter. Brainstorm about the way you use language or about any problems you have had learning or using language. When does language create problems for you? Do you ever feel inferior or threatened based on the way you use language? Identify why these features of language make you feel this way and how society promotes or discourages this view of language.

Write an essay that uses one of Jones's points about language as the basis for your own discussion. Look at the way she uses William Labov's view in her first paragraph and use a quote from her essay in the same way. Then, using this quote as an introduction, expand your essay from that quote to your main point, and use supporting details such as personal experiences or observations to persuade your reader.

When you have finished the first draft, read your introduction to see how effectively you have tied the quote from Jones's essay to your main point. If you have not linked them effectively, rewrite the introduction. Next, look for transitions and connections between your ideas throughout your essay. Rewrite wherever the ideas are not adequately linked. Finally, apply Safire's rules to your essay to make it as grammatical as possible.

## Assignment 3

Read the student essay by Melanie Broaddus in this chapter. Brainstorm about words that seem to be difficult to define or that seem to have many meanings. Choose one word and look up this word in several dictionaries. Also, do an informal survey where you ask at least ten people what they think this word means. Then write an essay that defines a word about which people have different perceptions. Demonstrate these perceptions, and then discuss which is the most accurate definition.

When you finish your first draft, highlight or underline each of the definitions you provide. How do you tie them together? Does each move easily into the next? Also, look for the main point and decide whether you have supported one definition over the others. Before rewriting, apply Safire's rules as a check on grammar and then rewrite the whole essay.

# *Appendix*

# *Grammar Reference Lists*

The following lists serve as references for many of the discussions in this text. Make a photocopy for easy reference when reading or when revising your writing. Each of the lists is discussed in detail in the text. Look in the index for page references if you are not sure about what the terms mean or how the lists may be useful to you.

## SUBORDINATING CONJUNCTIONS

| | | |
|---|---|---|
| after | how | unless |
| although | if | until |
| as | in order that | when |
| as if | since | whenever |
| as long as | so that | where |
| as though | that | wherever |
| because | though | while |
| before | | |

## COORDINATING CONJUNCTIONS

| | | |
|---|---|---|
| and | for | so |
| but | nor | yet |
| | or | |

## CONJUNCTIVE ADVERBS

| | | |
|---|---|---|
| accordingly | henceforth | nevertheless |
| also | however | otherwise |
| anyhow | indeed | still |
| besides | instead | then |
| consequently | likewise | therefore |
| furthermore | meanwhile | thus |
| hence | moreover | |

## PREPOSITIONS

| | | |
|---|---|---|
| about | during | off |
| above | for | on |
| across | from | out |
| ahead of | in | over |
| around | in addition to | regardless of |
| as | in back of | through |
| at | in front of | to |
| before | inside | together |
| below | in spite of | under |
| beneath | instead of | until |
| between | into | up |
| beyond | like | with |
| by | near | without |
| down | of | |

## Irregular Verb Forms

The list below includes the present, past, and future tense forms for many irregular verbs. Memorizing this list may be difficult, but if you keep a photocopy, or simply make notes about verb forms that you consistently have trouble with, it may help you learn to use these forms in your writing. The infinitive form is used with *to*; the present form listed here adds an -*s* ending in third person, such as "he chooses"; when the third person form is irregular, it is included here. The past participle forms can be used with a variety of helping verbs, but in this list they appear with the helping verb *have*.

| Infinitive (form with "to") | Present | Past | Past Participle (used with helping verbs; for example, *have*) |
|---|---|---|---|
| to be | am/is/are | was/were | have been |
| to begin | begin | began | have begun |
| to bite | bite | bit | have bitten |
| to blow | blow | blew | have blown |
| to break | break | broke | have broken |
| to bring | bring | brought | have brought |
| to build | build | built | have built |
| to catch | catch/catches | caught | have caught |
| to choose | choose/chooses | chose | have chosen |
| to come | come | came | have come |
| to cost | cost | cost | have cost |
| to deal | deal | dealt | have dealt |
| to dig | dig | dug | have dug |
| to do | do/does | did | have done |
| to draw | draw | drew | have drawn |
| to drink | drink | drank | have drunk |
| to drive | drive | drove | have driven |
| to eat | eat | ate | have eaten |
| to fall | fall | fell | have fallen |
| to fight | fight | fought | have fought |
| to find | find | found | have found |

*continued*

## IRREGULAR VERB FORMS *continued*

| Infinitive (form with "to") | Present | Past | Past Participle (used with helping verbs; for example, *have*) |
|---|---|---|---|
| to fly | fly/flies | flew | have flown |
| to forget | forget | forgot | have forgotten |
| to freeze | freeze | froze | have frozen |
| to get | get | got | have gotten |
| to give | give | gave | have given |
| to go | go/goes | went | have gone |
| to have | have/has | had | have had |
| to know | know | knew | have known |
| to lead | lead | led | have led |
| to lend | lend | lent | have lent |
| to lie (as in relaxing) | lie | lay | have lain |
| to make | make | made | have made |
| to ride | ride | rode | have ridden |
| to ring | ring | rang | have rung |
| to run | run | ran | have run |
| to say | say | said | have said |
| to see | see | saw | have seen |
| to set (as in put in place) | set | set | have set |
| to shake | shake | shook | have shaken |
| to sing | sing | sang | have sung |
| to sink | sink | sank | have sunk |
| to sit | sit | sat | have sat |
| to speak | speak | spoke | have spoken |
| to steal | steal | stole | have stolen |
| to swim | swim | swam | have swum |
| to take | take | took | have taken |
| to tear | tear | tore | have torn |
| to throw | throw | threw | have thrown |
| to wear | wear | wore | have worn |
| to write | write | wrote | have written |

# Index